Consent under Duress

Consent under Duress

TOM DOUGHERTY

OXFORD
UNIVERSITY PRESS

Great Clarendon Street, Oxford, OX2 6DP,
United Kingdom

Oxford University Press is a department of the University of Oxford.
It furthers the University's objective of excellence in research, scholarship,
and education by publishing worldwide. Oxford is a registered trade mark of
Oxford University Press in the UK and in certain other countries

Published in the United States of America by Oxford University Press
198 Madison Avenue, New York, NY 10016, United States of America

British Library Cataloguing in Publication Data
Data available

Library of Congress Control Number: 2024936051

ISBN 9780198922339

DOI: 10.1093/9780198922360.001.0001

Printed and bound by
CPI Group (UK) Ltd, Croydon, CR0 4YY

The manufacturer's authorised representative in the EU for product
safety is Oxford University Press España S.A. of el Parque Empresarial San
Fernando de Henares, Avenida de Castilla, 2 – 28830 Madrid
(www.oup.es/en).

Contents

PART 4. UNCERTAINTY ABOUT DURESS

Acknowledgments

In writing this book, I have been particularly indebted to Johann Frick, Hallie Liberto, and Victor Tadros. Their work has been an inspiration to me, I have learned an incredible amount about the issues covered in this book from conversations with them, they have generously provided critical feedback on much of this book, and their friendship has been invaluable to me.

For helpful comments and discussions, I would also like to thank Larry Alexander, Abdul Ansari, Olivia Bailey, Sam Berstler, Danielle Bromwich, Luc Bovens, Pascal Brixel, Sarah Buss, Tom Christiano, Shlomo Cohen, Nico Cornell, Michelle Dempsey, David Enoch, Kim Ferzan, Johann Frick, Mollie Gerver, Simone Gubler, Liz Harman, Alison Hills, Sukaina Hirji, Samia Hesni, Mike Huemer, Markus Kohl, Niko Kolodny, Zöe Johnson King, Quill Kukla, Adam Lerner, Matthew Liao, Hallie Liberto, Jordan Mackenzie, Sarah McGrath, Jeff McMahan, Carla Merino-Rajme, Joseph Millum, Sarah Moss, Andreas Müller, Véronique Munoz-Dardé, Ram Neta, David Owens, Tom Parr, Sumeet Patwardhan, Stella Rhode, Gideon Rosen, Geoff Sayre-McCord, Peter Schaber, Samuel Scheffler, Melissa Schwartzberg, Dan Shahar, David Shoemaker, Zofia Stemploska, Sarah Stroud, Gopal Sreenivasan, Victor Tadros, Will Tadros, Sergio Tenenbaum, Jonathan Way, Stephen White, and Andrew Williams.

I was very fortunate that Véronique Munoz-Dardé and Massimo Renzo organized a workshop on a draft of this book, under the auspices of the Institute for Philosophy and King's College London. I received invaluable feedback from them, my commentators Sophie Dandelet, Kate Greasley, Joe Horton, and David Owens, and the other workshop participants. I am also extremely grateful to Michelle Dempsey for co-organizing the *Coercion and Consent Workshop* at Villanova University, and for the workshop participants for helpful feedback on material from this book. For critical feedback, I would also like to thank the organizers of and audiences at talks at Virginia Tech, Massachusetts Institute of Technology, Princeton University, Oxford University, University of North Carolina at Chapel Hill, Northwestern University, Tulane University, New York University, University of Maryland at College Park, the 2019 *University of North Carolina Philosophy Politics and Economics Retreat*, and the 2022 Arizona *Workshop in Normative Ethics*, Birkbeck, the 2019 American Philosophical Association—Pacific Division Conference, the *Normative Powers in Morality, Politics, and Law Conference* at the Université de Montréal and McGill University, and an informal meeting of University Michigan law and philosophy faculty in Ann Arbor. Similarly, I am grateful for the critical feedback that I received from the participants in my "Coercion and Consent" graduate seminar at UNC Chapel Hill, the participants in Johann Frick's "Relational and Non-Relational Morality" graduate seminar at Princeton University, and Véronique Munoz-Dardé's "Remnants of Contractualism: Consent, Reasonable Rejection, Aggregation and Risks (Or: Fragments of Social Accord)" graduate seminar at the University of California at Berkeley.

The research for this book was supported by a 2018–2019 Faculty Fellowship at the Center for Ethics and Public Affairs at the Murphy Institute at the University of Tulane, and I am grateful to all involved for facilitating this.

I am grateful to Oxford University Press, Sage Publishing, the University of Chicago Press, and Wiley for permission to reprint previously published material. Specifically, parts of Chapters 1, 2, and 7 were published in *Nous* (Dougherty 2021b), parts of Chapters 4, 5, and 6 were published in *Ethics* (Dougherty 2021a), parts of Chapters 10 and 11 were published in *Philosophy and Phenomenological Research* (Dougherty 2021c), parts of Chapter 3 were published in *Oxford Studies in Normative Ethics* (Dougherty forthcoming), and parts of Chapter 9 were published in *Politics, Philosophy, and Economics* (Dougherty 2022). For comments on the reprinted material, I am grateful to anonymous referees and editors.

Thanks to Ripley Stroud for thorough proofreading that improved the readability of this book.

Finally, warm thanks to Peter Momtchiloff, who retired as Senior Commissioning Editor at Oxford University Press a few weeks before I submitted the final version of this book. Peter's contributions to the world of academic philosophy have been immeasurable, and I am personally grateful for Peter's support.

Introduction

This Book's Topic

Initially, the #MeToo movement concerned misconduct that paradigmatically falls under the categories of sexual assault and sexual harassment that have been established by the law. But subsequently, the movement broadened the focus of popular attention to include sexual misconduct that does not constitute a legal offense. A commonly discussed allegation was that a celebrity, without using threats or violence, pressured a reluctant young partner through repeated attempts to initiate sexual activity. The public debate about how to morally evaluate this alleged behavior largely divided into two camps, with some assimilating it to serious sexual assault that is on a par with rape and others viewing it as just "bad sex."[1] Regardless of which camp is right about this allegation, we should be struck by the absence of an intermediary position in the debate. Perhaps this just reflects the polarization of current thinking about sexual misconduct. But I suspect that this is also because we have yet to develop a sufficiently rich normative framework for capturing a spectrum of sexual misconduct that varies in its gravity.

We have also made little progress toward understanding the social constraints that people face when giving consent. To illustrate these, consider Kristen Roupenian's (2017) fictional short story, "Cat Person." Its protagonist is a twenty-year-old woman, Margot, whose date with an older man culminates in the following scene:

> Margot sat on the bed while Robert took off his shirt and unbuckled his pants, pulling them down to his ankles before realizing that he was still wearing his shoes and bending over to untie them. Looking at him like

[1] For the complainant's testimony, see Way (2018). For social commentary that categorizes the alleged incident as sexual assault, see Lindsey (2018) and Price (2018). As examples of social commentary that took a lenient view of the alleged incident, Bari Weiss (2018) claims that the encounter was just "bad sex," Caitlin Flanagan (2018) claims that the allegations "destroyed a man who didn't deserve it," and Lucia Brawley (2018) claims that the interactions were consensual and did not constitute sexual assault, suggesting that it is inappropriate to consider the complainant a "victim." For philosophical discussion, see Ferzan (2018) and Hänel (2018).

> that, so awkwardly bent, his belly thick and soft and covered with hair, Margot recoiled. But the thought of what it would take to stop what she had set in motion was overwhelming; it would require an amount of tact and gentleness that she felt was impossible to summon. It wasn't that she was scared he would try to force her to do something against her will but that insisting that they stop now, after everything she'd done to push this forward, would make her seem spoiled and capricious, as if she'd ordered something at a restaurant and then, once the food arrived, had changed her mind and sent it back.

Unusually for its genre, "Cat Person" went viral. Presumably, the story became an internet sensation partly because many readers' experiences resonated with Margot's. Indeed, not long after its publication, the *New York Times* ran an article, "45 Stories of Consent on Campus," which collated pseudonymous testimonies from college students about their sexual experiences. One student, Courtney, recalled reluctantly having sex to avoid being rude:

> Maybe we all have different reasons for saying yes when our bodies or hearts say no. The first time I had sex, the implication was that I would say yes. Not because I had to under some form of coercion, but simply because it was the polite, lady-like thing to do. (Bennett and Jones 2019, 68)

Another student related that once "icky encounters" had started, she felt "contractually obligated to take the guy to the end" (Bennett and Jones 2019, 67–8). Like Margot, these students had unwanted sex, not because of force or threats of violence, but because they faced various forms of social constraints: they inhabit social worlds in which refusing sex is marked as capricious, rude, or a breach of contract. Social pressures led them to consent.

In addition, there has been almost no philosophical discussion of the fact that sexual encounters involving duress typically unfold against a backdrop of ignorance. In particular, people can be unsure of how their partner will react if they refuse sex. In the case of misconduct, uncertainty can also arise if a perpetrator is unclear about their intentions. A perpetrator may have several reasons for leaving it ambiguous whether they are making a threat. They may aim to retain "plausible deniability" as to whether they are engaging in coercion. They may want flexibility about how to respond to refusal: by leaving things uncertain, they have both the option of doing nothing and pretending that they never made a threat and the option of punishing refusal with the rationale that they forewarned their victim. They may create uncertainty to tempt their victim to choose the "safe" option of compliance out of risk aversion. And sometimes, a perpetrator may have none of these ploys consciously in mind, as it may not be transparent to them whether they intend to be making a threat or not.

These issues are the central topics of this book. To capture a spectrum of sexual misconduct, I will argue that the severity of the duress that someone is under can modulate how bad it is for another person to act on the basis of their consent. To kick-start inquiry into the ethical significance of social constraints on consent, I will argue that the moral force of this consent can be undermined by these constraints—as indeed it can be by third-party coercion or natural forces. And to cover consent that someone gives while they do not know what will happen if they dissent, I will argue that their consent can be undermined by their subjective belief that they face duress—whether or not that belief is accurate. Accumulatively, these conclusions aim to make progress toward developing a theoretical framework that can capture more of the complexity concerning consent.

My hope is that these contributions are resources that will be helpful to people when understanding consent under duress. For example, if we are working only with the binary of rape or bad sex, then we will struggle to understand instances of sexual misconduct that are less grave than rape. But to avoid raising false hopes, let me stress upfront that this book's conclusions will often not by themselves yield verdicts about contentious cases. Reaching these verdicts requires further assumptions that go beyond what I will argue for here. So while I will offer a richer taxonomy within which to classify, for example, a celebrity pressuring a young person into sex, I will not argue for where this behavior should be located within the taxonomy. Accordingly, at the end of this book, there will remain a significant amount of work to be done toward understanding the ethics of consent under duress. This book offers progress on the journey, but it will not take us all the way to our destination.

This Book's Expansive Approach and Scalar Approach

This is a book about how duress undermines consent. Specifically, it focuses on "permissive consent"—the consent that can give other people moral permissions to act in certain ways. Permissive consent can be rendered morally insignificant when it is given under some types of duress. Suppose you let someone into your home because they are threatening you with a gun. Even though you give consent, it is still wrong for them to enter because you were responding to duress.

Duress can undermine all types of permissive consent, and I will defend an account that applies to all these types. But since duress has a particular practical importance for sexual misconduct, much of this book's discussion will focus on sexual consent. This discussion will include severe coercion that leads to sexual assault. It will also include less severe duress, such as a threat to behave angrily in response to sexual refusal or pressure from social norms. To include these constraints and pressures alongside interpersonal coercion, I am framing this book's topic as consent under duress.

In what follows, I will defend unorthodox claims like the following:

- Even minor duress can undermine consent and hence lead to sexual misconduct.
- Consent's moral efficacy comes in degrees.
- Consent can be undermined by duress arising from natural causes and social norms.
- Someone's consent can be undermined by their believing that they face duress, even though they don't in fact face this duress.

These claims are the upshot of two key approaches that I take in this book.

First, I adopt an expansive approach when it comes to recognizing behavior that constitutes misconduct as a result of someone's consent being given under duress. By contrast, the traditional approach to defining sexual misconduct in the law is a restrictive approach: it marks off as non-consensual a narrow class of egregiously wrongful behaviors, such as rape. Moreover, the traditional approach holds that these behaviors are committed only in virtue of severe interpersonal coercion, such as threats of physical violence. By contrast, I will argue that consent is also undermined by minor duress, by duress that comes from sources such as natural causes and social norms, and by duress that is merely apparent to the consent-giver with no objective basis in reality. In this way, I am expanding the class of behaviors that are wrongful in virtue of consent being undermined by duress.

Second, I adopt a scalar approach when thinking about how duress undermines consent. By advocating a scalar approach, I mean that many of the relevant moral phenomena come in degrees, and I mean that we should recognize these degrees as morally significant. For a start, duress comes in varying degrees. For example, a threat of physical violence is typically more severe than a threat of defamation. I will argue that in turn the severity of duress can affect the degree to which it undermines someone's consent. And I will argue that the degree to which an action is gravely wrongful is affected by the degree to which the consent to this action is undermined. Again, this contrasts with the traditional approach, which holds that consent is invalidated only by duress that reaches a threshold of severity. For example, in some jurisdictions' criminal law, the threshold is specified as the duress that a person of "ordinary firmness" would not be able to withstand. Threats of physical violence are paradigmatically taken to pass this bar, but minor duress is not taken to do so. Since the traditional view is centered around a binary of valid and invalid consent, it struggles to accommodate the significance of the fact that duress comes in degrees of severity and the fact that these degrees can shape the moral efficacy of the consent.

My expansive approach and my scalar approach work in tandem: each approach makes the other more plausible. To the extent that we expand the class of what constitutes misconduct, we need resources with which to draw moral distinctions within this heterogeneous class. By providing these resources, the scalar approach supplements the expansive approach. And when we make room for the idea that consent can be undermined in minor ways, with the result that certain actions are wrongful, we need to expand our view of what constitutes misconduct to include these actions. Thus, the expansive approach is a natural consequence of the scalar approach. In these ways, the two approaches are mutually reinforcing. By providing separate arguments for each approach, I hope that this book can offer a robust defense of their combination.

The Main Ideas of This Book

Before our discussion dives into the complexities surrounding consent under duress, let me take a step back and sketch the main ideas of this book.

Consent can be undermined by duress from many sources. One source is the consent-receiver themselves. In particular, the consent-receiver may coerce someone into consenting by penalizing withholding consent. For example, imagine that a bully is threatening to smash a victim's glasses unless they let the bully pinch them. Prior to the threat, the victim had the cost-free option of not consenting to the pinch. But the bully's threat imposes a penalty of smashed glasses on this option. If the victim consents to the pinch to avoid this penalty, then their consent is invalid.

When explaining how this duress invalidates consent, a satisfactory account has to track key differences between cases. Suppose that a customer threatens the owner of a club by saying, "Let me into your club's VIP room or you will lose $1000." Does this threat invalidate the club-owner's consent? We cannot answer this question until we hear more about why the club-owner will lose $1000 if they do not let the customer into the VIP room. On the one hand, if the customer is simply threatening to take their business elsewhere, with the result that the club misses out on profits from serving them, then the customer's threat would not invalidate the club-owner's consent. On the other hand, if the customer is threatening to spread false rumors about the club, with the result that fewer people come to the club, then the customer's threat would invalidate the consent. But whether the mechanism underpinning the threat is boycott or slander, we can imagine that the club-owner goes through a similar process of decision-making: they judge that a loss of $1000 is unaffordable and hence agree to let the customer into the VIP area. This brings out that the difference between the boycott and slander cases does not concern the features of the club-owner's agency that are "beneath their skin" (i.e., features that neither concern the individual's relations with other people nor concern the moral status of others' actions). Rather, the difference concerns the external, moral, features of the duress to which the customer subjects the club-owner.

I propose that we distinguish these cases by focusing on whether the club-owner has a legitimate *complaint* against the customer's threat. On the one hand, the club-owner cannot legitimately complain about the customer taking their business elsewhere. That is an acceptable form of market activity. If an establishment is not providing the services that a customer desires, then the customer is entitled to take their business elsewhere. And it is fine for the customer to announce in advance that this is how they will behave. On the other hand, the club-owner does have a legitimate complaint against the customer threatening to slander them. And importantly, this is a complaint that concerns how the threat is affecting their incentives for giving consent. The slandering itself is unjustifiable, and in turn, threatening slander is unjustifiable.

By focusing on the consent-giver's legitimate complaints, we can explain why this type of duress invalidates consent. My provisional idea is that four conditions are jointly sufficient for the consent being invalid. First, the consent-receiver is imposing a penalty on withholding consent. Second, the consent-giver consents to avoid this penalty. Third, the consent-giver has a legitimate complaint against the consent-receiver's imposing this penalty on withholding consent. And fourth, this complaint concerns how the penalty disincentivizes withholding consent. I formulate that provisional idea in a draft of a principle that I call the Consent-Receiver Principle.

Since we can have legitimate complaints against minor duress, the Consent-Receiver Principle has a striking feature: it implies that consent can be deprived of its moral efficacy by minor duress. For example, suppose that someone consents to sex to avoid angry behavior from their partner. If we fill in the background details of the case in the right way, then we can imagine that the prospect of angry behavior amounts to a minor form of duress. Accordingly, the draft of the Consent-Receiver Principle implies that the consent is invalid. That is potentially a welcome result insofar as it embodies this book's expansive approach to recognizing sexual misconduct. But we also now face a puzzle because the consent still seems to be having a moral effect. To see this, imagine a version of the case in which this person did not consent at all, and their partner proceeded to have sex with them. That would be an extremely grave type of misconduct. Since that misconduct is worse than having sex with someone who consents to avoid angry behavior, it seems that the latter person's consent is having a moral effect. I call the problem of explaining what this effect is the "Problem of Minor Duress."

My answer is that this consent has what I call an "ameliorative effect." The consent does not make it permissible for their partner to have sex with them. That remains a form of misconduct. But the consent does have the effect of making this a less grave type of misconduct. My rationale is that the presence of the consent at least means that their partner does not wrong them by disregarding their choices about whether to have sex. But their partner still wrongs them by acting on a sexual choice that was not free from illegitimate duress from their partner. This wronging is mitigated, but not eliminated, by the fact that the duress was minor.

This leads me to endorse the Ameliorative View of consent. According to this view, there are three types of consent. First, fully valid consent to an action releases the consent-receiver from their duty not to perform the action. (The action may still be wrongful on grounds unrelated to consent.) Second, fully invalid consent to an action has no moral effect at all: if the consent-receiver was under a duty not to perform the action, then the duty exists in full force. Third, partially valid consent to an action has an ameliorative effect: the consent does not eliminate the duty not to perform the action, but the consent does make it less gravely wrongful for the consent-receiver to perform the action. Further, consent can be partially valid to a greater or lesser degree, and this degree determines how great the ameliorative effect is. Since the degree to which the consent is partially valid can depend on the severity of the duress that the consent-giver is under, this view is helpful for understanding consent under duress. Once we have the Ameliorative View in hand, we should revise our earlier draft of the Consent-Receiver Principle so that it states a sufficient condition for consent not being fully valid.

Duress can also come from other sources besides the consent-receiver. For example, it can come from an agent who is a third party. Third-party duress is theoretically complex. On the one hand, it can prevent consent from being fully valid. For example, some threats of physical violence from a third party undermine consent in much the same way that violent threats from the consent-receiver do. On the other hand, there are also puzzling cases in which third-party duress does not prevent consent from being fully valid. Suppose that a bully tells a victim that they will smash the victim's vase unless a bystander smashes the victim's teapot. Since the victim cares more about the vase, they ask the bystander to smash the teapot. This request would constitute consent that is fully valid: the bystander would not wrong the victim by acting on their request.

I explain that puzzle case roughly as follows. The bystander only has two options available to them: smash the teapot or do nothing. Out of these two options, the victim is sincerely authorizing the bystander to smash the teapot: if the bystander were simply concerned to act exactly as the victim would like them to act, then they would smash the teapot. So we can see that action as an extension of the victim's agency. Generalizing from this, I defend the "Authorization Principle," which allows that consent under duress can be fully valid when it constitutes a suitable authorization from the consent-giver. Then I formulate a principle that governs third-party duress and leaves room for the Authorization Principle. I call it the "Third Party Principle." This is similar to the Consent-Receiver Principle insofar as it states that duress can prevent consent from being fully valid when the consent-giver has a legitimate complaint against the duress. But it leaves an exception for when the consent constitutes a suitable authorization from the consent-giver.

Natural forces could impose the same constraints on someone's consent as a third party does. Admittedly, the cases involving natural forces will be unrealistic. But they are certainly conceivable. When we compare these cases, I argue that it does not matter what the source of the constraints is. All that matters is how the constraints affect the consent-giver's and consent-receiver's options, as well as the consequences of these options. For this reason, I argue for the unorthodox view that consent can be invalidated by natural causes as well as human agency. That conclusion paves the way for my argument that social norms can also invalidate consent. I argue that social norms can place people in double-binds. For example, if refusing sex is socially marked as rude, then someone can be in a double-bind between refusing sex and being polite. I argue that people can be entitled to be free from certain double-binds. When they are entitled to be free from a double-bind, and when they consent because of the double-bind, their consent is not fully valid.

All of the preceding principles are "objective" principles in the sense that they govern consent that is given under conditions of full information. Under those conditions, the consent-giver knows what will happen if they do not consent. But a common scenario is that a consent-giver lacks this knowledge. They may be misled about what will happen if they do not consent, e.g., because they are the target of a bluffing threat. Or they may be uncertain about what exactly will happen if they do not consent. For these conditions of partial information, I argue for a recipe that allows us to generate subjective principles that are counterparts to all the objective principles that I endorse. Each objective principle specifies something in the world that undermines someone's consent. For example, this could be the worldly condition that the consent-receiver is imposing a penalty on withholding consent. For each of these worldly conditions, we can formulate a counterpart doxastic condition: the consent-giver believes that the worldly condition obtains or at least takes there to be a chance that the worldly condition obtains. Roughly, my subjective principles state that if these doxastic attitudes cause someone to consent, then their consent is not fully valid. My subjective principles are controversial insofar as they do not place any importance on whether the consent-receiver intends the consent-giver to have these doxastic attitudes. Similarly, my subjective principles do not place any importance on whether the consent-receiver has caused the consent-giver to have these doxastic attitudes or whether the consent-receiver has evidence that the consent-giver has these doxastic attitudes.

The Structure of This Book

This book grew out of a series of journal articles, which I wrote in an experimental spirit, trying out different ideas to see which work best (Dougherty

2021a, 2021b, 2021c, 2022, 2024). This experimentation meant that the journal articles are often not fully consistent with each other in their details (although they are animated by similar big-picture ideas). This book aims to settle on what I see as the most plausible consistent account that emerges from these experiments—an account that is supplemented by new ideas and arguments that have not been previously published.

There are a couple of ways to think of how this book is organized. The first way is in terms of the expansive approach and the scalar approach. In Parts 1, 3, and 4, I adopt the expansive approach when arguing for principles that state when consent is morally undermined. In Part 2, I adopt the scalar approach when considering how degrees of duress bear on the moral significance of consent. The second way to think of the book's organization is in terms of the four central questions that the book addresses.[2] Each question is addressed by one of the book's four parts. Each Part begins with an overview that provides some detail on what is covered by its chapters. So here I will offer only a brief sketch of each.

Part 1 addresses the question: Which types of duress from a consent-receiver prevent someone's consent from creating moral permissions for the consent-receiver? In Chapter 1, I focus on duress that takes the form of a consent-receiver imposing a penalty on withholding consent, and I ask why this duress invalidates consent. I survey candidate explanations that fail to give a satisfying answer to this question. This survey furnishes a set of cases that an adequate answer must handle. In Chapter 2, I defend my own answer in the form of the Consent-Receiver Principle and provide a foundation for this principle in the form of the Facilitative Duty Principle. In Chapter 3, I consider three types of duress from a consent-receiver, which at least in part do not fit the pattern of a penalty being imposed on withholding consent: emotional duress, paradoxical proposals, and exploitation.

Part 2 addresses the question: What moral difference is made by the severity of the consent-receiver's duress? This question becomes pressing in light of the fact that the Consent-Receiver Principle implies that consent can be undermined by minor duress. In Chapter 4, I introduce the "Puzzle about Minor Duress." This is the problem of explaining how consent has a moral effect when it is given because the consent-giver faces minor duress. In Chapter 5, I defend a solution to this puzzle. By preventing an especially

[2] I say that these Parts address these questions rather than answer them because I do not intend to offer a comprehensive characterization of all the ways in which consent is undermined by duress.

grave wrong of disregarding whether someone has made a choice to consent, consent given under minor duress can have an "ameliorative effect." By this, I mean that the consent does not prevent an action from being a wronging but the consent does make the action a less grave wronging. In Chapter 6, I show how this solution ushers in the tripartite "Ameliorative View" of consent. On this view, fully invalid consent has no moral effect at all; fully valid consent prevents an action from being a wronging; and partially valid consent has an ameliorative effect on an action. Further, I argue that consent to an action can be partially valid to a greater or lesser degree, and this can affect how gravely wrong the action is.

Part 3 addresses the question: Besides duress from the consent-receiver, which other forms of duress, if any, prevent consent from being fully valid? In Chapter 7, I explore a puzzling feature of third-party duress: it sometimes, but not always, invalidates consent. I argue that the duress does not invalidate consent when the consent-giver has appropriately authorized the consent-receiver's action. Leaving room for this scenario, I defend the Third Party Principle, which specifies when third-party duress invalidates consent. In Chapter 8, I argue for the unorthodox claim that consent can be deprived of its full validity by natural causes, and I defend the Natural Causes Principle. In Chapter 9, I defend the Social Norm Principle, which holds that someone's consent can be invalidated by social norms.

Part 4 addresses the question: Which normative principles explain why consent lacks full validity as a result of uncertainty about duress? Until this point in the book, our inquiry assumes that consent-givers and consent-receivers are fully informed of the morally relevant facts. But this assumption is relaxed in the fourth part of the book. In Chapter 10, I argue that what matters is the consent-giver's beliefs and credences about the duress they face. Accordingly, I defend what I call the "Subjective Principles," which are subjective counterparts to the Consent-Receiver Principle, the Third Party Principle, the Natural Causes Principle, and the Social Norm Principle. In Chapter 11, I argue against rival principles that state that what also matters are the consent-receiver's intentions regarding the consent-giver's beliefs and credences, the consent-receiver's causal contributions to these beliefs and credences, or the consent-receiver's evidence about these beliefs or credences.

Consent under Duress. Tom Dougherty, Oxford University Press. © Tom Dougherty 2024.
DOI: 10.1093/9780198922360.003.0001

Framing the Book's Inquiry

To frame our inquiry, some initial set-up will help. I will begin by explaining why I use the concept of consent to theorize certain types of sexual misconduct. Then I will explain key methodology that I will use in our investigation. Finally, I will state and explain substantive assumptions and terminological choices that I will be making throughout this book.

How Much Work Should Consent Do in Our Theory?

In this book, I will be defending an expansive approach to theorizing consent under duress: I aim to expand the class of sexual encounters that are categorized as misconduct on the grounds that the victim's consent was impaired. Such an approach has been criticized from different perspectives, particularly when it comes to sexual consent. On the one hand, there is a reactionary critique. This is a backlash to the trend in popular discourse toward recognizing as sexual misconduct behavior that had previously been socially accepted. On the other hand, there is a feminist critique. This critique shares the assumption that there is a lot more sexual misconduct than has been traditionally recognized. But it rejects the idea that this misconduct is to be explained in terms of victims' lack of morally efficacious consent.

I will not respond explicitly to the reactionary critique, but the arguments that I go on to offer in this book offer an implicit response. However, at the outset, I want to engage with the feminist critique in order to explain why I am framing our inquiry in the way that I do.

One version of the feminist critique arises from the work of Catherine MacKinnon (1989, 2003, 2016). While MacKinnon focuses on how we should frame laws against sexual misconduct rather than on the morality of this misconduct, their work has been so influential that it has resonated throughout moral philosophy. MacKinnon (2016, 442) argues that in general sexual misconduct must be understood "in the context of historically unequal power relations, in which members of one group have more power than members of another." These "inequalities of power, meaning social hierarchies," include:

> age (middle over young and old), family (husband over wife, parents over children, older children over younger children), race (in the United States, white over people of color), authority (educational, medical, legal, spiritual among them); law (police and prison guards over citizens and inmates), as well as illegal statuses such as those created by the law of immigration, homosexuality, and prostitution; and economics (poverty, and employers over employees). (MacKinnon 2003, 270)

MacKinnon further argues that the law has typically served to facilitate intergroup domination by construing sexual assault as legal. For example, if a law holds that legally efficacious consent is absent only when a victim resists to the utmost, then the law grants legality to misconduct perpetrated against a victim who refuses sex without this resistance. In this way, the notion of "consent" has historically been employed to legitimate and normalize sexual domination.

This critique is intentionally a close cousin of a Marxist critique of liberalism. The Marxist critique views liberalism as an ideology that serves to justify unequal class relations, particularly those between owners of capital and workers. The Marxist critique continues that the problematically exploitative nature of these working arrangements is masked by liberal ideology's tenet that workers' consent makes these arrangements pass the bar of justice. Similarly, MacKinnon claims that sexual misconduct is masked by the legal ideology that sexual consent makes sexual domination pass the bar of the law. To reveal this misconduct for what it is, MacKinnon urges us to reform the law without using the notion of consent to characterize sexual offenses.

I am more optimistic than MacKinnon about the possibility of liberating the notion of consent from problematic ideologies and re-constructing it so that it can fit into a feminist ethical theory. I believe that this is in effect what has been happening with progressive grass-roots approaches to sexual ethics in recent decades. These approaches have been progressive precisely because they have been demanding about what is required for morally and legally efficacious consent. Indeed, that is the spirit of this book: my hope is that by adopting an expansive approach toward consent under duress, we can uncover forms of sexual misconduct that have been hidden. And crucially, with one exception, this book does not make claims about when consent justifies behavior.[1] Instead, this book focuses on defending claims about when consent fails to justify behavior. Moreover, since I offer sufficient conditions rather than necessary conditions in this regard, I do not mean to close the list on sexual misconduct to include only the behaviors that I discuss. As such, this book does not put consent in the role of defender of sexual misconduct, but rather that of prosecutor.

There is another version of the feminist critique. Some people object that consent theorists ask the notion of consent to do too much work in our ethical theories, particularly when it comes to sexual consent.[2] They think that certain sexual encounters are consensual but problematic in other ways: for example, the encounters involve harm or disrespect. Consequently, they maintain that insofar as we rely on consent as our only—or primary—standard for evaluating sexual encounters, we will miss what is problematic in these encounters and hence fail to take them as seriously as we should. I suspect that they may feel that I am asking too much of consent when I discuss encounters involving minor coercion or encounters involving duress that comes from social norms, such as norms of politeness. I predict that they may be inclined to diagnose what is wrong with these encounters not in terms of defects in people's consent but instead in terms of the presence of other morally significant factors. After all, if someone has sex to avoid being rude, then this is likely going to be a sexual encounter that is bad for them.

In response to these concerns, I fully agree that harm, risk, and other considerations matter a great deal independently of consent and hence that consent plays only a circumscribed role in sexual ethics. For example, I agree with Quill R Kukla (2018, 72), writing as Rebecca Kukla, that "We can consent to all sorts of lousy sex, including demeaning, boring, alienated, unpleasantly painful or otherwise harmful sex." As consent theorists have stressed, consent is a necessary but not sufficient condition for ethical sex (West 2010). But despite that point of agreement, I want to hold my ground and insist that consent is among the primary moral considerations in the encounters that I discuss. Why do I think this? Well, I start by assuming that our theory needs to explain why it is wrong for the consent-receiver to proceed with sex in these encounters. Insofar as these encounters are shaped by both minor duress and social norms, this explanation will at least

[1] The exception is the Authorization Principle defended in Chapter 8. As we will see, the principle is needed to qualify—and hence make defensible—several principles that specify sufficient conditions for misconduct.

[2] For a recent work that takes this position, see Ichikawa (2020).

partly concern how the consent is given under problematic constraints and hence the consent-giver's reasons for consenting. For example, it is wrong to have sex with someone because they are consenting in response to minor coercion or because they are consenting to be polite. In the respect that all these phenomena concern the consent-giver's reasons, I see these phenomena as theoretically unified. And since this theoretical unity concerns the constraints that someone faces when consenting and how these constraints shape their reasons for giving consent, I see all these phenomena as concerning consent.

Substantive Assumptions

As I mentioned in the Introduction, this book is about permissive consent. I am going to use "consent" throughout to refer to this type of consent. This usage is both narrower and broader than other usages of the term "consent." It is narrower than the usage of "consent" to refer to agreements, like contracts or promises, which bring about other normative changes such as the creation of new duties. It is broader than the usage of "consent" to refer to speech-acts that are performed in response to requests (Kukla 2018). I am not concerned with which of these usages best tracks the English word "consent," as I do not think that the contingencies of a natural language like English have implications for what we morally owe each other. Instead, I am engaging in an inquiry in normative ethics, and I am adopting the terminology that is most helpful for carrying out this inquiry.

To understand the effects of consent, we need to make assumptions about the moral status quo that is altered by this consent. I will assume that we have "directed duties" or "bipolar obligations" (Sidgwick 1893; Thompson 2004; Darwall 2006; Sreenivasan 2010). For simplicity, I will focus on duties to omit actions, but everything that I will say applies equally to duties to perform actions. These duties constitute dyadic moral relationships with the structure, "X owes Y a duty that X not perform action A." A characteristic feature of these duties is that their breach often constitutes a wronging.[3] For example, if a stranger culpably breaches their directed duty

[3] Traditionally, ethicists had assumed that directed duties line up neatly with wrongings and claim-rights. But there have been important recent challenges to this orthodoxy (Cornell 2015; Martin 2021). Even if these challenges are right, there remains a noteworthy pattern insofar as the breach of a directed duty often constitutes a wronging.

not to pinch you, then they would wrong you by pinching you. Prospectively, the fact that they would wrong you means that you are entitled to demand that they do not do so. Similarly, it means that you are entitled to take reasonable measures to prevent them from doing so. For example, you would be entitled to grab their wrist to prevent the pinch. Retrospectively, if they have wronged you, then you have suffered a moral injury. As a wronged party, you would have a special status with respect to the stranger's action, entitling you to adopt an attitude of resentment toward them and hold them accountable (Strawson 1962; Darwall 2006; Wallace 2019). Consequently, they would be obliged to acknowledge their mistreatment of you and apologize. They may also have to offer compensation that makes up for, or at least mitigates, harm that you have suffered (Thomson 1990, 82–98). Importantly, these phenomena are rooted in aspects of your relationship with the stranger. You are not objecting to the mere impermissibility of their action, but the fact that *they* have wronged *you*.

Consent can release someone from at least many of these directed duties. (For our purposes, we need not get into the controversy about whether there are some directed duties that cannot be released by consent.) Consequently, consent is a three-place relation between the consent-giver, the consent-receiver, and the action. As such, it is not a two-place relation between the consent-giver and an action, even though it is natural to talk of, e.g., "consent to a pinch." When the consent has its full moral efficacy, it can make it the case that the action does not breach a certain duty of the consent-giver. But that does not mean that the action is all things considered permissible. For example, an act of adultery can be fully consensual and yet also be impermissible in virtue of breaching a monogamy agreement. Indeed, the consent-giver's own interests can make it impermissible for the consent-receiver to perform the act to which consent has been given. Consider:

> *Sibling Invitation.* Sister is visiting town and so out of a sense of familial obligation Brother has invited her to stay. However, Sister knows that her stay would cause considerable inconvenience for Brother: he and his partner are already struggling with busy periods at work, boisterous children, and limited living space. In the circumstances, there would be no redeeming benefit to Sister's and Brother's relationship, and it is an open secret that Brother is hoping that Sister can stay elsewhere. Meanwhile, Sister also has the option of staying with an old friend, who would enjoy hosting her and would find no inconvenience in doing so.

Since Sister has a better alternative that has no cost, she would unjustifiably set back Brother's interests without a redeeming benefit by staying with him. In light of this setback to his interests, Sister should not stay with Brother. I will put this point by saying that the stay is impermissible for Sister. But while it is impermissible for Sister to stay with Brother, she nonetheless has his fully valid consent to stay. This illustrates that it is possible that even though fully valid consent has been given to an action, the action is impermissible in virtue of setting back the interests of a consent-giver. Indeed, there is a further question, which I will not try to answer here, of whether it is possible for an action to wrong a consent-giver even though they have given fully valid consent. This possibility would arise if the consent-receiver is under two directed duties not to perform the action, and the consent releases them from only one of these duties. For example, suppose that Sister has a directed duty not to unjustifiably set back Brother's interests and a directed duty not to enter Brother's property. If Brother's consent releases her from the latter duty but not the former, then she may still wrong him by staying with him.

That general view of consent is widely shared in contemporary discussions of consent in philosophical ethics. Less shared is a theoretical framework for consent that draws on Thomas M. Scanlon's (1986, 1998, 2013) work on interpersonal justifiability and the moral significance of choice. In this book, I sometimes frame issues of consent in terms of interpersonal justifiability, such as when I ask whether a consent-receiver can justify acting in a certain way by appealing to a particular instance of consent. Here I am typically assuming that consent is constituted by an expression of the consent-giver's will—an assumption that I defend at length in my other book on consent (Dougherty 2021d). This assumption leads us to consider how someone can justify their behavior to another person by appealing to that person's expressed choices. As I will discuss more fully in due course, I follow Scanlon in holding that the success of this appeal depends on whether the consent-receiver has done all that they should to put the consent-giver in a good position for making and expressing this choice. I then depart from Scanlon's view—though I like to think that I remain in its spirit—by adding that the consent-giver must also be in a sufficiently good position for making and expressing this choice, even if the consent-receiver can do nothing to improve this position. Since I anticipate that some readers will be disinclined to accept the interpersonal justifiability approach, and some may see it as in tension with an approach based on directed duties, I have tried as far as possible to offer multiple arguments for my conclusions.

Methodology

In the last Section, I made an argument by appealing to a particular case—the *Sibling Invitation* case. This was the first of many uses of the method of cases. The primary point of this method is to draw out the implications of views and principles. This allows us to test these views and principles by considering whether we find these implications independently plausible.[4] This method can also have the advantage of making a discussion easier to follow. In philosophy, we are often dealing with abstract ideas. We can make our inquiry more concrete by considering particular cases that illustrate these abstract ideas. This is of a piece with the common advice that authors should use examples to make their writing clear and easy to follow.

Some of these cases will be somewhat unusual. Often, this serves a philosophical purpose. One purpose is to bracket off orthogonal considerations so that we can focus on one moral factor in isolation. Another purpose is to consider logically possible phenomena with unusual causal structures. I hope to show that we can make theoretical progress by considering cases with these causal structures. For example, these cases will turn out to be particularly helpful when considering duress from third parties and natural causes. Consequently, if we restrict ourselves to considering only common cases, then we will miss out on the insights that we can get from considering the unusual cases.

Besides using the method of cases, I will also offer arguments that appeal to bigger-picture ideas. Examples include my arguments concerning how we can appeal to people's expressed choices in order to justify our behavior toward them. Not only does this mode of argument open up new avenues of progress, but it also helps us see the wood for the trees. Rather than just seeing multiple details in isolation, we get to see how these details hang together in a bigger-picture view.

[4] Philosophers often mark this independent plausibility by describing a claim as "intuitively" correct or supported by "intuition." By doing so, they need not be presupposing any moral epistemology. Rather, they are frequently flagging a claim as an argument's premise—typically, a premise that does not receive further defense.

Terminological Choices

I mentioned earlier that I see a theoretical unity concerning misconduct that results from different forms of coercion and pressure. It is because of that theoretical unity that I have framed this book in terms of "duress." For many of the phenomena that I discuss, people talk more often in terms of "coercion." For example, if someone threatens to shoot a driver unless they let them enter their vehicle, then it is natural to describe this as an instance of coercion. For a case like this, I do not mind that description, and you should feel free to mentally substitute "coercion" for "duress." However, I will also consider cases in which people are pressured by warnings or by others' menacing reputations. To my ear, it sounds odd to describe someone as coercing another person simply in virtue of having a menacing reputation. In addition, it sounds to me as if coercion always comes from an agent. Consequently, it sounds jarring to me to talk of natural forces or social norms coercing people. However, it does sound fine to me to talk of someone being under duress from natural forces, social norms, warnings, and reputations. Because I see these phenomena as theoretically unified, I have sought an overarching term that covers them all. That term is "duress."

Another terminological choice that I have made is to discuss "valid" and "invalid" consent. Or, in terms of the ameliorative approach that I go on to defend, I discuss "fully invalid," "partially valid," and "fully valid" consent. The terminology of valid and invalid consent is standard in bioethics and common in normative ethics.[5] However, within the criminal law, the term "consent" is commonly used as a "success term," in the sense that it is used to refer to an act that is necessarily normatively efficacious. On that terminology, what I call "invalid consent" would be described as, e.g., merely "*prima facie* consent" (Hurd 1996), the absence of consent (Alexander 1996), or "assent" (Ferzan and Westen 2017). Nothing substantive hangs on which terminology we choose, but the former terminology is more helpful than the latter. The problem with the latter success term terminology is that it makes it harder to separate two types of interactions. In the first type of interaction, someone does not express any agreement to an encounter. In the second type of interaction, someone's expressed agreement is not

[5] For example, it is used in twelve of the fifteen essays in the most recent edited collection on the ethics of consent: (Miller and Wertheimer 2010). The terminology is also used in Wertheimer (2003, 121); Conly (2004); Manson and O'Neill (2007); Owens (2007, 2012); Pallikkathayil (2011, 7); Millum (2014); Tadros (2016, 204); Bromwich and Millum (2018); and Bolinger (2019, 80).

morally significant, e.g., because of the duress they face. On the success term terminology, both of these are described as interactions in which consent is not given. Since these interactions are morally different, it is a shame that they are both described with this same phrase. By contrast, the valid/invalid terminology allows us to sharply distinguish these interactions. That terminology lets us say that when someone does not express agreement, they do not give consent at all. And this terminology allows us to say that when someone expresses agreement because of duress, they do give consent, just consent that is invalidated by the duress.

Finally, a quick word on pronouns. I use gender-neutral they/them pronouns when referring to other scholars. I do so partly to embody and promote this as a general norm for academic scholarship. For the long explanation of why I do so, please see Robin Dembroff and Daniel Wodak's (2018) excellent essay on this topic. But let me give a short explanation here. Much of the time, academics write about each other without knowing each other's genders or preferred pronouns. As a result, if we use gender-specific pronouns for each other, then we must make guesses about the right pronouns to use—often guesses based on our latest knowledge of others' gender presentations or first names. Since these are not reliable bases for guessing, this approach inevitably leads to misgendering, and consequently I do not want to adopt this approach. Moreover, I want a uniform policy that treats all scholars the same, regardless of how well I know them personally. As a result, I have decided to use gender-neutral pronouns that cannot misgender anyone since they imply nothing about anyone's gender. At the time of writing, this is not a standard approach, and I realize that this choice may come to look outdated if the academic community settles on a better convention for how to solve the problem of referring to other scholars without risking misgendering.

DOI: 10.1093/9780198922360.003.0002

PART 1
DURESS FROM THE CONSENT-RECEIVER

In Part 1, we examine consent given in response to duress from the consent-receiver. We begin by considering how a consent-receiver can penalize withholding consent. This duress features in the following example:

> *Threat.* Bully sincerely threatens to smash Victim's glasses unless Victim lets Bully pinch them.

Bully's duress means that Victim's consent fails to release Bully from their duty not to pinch them. This is a datum that we have to explain.

Chapter 1 considers how various claims might be offered as an explanation:

- Consent is undermined by threats but not offers.
- Duress prevents the consent from being given voluntarily, autonomously, or responsibly.
- Consent is invalidated by attempts to illegitimately manipulate the consent-giver.
- Consent is invalid when the consent-giver is choosing to consent instead of submitting to an action that would infringe their rights or wrong them.

I argue that these claims fail to provide adequate explanations of various cases. Perhaps the most important pair is the following:

> *Boycott.* Uncool says that if Club-Owner does not let Uncool into the VIP area, then they will stop coming to the club, and it will lose $1000 in profit. Since the club's finances are in dire straits, Club-Owner lets Uncool into the VIP area.

> *Slander*. Uncool says that if Club-Owner does not let Uncool into the VIP area, then they will spread false rumors, and the club will lose $1000 in profit. Since the club's finances are in dire straits, Club-Owner lets Uncool into the VIP area.

In the latter case but not the former, Club-Owner gives invalid consent. However, in both cases, Club-Owner goes through the same process of decision-making: they judge that the club cannot afford losing $1000 and consequently consent to Uncool entering the VIP area. In that respect, the features of Club-Owner's agency that are "beneath their skin" are the same in both cases. By this, I mean that the features neither concern the individual's relations with other people nor concern the moral status of others' actions. Therefore, these features cannot explain why the consent is valid in *Boycott* but not *Slander*. To explain this, we must focus on the moral acceptability of the duress to which Uncool subjects Club-Owner.

In Chapter 2, I defend a moral principle that can track the difference between the *Boycott* and *Slander* cases. This is the Consent-Receiver Principle. I introduce a draft of the principle, which states that someone's consent is invalid when the following four conditions are met. First, the consent-receiver imposes a penalty on withholding consent. Second, the prospect of this penalty causes the consent-giver to consent. Third, the consent-giver has a legitimate complaint against the way that the consent-giver imposes this penalty on withholding consent. Fourth, this complaint concerns the way that the penalty alters the consent-giver's incentives for withholding consent. I offer three lines of defense of this principle. First, I consider how the consent-receiver might try to justify their behavior to the consent-giver. Specifically, they might try to appeal to the consent to justify their behavior. I argue that this appeal would not be successful when the consent-giver has a legitimate complaint against the way that the consent-receiver has obtained this consent. Second, I argue that the Consent-Receiver Principle has the correct implications for the cases that we consider in Chapter 1. For example, Club-Owner has a legitimate complaint against a threat of slander but lacks a legitimate complaint against a customer's threat to take their business elsewhere. Third, I argue that the consent-receiver has certain facilitative duties to put the consent-giver in a sufficiently good position to give consent. The consent-receiver breaches a facilitative duty when they impose a penalty on withholding consent and the consent-giver has a complaint against the imposition of this penalty.

In Chapter 3, I consider three types of duress that the consent-receiver can subject the consent-giver to. First, there is emotional duress: the consent-receiver issues a threat that frightens the consent-giver, who is consequently unable to deliberate properly. Since the effect of the fear is to incapacitate the consent-giver, I argue that this phenomenon is best understood in terms of the capacity or competence conditions on valid consent. Second, there is what I call a "paradoxical proposal." Roughly, this is a proposal that is wrongful even though it is a proposal to perform an otherwise permissible action in response to consent being withheld. For example, a law enforcement official would make a paradoxical proposal by threatening to pass on evidence proving a criminal's guilt unless the criminal's spouse has sex with the official. Normally, it would be permissible to pass on the evidence, but the criminal's spouse has a legitimate complaint against this proposal. I analyze paradoxical proposals by paying attention to what the consent-receiver plans to do independently of the proposal. Third, there are cases of exploitation. For example, an affluent tourist could offer sex to an economically desperate person who has significant objections to sex work. While I have not found a principle that establishes that exploitation invalidates consent, I argue that we can diagnose what is wrong with this behavior without appealing to consent.

1
Why does Duress Undermine Consent?

Let's begin our inquiry by focusing on consent given in response to duress from the consent-receiver. Here is an illustrative example:

> *Threat.* Bully sincerely threatens to smash Victim's glasses unless Victim lets Bully pinch them.

I am assuming that Bully would successfully follow through on their sincere threat. For concision, I am leaving this assumption implicit in the description of this case. Similarly, with subsequent cases throughout this book, I will also implicitly assume that the penalty would in fact be imposed. In the *Threat* case, Bully's duress means that Victim's consent fails to release Bully from their duty not to pinch them. This is a datum that we have to explain.

We need some terminology to describe this datum. Within normative ethics, the most common way to do so is to distinguish valid consent from invalid consent. By the orthodox definition, consent is valid when it succeeds in releasing someone from a duty and invalid when it fails to do so. For the purposes of Part 1 of this book, I will adopt this definition. Hence, I will say that Victim's consent is not valid and that Bully's threat invalidates Victim's consent. However, in Part 2, I will depart from this orthodoxy and defend a three-part taxonomy of fully valid consent, partially valid consent, and fully invalid consent. But since it would take an excessively lengthy detour to explain and motivate that taxonomy, I will talk in terms of valid and invalid consent for now.

Bully's duress operates by conditionally imposing a penalty on Victim's decision to withhold consent. Some people call this "volitional coercion" (Pallikkathayil 2011, 1). In Chapters 1 and 2, I will address the question of why this type of duress invalidates consent. In doing so, I am going to limit our discussion in two ways. First, I am going to focus on duress that involves the consent-receiver attaching a penalty to the withholding of consent. This sets to one side the topic of duress from third parties and social norms—a topic that we will discuss in Part 3. It also means that in Chapters 1 and 2 I will not discuss forms of pressure that undermine someone's agency without affecting their options, e.g., by overwhelming them with emotions like fear. We will consider this pressure in Chapter 3. Second, I am going to make an idealizing assumption that the consent-giver has accurate beliefs about the consequences of their withholding consent. We will relax this assumption of full information in Part 4.

In this Chapter, I will begin by looking at reasons to reject various explanations of why duress invalidates consent. Some of these contain insights that I will incorporate into my own proposal, which I develop in Chapter 2. But as comprehensive explanations of why consent is invalidated by duress from a consent-receiver, these candidates fail to handle certain cases. As we will see, often the problem is not that the explanations are down the wrong track so much as that they do not go far enough. Since there are many candidates and I want to keep our discussion to a reasonable length, I will not attempt to show that these challenges deliver knockout blows. Instead, I will move swiftly through the terrain, with the primary purpose of setting up and motivating my own proposal, as well as getting on the table a range of problem cases that ought to be explained by a satisfactory account of consent under duress.

1.1 Threats and Offers

Let us start by comparing a pair of cases:

> *Theft.* Bully proposes to steal Victim's sunglasses unless Victim loans Bully the use of their phone. Victim agrees.
>
> *Trade.* Merchant proposes to trade their pair of sunglasses in exchange for using Contractor's phone. Contractor agrees.

Victim and Contractor are moved by the same consideration—a pair of sunglasses. Yet only Victim's consent is invalid. Why?

Since it is natural to call Bully's proposal "a threat" and Merchant's proposal "an offer," it is tempting to answer that threats invalidate consent. But we should resist this temptation for two reasons. First, insofar as we rely on linguistic intuitions about "offers" and "threats," the distinction is fraught. Consider:

> *Return.* Bully has already stolen Victim's sunglasses. Bully proposes to return the sunglasses if and only if Victim lets them use their phone. Victim agrees.

Ordinary English lets us say both that Bully is "offering" to return Victim's sunglasses and that Bully is "threatening" not to return them. Either way, these linguistic facts tell us little about the normative features of Bully's proposals in the *Theft* and *Return* cases. Both proposals invalidate Victim's consent.

Second, some threats are acceptable ways to obtain consent:

Steroids. Coach proposes that unless Player agrees to take a steroids test, Coach will drop Player from the team.

Whether or not Coach's threat is coercive, it does not invalidate Player's consent to the test. So it is not accurate to say that threats invalidate consent. Instead, only some threats have this effect. What we need to do is to characterize the ones that do.

1.2 Voluntariness

What other explanations can we give of why duress invalidates consent? A popular thought is that duress undermines consent by making the consent insufficiently voluntary.

This thought needs to be treated carefully. When some people say that behavior is voluntary, they mean nothing more than that it is free from coercion and misunderstanding (Hyman 2015, 77). On that use of the term "voluntary," we cannot explain why duress undermines consent with the claim that the consent is not voluntary: that claim would simply express the fact that the consent is given under duress. In other words, the claim is pointing to what needs to be explained rather than giving an explanation of it.

Instead, to give an explanation, we would need to understand voluntariness in a different way. One way is to assume that voluntariness concerns the internal features of an individual's agency that are "beneath the skin," so to speak. By this, I mean that the features neither concern the individual's relations with other people nor concern the moral status of others' actions. So, these are metaphysical features of an individual's agency rather than moral features.

But if we understand voluntariness in terms of the internal, metaphysical features of an individual's agency, then this proposal struggles to handle the differences between the following cases:

Boycott. Uncool says that if Club-Owner does not let Uncool into the VIP area, then they will stop coming to the club, and it will lose $1000 in profit. Since the club's finances are in dire straits, Club-Owner lets Uncool into the VIP area.

Slander. Uncool says that if Club-Owner does not let Uncool into the VIP area, then they will spread false rumors, and the club will lose $1000 in profit. Since the club's finances are in dire straits, Club-Owner lets Uncool into the VIP area.

Club-Owner's consent is valid in *Boycott* but not in *Slander*. But the internal features of Club-Owner's decision-making are the same in each case. In both cases, the club's poor finances lead Club-Owner to take the deal offered, and the duress equally undermines their agency. The difference between the cases does not concern the internal features of Club-Owner's agency, but rather the external, moral, features of the duress that Uncool subjects Club-Owner to.

I said that the internal features of Club-Owner's decision-making are the same in both cases because Club-Owner is motivated only by financial considerations and these considerations are the same. However, it is true that Club-Owner's psychology differs in other respects. For example, in only one case Club-Owner believes that they will be slandered if they withhold consent. By tweaking the cases, we could eliminate these psychological differences (although these tweaks would involve momentarily relaxing our assumption of full information). For example, we could revise both cases as follows:

Indirect Boycott. Uncool does not speak directly to Club-Owner but instead to Employee. Uncool says that if Club-Owner does not let Uncool into the VIP area, then Uncool will stop coming to the club, and it will lose $1000 in profit. Since Employee is not authorized to let people into the VIP area, Employee goes to Club-Owner's office to pass on the message. Employee says, "There's a customer saying we'll lose money if we don't let them into the VIP area." Club-Owner says, "I'm busy. Don't waste my time with extraneous details. Just tell me how much we'll lose." Employee says, "$1000." Club-Owner says, "We can't afford to lose that. Let the customer into the VIP area." Employee leaves and tells Uncool they can enter the VIP area.

Indirect Threat. Uncool does not speak directly to Club-Owner but instead to Employee. Uncool says that if Club-Owner does not let Uncool into the VIP area, then Uncool will spread false rumors, and the club will lose $1000 in profit. Since Employee is not authorized to let people into the VIP area, Employee goes to Club-Owner's office to pass on the message. Employee says, "There's a customer saying we'll lose money if we don't let them into the VIP area." Club-Owner says, "I'm busy. Don't waste my time with extraneous details. Just tell me how much we'll lose." Employee says, "$1000." Club-Owner says, "We can't afford to lose that. Let the customer into the VIP area." Employee leaves and tells Uncool they can enter the VIP area.

With these revisions, the intrinsic features of Club-Owner's psychology would be the same in both cases. And yet Club-Owner's consent would be valid in the *Indirect Boycott* case but not in the *Indirect Threat* case. Therefore, the validity of Club-Owner's consent does not turn on what the intrinsic features of their psychology are like.

As an aside from our main line of inquiry, we can draw an interesting conclusion from reflecting on the *Indirect Boycott* and *Indirect Threat* cases. In these cases, Club-Owner's psychology is the same and they have been provided with the same testimony from Employee. As a result, Club-Owner is in an identical epistemic position in each case. That means that Club-Owner does not know whether Uncool's threat is a threat of boycott or slander. Since only the threat of slander invalidates Club-Owner's consent, it follows that Club-Owner does not know whether their consent has been invalidated. So we have reached the following result: sometimes, a consent-giver is not in a position to know whether their own consent is valid.

1.3 Autonomy

The *Boycott* and *Slander* cases do not just cause trouble for appeals to voluntariness. The cases also cause trouble for Harry Frankfurt's (1988) view that coercion undermines autonomy because the victim does not want to act on the motivation on which they act. Frankfurt's conception of autonomy can be independently motivated by considering an unwilling addict who succumbs to the temptation to take a drug. Frankfurt would say that the addict does not take the drug autonomously for the following reason: they have a first-order desire to take the drug, but they lack a second-order desire to have this first-order desire. If it were down to the addict, then they would free themselves of their first-order desire for the drug. That is the sense in which they are an unwilling addict.

To see how Frankfurt intends this account to handle coercion, consider the *Threat* case. In this case, Victim acts on a desire to consent. But Frankfurt would say that Victim would prefer not to act on this desire. Victim would prefer not to have this desire to consent because Victim would prefer to be free from the coercion, and this freedom would eliminate their desire to consent. Since Frankfurt holds that someone acts autonomously only when they have a second-order desire to act on the first-order desires that guide their action, Frankfurt would infer that Victim does not act autonomously and conclude that Victim does not give valid consent.

To assess Frankfurt's explanation of why duress invalidates consent, we should distinguish two questions. The first question is: given the external circumstances that the consent-giver faces, do they wish to act on their motivation to consent? For both the *Boycott* and *Slander* cases, the answer to that question is "yes." Given the threat, it really is best for Club-Owner to comply with the threat. And so, given the threat, Club-Owner wants to be motivated to comply. The second question is: if the consent-giver were able to alter the external circumstances that they face, would they wish to act on their motivation to consent? For both cases, the answer to that question is "no": left to their own devices, Club-Owner would alter Uncool's behavior so that Uncool does not make the club's finances conditional on Uncool's entry into the VIP room. (This could be achieved by handing over the money for free in *Boycott* or by refraining from slander in *Slander*.) Thus, when we are precise when assessing Frankfurt's explanation, we will see that the explanation problematically treats both the *Boycott* and *Slander* cases alike. The reason why is that Frankfurt's explanation focuses on the internal aspects of the consent-giver's psychology. Namely, Frankfurt's explanation focuses on whether the consent-giver has a higher-order desire for the desire on which they act. But we have noted that there is a moral difference between the cases, in that Club-Owner gives valid consent in *Boycott* but not *Slander*. Since Frankfurt's explanation fails to track this moral difference, we should reject it.

1.4 Responsibility

The difference between the *Boycott* and *Slander* cases also cannot be accommodated by Heidi Hurd's (1996, 138–40) view that duress invalidates consent by excusing someone from responsibility for giving consent. Hurd motivates this view by claiming that duress undermines consent in the same way that duress excuses someone from responsibility for wrongdoing.

Hurd's idea is that certain types of duress undermine our voluntary agency quite generally. So when our agency is undermined in such a way that we are not responsible for acting wrongly, we are also not responsible for giving consent. And vice versa.

For our purposes, Hurd's view does not get us very far: just as we are curious why duress undermines consent, we would be equally curious about why duress undermines responsibility. More problematically, responsibility is the wrong concept to bring to bear here. In both the *Boycott* and *Slander* cases, Club-Owner is responsible for inviting Uncool into the VIP room. It is simply that in *Boycott*, Club-Owner is responsible for giving valid consent while in *Slander*, Club-Owner is responsible for giving invalid consent. This point is particularly clear if we consider the *Indirect Slander* and *Indirect Threat* versions of the cases.

More contentiously, I claim that coercive threats do not excuse someone from responsibility for wrongdoing. Instead, a coercive threat makes it the case that the threatened person does not perform a wrongful action (or at least performs an action that is less gravely wrongful). For example, if you break a shop window to prevent a villain from breaking your foot, then you are still responsible for your action of breaking the window. It is just that in the circumstances, your action was morally permissible. In other words, the action was not wrong. What this brings out is that when we say someone is not responsible for a wrongful action that they have performed, we are saying that they either have a particular type of excuse for their action or are exempt from responsibility altogether. These excuses and exemptions arise because either they are innocently ignorant of relevant facts or they are in a certain respect incompetent.[1] But ignorance and incompetence are internal features of someone's agency. And yet the internal features of Club-Owner's agency are the same in the *Boycott* and *Slander* cases. Thus, responsibility is the wrong concept to use to explain why Club-Owner's consent is valid only in *Boycott*.

1.5 Illegitimate Manipulation

Instead, the moral difference between the *Boycott* and *Slander* cases concerns the legitimacy of the threat that Uncool uses. This could lead us to hypothesize that Club-Owner's consent is invalidated because Uncool is

[1] In the literature on responsibility, the competence condition is standardly theorized in terms of control.

attempting to illegitimately manipulate Club-Owner. Since this hypothesis focuses on what the consent-receiver is attempting, it places moral significance on the consent-receiver's intentions. Indeed, it is plausible to think that someone engages in manipulation only if they have certain intentions.

There are several discussions of coercion and consent that suggest that these intentions matter. For example, when theorizing which sexual wrongs constitute rape, Sarah Conly (2004, 104) claims that a manipulative intention is a necessary condition for coercion. Similarly, Danielle Bromwich and Joseph Millum (2018, 456) propose that consent is invalidated when someone exercises illegitimate control over another person's decision. It is not fully clear to me whether Bromwich and Millum hold that someone's consent is undermined partly because someone intends to control them. But I take the natural interpretation of an "exercise of control" to be an intentional endeavor, and Bromwich and Millum mention attempts at control at various points in their discussion. Finally, a familiar idea in Kantian ethics is that coercion involves imposing one's will on another, making their choice for them, or using them as a mere means. These are examples of intentional manipulation.

But for the purposes of understanding how duress undermines consent, we should not focus on whether a consent-receiver has certain *intentions* when creating the duress. Certain warnings undermine consent in the same way that certain threats do. And a consent-receiver need have no manipulative intention when issuing a warning. Consider:

> *Warning.* Angry knows that they will lose control and smash Victim's glasses if Victim does not let Angry pinch them. Not wanting Victim to have smashed glasses, Angry warns Victim about this.[2]

When Angry gives the warning, they are not trying to control Victim's behavior. Instead, Angry is motivated by an altruistic concern for Victim's best interests. Yet Victim's consent would be invalidated all the same.

The same can be true when someone consents because of another person's reputation for imposing penalties. Consider:

> *Reputation.* Fearful receives accurate testimony from Trustworthy that Menace is disposed to smash people's glasses if they do not let Menace

[2] This case is inspired by one of Niko Kolodny's (2017), who credits A. J. Julius (2013, 362). I am indebted to Kolodny's essay for the insight that warnings constitute duress. For a discussion of the difference between threats and warnings, see Scanlon (2008).

> pinch them. Menace is aware that Fearful knows of their reputation. Menace asks to pinch Fearful. Fearful lets Menace pinch them to avoid having their glasses smashed.

Menace did not develop their reputation with any aim of controlling Fearful. Indeed, the case's description does not specify anything about Menace's intentions in this regard. Yet because Fearful is consenting to avoid Menace smashing their glasses, Fearful's consent is invalid.

This point is particularly important when it comes to consent that is given within the context of relationships that involve asymmetries of power. Hallie Liberto (2022, 240–1) considers a case in which a senior faculty member, Professor P, sexually propositions a postdoc, Sandra. Liberto notes that:

> people rarely plan or even predict that they will act vengefully toward another who has refused them sexually. Before facing sexual rejection, they might not consider what their subsequent behavior might be at all, especially if they do not expect to be rejected. Yet, bad behavior is common after sexual rejection. P would not have to go to any great, vengeful lengths to harm Sandra due to his prominence in the field.

And Liberto (2022, 241) notes that Sandra may also be subject to unfair treatment by Professor P, even if Professor P is not intentionally seeking revenge since

> rejection often causes an unpleasant feeling, which can manifest itself in unrelated professional decisions and discussions, even if P is not acting vengefully. P might scowl contemptuously or roll his eyes when Sandra is being considered for a job or an award. This might give those around him the impression that he is professionally unimpressed by Sandra, rather than feeling unpleasantly toward her because of the sexual rejection.

This is a complex case for several reasons. First, insofar as Sandra's job opportunities are affected at a critical stage of her career, refusing sex is potentially life-altering for her. Still, the consequences are less severe than a death threat. How is the validity of Sandra's consent affected by the degree of duress that she is subject to? I will postpone addressing degrees of duress until Part 2 of this book. Second, Sandra does not know if Professor P will penalize her for withholding consent. How does her uncertainty affect the validity of her consent? I will postpone discussing the issue of uncertainty until Part 4. For now, I am only pointing out that it makes no difference to the validity of Sandra's consent that, at the time of proposing sex, Professor P is not planning to penalize her in these ways. To screen off the issue of uncertainty and degrees of duress, we might suppose that Sandra knows for sure that Professor P will retaliate with physical violence against her. On that supposition, Sandra's consent would be invalid even if, at the time of proposing sex, Professor P does not intend to inflict violence in response to her withholding consent.

In passing, we should note that it sounds wrong to some people's ears, including my own, to describe at least some of these proposals as constituting coercion. For example, in *Warning*, if Angry is issuing a warning for Victim's sake, then it sounds odd to describe Angry as coercing Victim into consenting. Nonetheless, Angry's warning invalidates Victim's consent in a morally similar way to how Bully's threat does in the *Threat* case. It is partly to include these sorts of warnings that I frame our topic as consent under *duress* rather than coerced consent.

1.6 Proposals to Violate Rights

Instead of focusing on the consent-receiver's intentions, we could focus on the consent-giver's rights. For example, we might say that Victim's consent is invalid because Bully is threatening to smash their glasses, and Victim has a right that their glasses not be smashed.

Along these lines, Alan Wertheimer (2010, 198) proposes two jointly sufficient conditions for invalid sexual consent:

> (1) A proposes to make B worse off relative to the appropriate baseline if she does not acquiesce to the act *and* (2) it is reasonable for B to succumb to A's proposal rather than suffer the consequences.

Wertheimer (2010, 200) goes on to define the baseline of the first condition in terms of B's rights—the proposal is coercive when it is a proposal to "make B worse off than she has a right to be."

But it would be too narrow to say that consent is invalidated only when the consent-giver's decision-making is constrained by threats to perform actions that would violate the consent-giver's rights. In addition, some forms of duress illegitimately constrain a consent-giver, even though the duress does not involve a threat to the consent-giver's rights. Consider:

Distant Bomb. Terrorist has placed a bomb in the city center. Terrorist threatens to detonate the bomb unless Farmer lets Terrorist pinch them. Farmer lets Terrorist pinch them.

Since Farmer's rights are not violated by the explosion, Terrorist is not threatening to violate Farmer's rights. Yet Terrorist's threat invalidates Farmer's consent.

1.7 Implicitly Communicating Rankings

The *Distant Bomb* case also causes trouble for Liberto's (2021, 2022) view of why coercion undermines consent. Liberto's (2022, 224–32) full view is complex. For our purposes, the view's key part is the idea that someone gives invalid consent to an action when they are complying with the action instead of submitting to another action that would wrong them.[3] This makes Liberto's view similar to Wertheimer's: the issue of whether an action violates a consent-giver's rights is similar to the issue of whether the action wrongs the consent-giver. As a result, Liberto's view faces a similar problem to that faced by Wertheimer's view: Terrorist would not be wronging Farmer by detonating the bomb in the *Distant Bomb* case, and so Liberto's view does not explain why Farmer's consent is invalid.

Liberto (2022, 234–5) is aware of this problem and offers the following response. Liberto claims that we do not understand Farmer as performing a speech-act that constitutes permission-giving consent. Instead, Liberto claims that Farmer performs a speech-act of offering to exchange their victimhood for the victimhood of the inhabitants of the city center. The idea is that Farmer is not saying, "You have my permission to pinch me." Instead, Farmer is implicitly communicating, "Take me instead!" Thus, on the grounds that Farmer is not actually giving consent, Liberto claims that it is no shortcoming in their account that the account fails to explain why Farmer's consent is invalid.

But this response is unconvincing. In general, it is possible that the same utterance constitutes multiple speech-acts. Applying this point to the

[3] Liberto's thought is that when someone consents to the consent-receiver's action A1 when faced with a coercive threat that the consent-receiver will otherwise perform another action A2, they are implicitly communicating that they are consenting to A1 rather than A2. Liberto claims that this consent to A1 is invalid if A2 wrongs the consent-giver in virtue of the consent-giver's authority over their personal domain.

Distant Bomb case, it is possible that Farmer's utterance is both an instance of consent and also an offer to exchange their victimhood for another person's victimhood. Liberto directs us away from that possibility by claiming that we do not understand the relevant individual as giving consent. But that claim has plausibility only if we focus on a narrow range of cases in which someone is communicating implicitly. When we construct the *Distant Bomb* case, it is open to us to make the relevant communication explicit. So we could stipulate that Farmer explicitly says to Terrorist, "You have my permission to pinch me. I hereby consent to your doing so." When this stipulation is made, we should understand Farmer as giving consent. Of course, this consent is invalid and hence does not genuinely give Terrorist any new moral permission. But that invalidity is what we need an account to explain. Liberto's account does not provide this explanation.

1.8 Summary

In this Chapter, we have seen the limitations of various attempts to explain how duress undermines consent. We considered the following candidate explanations:

- Consent is undermined by threats but not offers.
- Duress prevents the consent from being given voluntarily, autonomously, or responsibly (where these notions are understood in terms of the internal, metaphysical features of a consent-giver's agency).
- Consent is undermined by attempts to illegitimately manipulate the consent-giver.
- Consent is invalid when the consent-giver is choosing to consent rather than submit to an action that would infringe their rights or wrong them.

These views could not explain at least one of the following:

- Some threats do not invalidate consent (the *Steroids* case).
- An utterance that invalidates consent can be classed as either a threat or offer (the *Return* case).
- The moral features of a proposal determine whether it undermines consent (the *Boycott* and *Slander* cases).

- A consent-receiver's duress can invalidate consent even if the consent-receiver does not intend to incentivize the consent-giver to consent (the *Warning* and *Reputation* cases).
- A threat to harm a third party can invalidate a consent-giver's consent (the *Distant Bomb* case).

We need a view that can accommodate all these points and handle all of the cases that we have encountered. In Chapter 2, I will develop such a view.

Consent under Duress. Tom Dougherty, Oxford University Press. © Tom Dougherty 2024.
DOI: 10.1093/9780198922360.003.0003

2
The Consent-Receiver Principle

In Chapter 1, we considered candidate explanations of why someone's consent can be invalidated by duress that comes in the form of a consent-receiver imposing penalties on withholding consent. The problem with several of these candidate explanations is that they were insufficiently general: they lacked the explanatory power to cover all the cases in which consent is invalidated by duress from the consent-receiver. In responding to this shortcoming, it would be an overreaction to jettison these explanations altogether. Rather, we should be interested in whether we can work their materials into a more comprehensive account.

That is my goal in this Chapter. I aim to develop a defensible version of the principle that duress invalidates consent because it illegitimately constrains the consent-giver's decision-making.[1] Specifically, I will defend and develop the Consent-Receiver Principle. This implies that, under conditions of full information, someone's consent is invalid when the following four conditions are jointly met:

> First, the consent-receiver will impose a penalty on withholding consent.
> Second, the prospect of this penalty causes the consent-giver to consent.
> Third, the consent-giver has a legitimate complaint against the way that the consent-giver has imposed this penalty on withholding consent.
> Fourth, this complaint concerns the way that the penalty alters the consent-giver's incentives for withholding consent.

[1] In key respects, my principle builds on and borrows from David Owens's (2012) "Injury Account," according to which duress invalidates consent because the duress wrongs the consent-giver. My account aims to avoid two shortcomings of Owens's account. First, Owens's account does not pin down the type of wronging that would invalidate consent and consequently faces counterexamples. (See the subsequent discussion of the *Humiliation* case and the *Promise* case in the main text.) Second—and more importantly—Owens's account leaves unclear why the fact that consent is invalidated by duress is explained by the fact that the duress wrongs the consent-giver.

My principle is also similar to Japa Pallikkathayil's (2011) view that coercion invalidates consent by removing options that the consent-giver is entitled to have open to them when deliberating. In Part 3, we will see that Hallie Liberto (2021, 2022) has criticized Pallikkathayil's view on the grounds that it implies that coercion morally debilitates a consent-giver. My view does not invoke the idea of moral debilitation and hence differs from Pallikkathayil's by avoiding Liberto's criticism.

Before we dive into the details, let me flag that a key feature of this principle is that it explains the invalidity of the consent in terms of what is morally problematic about the way that the consent was induced. Since we can have legitimate complaints against minor duress, a striking feature of this principle is that it implies that consent can be deprived of its moral efficacy by minor duress. In that respect, this Chapter embodies this book's expansive approach to recognizing misconduct. We will discuss minor duress in Part 2 of the book.

2.1 Consent, Complaints, and Rebuttals

Since my plan is to develop a principle that states that duress invalidates consent when it illegitimately constrains the consent-giver's decision-making, I will begin by saying what I mean by an illegitimate constraint. To do so, I will introduce the notion of a personal complaint against another person's behavior and the notion of a rebuttal of such a complaint. Since these notions will play central roles in my view, I will start by saying a little about how I am understanding each notion.

As we noted earlier, valid consent releases the consent-receiver from a duty that they owed to the consent-giver. A characteristic feature of these duties is that if an agent culpably breaches a duty that they owed to you, then they would typically wrong you and you would suffer a moral injury.[2] As a wronged party, you would have a special status with respect to the stranger's action, entitling you to hold them accountable. There are various ways that you can hold them accountable. You can do so expressively by performing certain speech-acts, such as a speech-act of complaining. But underlying this speech-act are legitimate grounds for complaining. These grounds specify the respect in which you have been morally injured. For example, you would have grounds for complaining about a stranger pinching you. These grounds exist whether or not you perform any speech-act. If you are unable to communicate, then you still have the grounds for complaining. I will have in mind these grounds, rather than their expressions in speech-acts, when I say that you would have a "complaint" against a stranger for pinching you.[3]

[2] There is room for disagreement about whether the breach must be culpable in order to result in a wronging. In addition, there is disagreement about whether culpable breaches necessarily wrong victims. For a view that denies this, see Cornell (2015).

[3] In invoking complaints, my approach is indebted to the work of Thomas Scanlon (1986, 1998, 2013) and Johann Frick (2016) on interpersonal justification, choice, and deliberation.

The contours of our rights at least partly determine when we have complaints against others' actions. I will not offer anything like a full theory of rights here, but I will note that often our default rights protect us from harms or trespass by others. In this way, these rights give us spheres of freedom from others' interference, within which we can go about living our own lives. Put another way, we end up with personal domains that protect critical interests of ours. But since we are social creatures that live alongside each other, this protection comes at the cost of restricting their liberty, and so it is inappropriate for us to enjoy unlimited protection. As a limit to this protection, there are some situations in which others harm us without infringing our rights. Consider:

> *Crush.* Aidan has a crush on Bev, and so Aidan is heartbroken when Charlie partners up with Bev.

Even though Charlie's action causes Aidan emotional or psychological harm, Charlie's action does not wrong Aidan. Charlie has their own valid interest in pursuing relationships of their own choosing. This limits the extent of Aidan's rights with respect to the harms that they suffer as a result of Charlie's interactions with Bev. Consequently, Aidan would not have a complaint against Charlie causing them this harm. In light of Charlie's own valid reasons, Charlie has a *rebuttal* of a putative complaint from Aidan.

In that example, Charlie's rebuttal appeals to the fact that Aidan has no right over how Charlie interacts with Bev. Other rebuttals can justify rights infringements. Consider:

> *Kick.* Devi is about to fall asleep in an important meeting, and they will be hauled over the coals by their boss if they do. Sitting across from Devi, Eli notices this. Eli sees that the only unobtrusive way to prevent Devi from falling asleep is to kick Devi under the table, and so Eli kicks Devi.

Since Devi has a right against being kicked by others, Eli thereby infringes Devi's right. But Eli does not thereby wrong Devi because Eli acts for Devi's sake in a manner that Devi would authorize. In light of this, Eli has a rebuttal of a putative complaint from Devi against being kicked.[4]

[4] Eli's valid rebuttal of a putative complaint is also a justification of their behavior: Eli could invoke this rebuttal to justify the kick to Devi. But not all interpersonal justifications constitute rebuttals of complaints. Consider:

For our purposes, the most important rebuttal of a putative complaint is that the individual has given valid consent. By giving this consent, the individual chooses to relax some of the protection that they enjoy from another person. There are various self-centered and altruistic reasons that the individual may have for relaxing this protection. But as the phenomenon of duress makes clear, there are cases in which consent is invalid and hence fails to waive a right. In those cases, the fact that consent is given does not constitute a rebuttal against a putative complaint. Instead, the original complaint remains on the table.

Framing our topic in this way, the salient question becomes: why does consent under illegitimate duress from the consent-receiver not constitute a rebuttal of a putative complaint? At a high level of abstraction, we can say that the consent does not constitute a rebuttal because the consent-receiver induced the consent in a problematic way. The consent-giver can then counter-rebut the putative rebuttal by saying that it was inappropriate for the consent-receiver to rely on their consent in the usual way, given that the consent-receiver had induced this consent in a problematic way. To illustrate, take the simplest case with which we began:

> *Threat.* Bully sincerely threatens to smash Victim's glasses unless Victim lets Bully pinch them.

Suppose that Victim consents to the pinch and Bully pinches Victim. Victim would have a legitimate complaint against the pinch. Bully could try to rebut this complaint by saying that they had Victim's consent. But Victim has a successful counter-rebuttal. Victim can say that they gave this consent because they were being illegitimately threatened. And Victim can say that Bully was wronging them by inducing their consent with the threat. Since

> *Coerced Kick.* Frankie credibly threatens to shoot Grayson unless Grayson kicks Harley, and so Grayson kicks Harley.

In light of the threat, Grayson would be able to justify their behavior to Harley: Grayson could point out that although they gave full moral consideration to Harley's right against being kicked and to the harm that Harley thereby suffered, there were weightier moral considerations in play. Since Harley would have to accept that Grayson was justified in acting in this way, Harley could not reasonably demand that Grayson have acted otherwise. But this does not take away from the fact that Harley retains a legitimate complaint against this treatment. Grayson is still obliged to recognize that they have infringed Harley's right and apologize for this. If it were possible for Grayson to compensate Harley, then they ought to do so, since Grayson is prohibited from transferring onto Harley the costs of Grayson escaping Frankie's threat. Therefore, even though Grayson was justified in their behavior, they have still morally injured Harley.

Bully was wronging them by inducing their consent with a threat, Victim has an independent legitimate complaint against Bully threatening them in this way. In light of this independent complaint against the way that the consent has been induced, Victim is able to counter-rebut Bully's appeal to their consent and thereby insist on their original complaint against being pinched.

This counter-rebuttal relies on an independent rationale of why it is wrong to issue illegitimate threats that induce consent. In this way, my account of why certain forms of duress invalidate consent passes the buck onto an independent account of why it is wrong for consent to be induced by certain forms of duress. But this does not make the account circular, since these accounts address different questions. The question of whether someone's consent is valid is a question concerning whether the consent creates a new moral permission for the consent-receiver to perform an action. The question of whether it is wrong for the consent-receiver to use, e.g., a certain threat to induce the consent is a question concerning the permissibility of inducing consent with the threat. Importantly, we will often address the latter question by subsuming it under the more general question of which actions are wrong in virtue of being illegitimate ways to influence each other's conduct. For example, with respect to the *Threat* case, we can say that quite generally it is wrong for Bully to control Victim's behavior by threatening to smash their glasses, and so *a fortiori* it is wrong for Bully to control whether Victim consents with this threat.

While our explanation would be relying on an independent explanation of why, in general, someone wrongs another person by coercing them, this reliance does not increase the overall theoretical debts of our moral theory. Our moral theory already has this debt, as we need this independent explanation to account for the wrongfulness of coercion in cases where consent is not involved. While I will not take a stance on this explanation here, there is already a mature debate in moral philosophy about this explanation—a debate that largely operates independently of the issue of consent (Scanlon 2008; Shaw 2012; Kolodny 2017; White 2017). And even in the absence of an independent account, we can rely on intuition to spot clear cases: we do not need a general theory to be confident that a perpetrator mistreats a victim by influencing their conduct with a threat to smash their glasses.

2.2 The Consent-Receiver Principle

Our discussion suggests that someone's consent is invalidated when they have a legitimate complaint against the consent-receiver conditioning a penalty on withholding consent. This idea needs to be made more precise in two ways.

First, as it stands, the idea is too broad, as it would catch in its net orthogonal complaints that are irrelevant to whether someone's consent is invalidated by duress. Consider variants of our earlier *Boycott* case:

> *Humiliation.* Spouse and Club-Owner are married. Spouse says that if Club-Owner does not let Spouse into the VIP area, then Spouse will stop coming to the club and it will lose $1000 in profit. Given the social context, Spouse humiliates Club-Owner by making this threat.
>
> *Promise.* Uncool promises that they will not make any legitimate threats to Club-Owner. Uncool breaks this promise by saying that if Club-Owner does not let Uncool into the VIP area, then they will stop coming to the club, and it will lose $1000 in profit.

By humiliating Club-Owner, Spouse wrongs Club-Owner in *Humiliation.* As a result, Club-Owner would have a legitimate complaint against the way that Spouse has induced Club-Owner to consent. Similarly, Uncool wrongs Club-Owner by breaking the promise in *Promise*, and again Club-Owner would consequently have a legitimate complaint against the way that Uncool has induced Club-Owner to consent. Yet in both the *Humiliation* and *Promise* cases, Club-Owner validly consents.[5] The reason why is that the wrongs of humiliation and promise-breaking are irrelevant to the validity of Club-Owner's consent.

In light of this, we should specify that the complaint must concern the way that the imposed penalty affects the consent-giver's incentives for withholding consent. As well as handling the *Humiliation* and *Promise* cases, this point is also motivated by considerations concerning the counter-rebuttals that a consent-giver can make. If an individual attempts to complain about an agent performing an action, then the agent can attempt to rebut this attempt by pointing out that the individual consented. In response, the individual could now attempt to counter-rebut this rebuttal by pointing out that the agent wronged the individual when inducing their consent. The success of this attempted counter-rebuttal depends on whether the wrong is grounded in how the consent was induced. In other words, the attempt's success depends on whether the wrong is incidental to the incentives bearing on the individual's decision to consent.

[5] Views like Owens's (2012) and Pallikkathayil's (2011) also imply otherwise and hence need revision.

With all that in mind, let us formulate a draft of our principle as follows:

Consent-Receiver Principle (Draft). Under conditions of full information, X's consent to Y performing action A is not valid if:

(i) Y will impose a penalty on X's withholding consent to A;
(ii) the prospect of this penalty causes X to consent to A;
(iii) X has a legitimate complaint against Y conditioning this penalty on X's withholding consent; and
(iv) this complaint concerns the way that the penalty alters X's incentives for withholding consent.

We can view the principle as specifying the respects in which the consent-giver's decision-making must be constrained in order for their consent to be invalidated by the consent-receiver's duress. I call this the "Draft" of the principle to flag that we will need to make a small revision to it in Chapter 6. Once this small revision has been made, I will endorse the final draft of the Consent-Receiver Principle.

But first let me say a little about the principle's conditions. Condition (iv) is included in light of the aforementioned need to specify the type of complaint that invalidates consent. Condition (iii) specifies that the penalty must be such that the consent-giver has a legitimate complaint against the consent-receiver imposing this penalty conditionally on the consent-giver's decision to withhold consent. Condition (ii) specifies that the constraint must play a causal role in the giving of consent. This causal chain would have to involve the consent-giver's reason for consenting being that they aim to avoid this disincentive. The mere existence of a so-called deviant causal chain between the threat and the consent-giver's decision would not invalidate the consent.[6] That said, the causal role should be understood capaciously. We should include threats to perform actions that impose penalties. We should also include threats to omit obligatory actions that would prevent bad consequences. For example, consider:

Stranded. Tracy and their partner have been hiking in a remote part of the countryside and night is falling. Tracy's partner says that they will not give Tracy a lift unless they have sex.

[6] For discussion of causation and consent, see Tadros (2021).

Since Tracy's partner gave them a lift to get there and there is no other way home, Tracy is entitled to a lift home. This threat means that if Tracy withholds consent, then this will cause their partner to omit giving Tracy a lift. By omitting this, Tracy's partner would make it the case that Tracy is stranded. Therefore, if Tracy consents to avoid being stranded, then the Consent-Receiver Principle implies that Tracy's consent is not valid.

It is important that the Consent-Receiver Principle be interpreted in terms of the personal complaints that the consent-giver would have. The principle is not invoking the general complaint that the duress is all things considered impermissible. To see why this makes a difference, consider:

> *Chained Threat.* Mafioso threatens to kill Pawn unless they sincerely threaten Club-Owner by saying, "If you do not let me into the VIP area, then I will smash the club's windows." Mafioso makes clear that, to save their life, Pawn must make the threat and be prepared to follow through on the threat by smashing the windows. But Mafioso also makes clear that Pawn need not actually enter the VIP area to save their life. Pawn makes the threat, and Club-Owner consents to Pawn entering the VIP area.

Given the alternative of death, it is permissible for Pawn to make the threat. Yet the threat invalidates Club-Owner's consent. The reason why is that Club-Owner has a personal complaint against Pawn's threat, since Pawn is threatening to infringe Club-Owner's rights over their windows. Club-Owner has this personal complaint even though they lack the general complaint that the threat is all things considered impermissible.

Finally, I have gone with the title "Consent-Receiver Principle" for brevity. But a more accurate, though more cumbersome, title might be "Objective Consent-Receiver Principle" because it is a principle that covers consent given under conditions of full information. As a result, the principle does not apply to cases in which it is unclear what the consent-receiver will do. Consider the following variant on an earlier case:

> *Disjunctive Threat.* Bully sincerely threatens either to smash Victim's glasses or to smash Victim's phone unless Victim lets Bully pinch them.

There is no single penalty that is definitely threatened by Bully. Instead, Bully threatens a disjunctive set of penalties. Of course, *Disjunctive Threat* is a stylized case. But it exemplifies an issue that has real-world importance with respect to vague threats. It is possible that a consent-receiver behaves in a menacing way that leaves the consent-giver in a generalized state of fear that lacks a specific object. For example, consider abusive relationships, in which the perpetrator engages in multiple types of abuse. Their victim may have the general fear that something bad will happen if they do not give consent. But there may be no specific consequence that they are fearful of because they are unsure what will happen. We will discuss cases involving uncertainty in Part 4, where we will introduce the "Subjective Consent-Receiver Principle" to govern cases of partial information.

2.3 The Consent-Receiver Principle's Implications for Cases

So far, I have motivated the Consent-Receiver Principle by considering the complaints that people have. In addition, we can motivate the Consent-Receiver Principle on extensional grounds: it has the explanatory power to handle the cases that we have considered so far. Recall the *Threat* case and the *Slander* case:

> *Threat.* Bully sincerely threatens to smash Victim's glasses unless Victim lets Bully pinch them.
>
> *Slander.* Uncool says that if Club-Owner does not let Uncool into the VIP area, then they will spread false rumors and the club will lose $1000 in profit. Since the club's finances are in dire straits, Club-Owner lets Uncool into the VIP area.

In these cases, the consent-giver has a legitimate complaint against the threatened consequences being attached to their withholding consent. The same is straightforwardly true of the *Warning* case and the *Reputation* case:

> *Warning.* Angry knows that they will lose control and smash Victim's glasses if they do not let Angry pinch them. Not wanting Victim to have smashed glasses, Angry warns Victim about this.
>
> *Reputation.* Fearful receives accurate testimony from Trustworthy that Menace is disposed to smash people's glasses if they do not let Menace pinch them. Menace is aware that Fearful knows of their reputation. Menace asks to pinch Fearful. Fearful lets Menace pinch them to avoid having their glasses smashed.

In these cases, the consent-giver faces the same penalties for withholding consent as the consent-giver faces in the *Threat* case. The grounds for all these complaints are simply that the penalty would infringe one of the consent-giver's rights. In these circumstances, this fact makes it the case that the consent-giver has a legitimate complaint against the consent-receiver in virtue of the consent-receiver inducing consent by means of conditionally attaching this penalty to withholding consent.

But rights are not the only grounds for complaints, and that is why the Consent-Receiver Principle can also handle cases in which a third party will suffer the penalty imposed on consent being withheld. Our earlier example was the *Distant Bomb* case:

> *Distant Bomb*. Terrorist has placed a bomb in the city center. Terrorist threatens to detonate the bomb unless Farmer lets Terrorist pinch them. Farmer lets Terrorist pinch them.

By itself, the detonation of the bomb would not wrong Farmer. But Terrorist does wrong Farmer by making this the consequence of not letting Terrorist pinch them. Farmer has good reasons for not wanting their actions to causally contribute to the detonation. For a start, Farmer has altruistic reasons not to want their actions to contribute to others' suffering. Moreover, were Farmer to contribute to others' suffering, they would perform an action that is morally bad in a respect—in the respect that the action led to harm to others. Indeed, in these circumstances, this bad-making feature will almost certainly make it morally wrong of Farmer to withhold consent. Farmer has good reasons to avoid performing actions that hurt others, actions that are morally bad in a respect, and actions that are wrong. So, by making the detonation conditional on Farmer's refusal, Terrorist is limiting Farmer's options concerning what they can do without penalties that they have good reasons to avoid. In these respects, Farmer has a legitimate complaint against Terrorist making the harm to the city-dwellers a condition on their withholding consent. And this is not a special claim about consent. Farmer would have a similar complaint against Terrorist imposing this condition on, e.g., Farmer's decision whether to grow barley in their fields.

In analyzing these cases, I have been assuming that it is uncontroversial that the relevant consent-givers have legitimate complaints against the imposition of the penalties that they face. But there will be cases in which we do not feel sure whether the consent-giver has the relevant legitimate complaint. Our uncertainty could be resolved by an account that specifies when people have legitimate complaints. Since I have not offered this account, there is a limit to our ability to apply my account to certain cases.

Still, it is important not to exaggerate this limit. Often, we will be able to apply my account. This is because often it will be intuitively clear to us which legitimate complaints people have. Earlier, we considered the *Stranded* case, in which Tracy's partner says that they will not give Tracy a lift home from a remote location unless they have sex. Suppose that someone asks, "Does Tracy have a legitimate complaint against their partner making it the case that withholding consent will leave Tracy stranded in a remote part of the countryside as night falls?" I assume that each of us will quickly and confidently answer, "Yes." This illustrates that for some cases we have clear intuitions about people's legitimate complaints. In these cases, it is straightforward how to apply my account.

Moreover, even in the absence of comprehensive principles that tell us which legitimate complaints people have, we can often engage in casuistical reasoning about particular cases. Without offering a full defense of this proposal, I suggest that this reasoning will typically appeal to the interests of the relevant parties. In particular, we should consider the consent-giver's interest in withholding consent not leading to a penalty. Then we compare this interest with the interests of others, including the consent-receiver and third parties. In making this comparison, we should morally weight these interests by partially or wholly discounting morally illegitimate interests, such as an individual's interest in taking sadistic pleasure in another person's suffering. This comparison will at least partly determine whether the consent-giver has a legitimate complaint against withholding consent leading to the penalty.

To illustrate this, consider the following testimony from a college student, Livia:

> I'm bad at saying no to people…Like, with men, when they want sex. I don't want to disappoint them, but I'm also not usually into it…I mean, the last time I had sex with a guy, he was like, "I don't have a condom, is that okay?" And I knew it wasn't, but I said yes anyway…Because I didn't want him to be mad at me. Or yell at me. And I wasn't sure I didn't want it. I was already there, so I just let it happen. (Bennett and Jones 2019, 67–8)

To bracket issues concerning uncertainty, let us assume that Livia's partner would in fact be mad at her and yell at her if she refused to have unprotected sex. I claim that Livia would have a legitimate complaint against this angry behavior. Why would she have this complaint? My answer is that this is explained by the various interests that Livia and her partner have and lack. On the one hand, Livia has a powerful interest in sexual freedom, which includes a powerful interest in withholding consent to unprotected sex without this leading to angry behavior from her partner. On the other hand, her partner lacks a legitimate interest in behaving angrily in response to her withholding consent. (For the purposes of the explanation, it would be enough to say that he has only a very weak legitimate interest in this.) Since these are all the relevant interests, and Livia's interest in sexual freedom is the strongest interest, she has a complaint against her partner behaving angrily in response to her withholding consent.[7]

For an illustrative case for which we should give the opposite verdict, consider:

> *Ultimatum*. Sam and Riley are in a long-term relationship. Both Sam and Riley are willing to be in this relationship only if it is sexually exclusive—i.e., neither has sex with third parties. Over time, Sam and Riley have gradually stopped having sex. For Sam, a sexless relationship is a deal-breaker: if the relationship will no longer involve sex, then Sam prefers to exit the relationship. Consequently, Sam says to Riley that they need to break up unless they start having sex again at some point in the future.

Does Riley have a complaint against Sam imposing the consequence of a breakup on withholding sexual consent? On my proposal, we need to survey the interests that each person has. Riley does have an interest in being free from this constraint. But Sam has a weightier interest in pursuing the types of relationship that they wish to pursue. Consequently, it is reasonable for Sam to propose a choice between a sexual relationship or breaking up. Note that this conclusion holds only because Sam's proposal is that the relationship becomes sexual at some point or another in the future. If we

[7] That analysis concerns angry behavior—yelling and getting mad. I am not sure what to say about a hidden emotion of anger. Other emotional reactions, like disappointment, would not invalidate consent. Consider:

> *Jetlag*. Dee has returned from a long trip, and their sexual partner Parker is looking forward to having sex with them. Dee is tired from jetlag but realizes that Parker would feel disappointed if they did not have sex. (Parker will hide this, but Dee knows Parker will privately feel disappointment.) Dee consents because they do not want to disappoint Parker.

Dee is consenting because refusing would lead to Parker's disappointment. But it seems to me that Dee wouldn't have a legitimate complaint against Parker being privately disappointed in response to refusal.

modified the case so that Sam is proposing that either they have sex right now or they break up, then this proposal would infringe Riley's entitlements. This is because while Sam has a weighty interest in pursuing a sexual relationship, Sam does not have a legitimate interest in having sex on this specific occasion. The lack of this legitimate interest explains why Morgan is entitled to withhold consent on this occasion without this leading to the break-up of their relationship.

Or so I maintain. I discuss these cases not to insist on my verdicts about them but rather to illustrate the type of moral argument that could resolve whether a consent-giver has a legitimate complaint. This argument proceeds by comparing the interests that the various parties have and the relative strength of these interests. The overall balance of these interests determines what complaints the consent-giver would have. This type of argument is somewhat imprecise insofar as it neither appeals to specific principles nor theorizes in detail what an interest is. But even somewhat imprecise reasoning can lead us to conclusions about which we are at least reasonably confident.

2.4 The Facilitative Duty Principle as a Rationale for the Consent-Receiver Principle

So far, I have motivated the Consent-Receiver Principle by considering the complaints that people may have in interpersonal justification and by considering the principle's implications for cases. Next, I want to provide a further motivation for the principle by considering a general view of how our communication of our choices affects how others may treat us.

Here, I will be drawing on Thomas Scanlon's (1986, 1998, 2013) view of the significance of choice. Consider an abbreviated version of a running example of Scanlon's:

> *Hazardous Waste.* Officials have dug up hazardous waste in order to relocate it. Pedestrian chooses to take a shortcut through the excavation site and suffers an injury from the waste.

Officials' actions have causally contributed to Pedestrian's harm. But the causation is mediated by Pedestrian's choice. Does this transfer responsibility for the harm from Officials to Pedestrian? One of Scanlon's insights is that we cannot answer this question simply by looking at Pedestrian's psychology when they made their choice. In other words, it is not enough to look at Pedestrian's beliefs and motivations. We must also consider the background events. Did Officials have a good reason for digging up the waste? Did they take reasonable steps to minimize the danger? Did Officials adequately publicize the risks of entering the site? These questions make clear that the responsibility for the harm can depend on whether Officials have discharged duties that are relevant to Pedestrian's choice. These duties include "facilitative duties" to put Pedestrian in a sufficiently good position to choose whether to enter the site. These duties include both duties to improve and duties not to worsen Pedestrian's position for making this choice. Whether Officials have discharged these facilitative duties bears on the moral significance of Pedestrian's choice to enter the site.

This analysis of the example illustrates a general moral principle:

> Facilitative Duty Principle. If Y's expressed choice is explained by X's failure to discharge their duties to put Y in a sufficiently good position for making and expressing this choice, then X cannot appeal to this expressed choice in order to justify interfering with Y's personal domain.

By "personal domain," I mean the area over which someone has authority, including their person and property, and I intend "interference" to be interpreted broadly. For the purposes of interpreting this principle, I will say that there are exactly two ways that an agent fails to discharge their duties to put an individual in a sufficiently good position for making and expressing a choice: either the agent breaches a duty to improve the individual's position, or the agent breaches a duty not to worsen the individual's position. In the *Hazardous Waste* case, the Facilitative Duty Principle implies that Officials can justify causally contributing to Pedestrian's harm only if the harm does not result from Officials' failure to discharge their facilitative duties with respect to Pedestrian's position to decide whether to enter the site.

Since consent consists in an expressed choice, this picture fits consent.[8] When someone gives consent, they attempt to release someone from a duty not to perform an action. Whether this attempt succeeds can depend on

[8] I defend the view that consent consists in an expressed choice (Dougherty 2021d). Some hold that expression is not required, and a mere choice is sufficient (Ferzan 2016). If you think that a choice is sufficient for consent, then feel free to omit "expressed" and "and expressing this" from the Facilitative Duty Principle.

whether the consent-receiver has discharged their facilitative duties toward the consent-giver. If the attempt results from the consent-receiver breaching these duties, then the consent-receiver cannot justify performing the action by appealing to the attempt.

As such, we can apply the Facilitative Duty Principle to explain why certain instances of consent are invalid.[9] To discharge their facilitative duties, a consent-receiver must not withhold certain information from the consent-giver. Consider:

> *Uninformed.* Physician fails to disclose that prostate removal will cause sterility. Although Patient is unwilling to become sterile, he signs the consent form and undergoes the operation.

The Facilitative Duty Principle allows us to give the following explanation of why Patient does not give valid consent. This principle implies that an agent cannot justify their behavior to a patient by appealing to the patient's expressed choice when the expressed choice results from the agent failing to discharge their facilitative duties to put the patient in a good position for making the choice. By failing to disclose information to Patient, Physician breached their facilitative duties to put Patient in a good position to give consent, and the breach caused the consent. Accordingly, the Facilitative Duty Principle entails that Physician cannot justify the surgery by appealing to the fact that Patient signed the consent form. On the assumption that the consent is invalid when Physician cannot justify acting on it, it follows that the consent is invalid.

Similarly, to discharge their facilitative duties, a consent-receiver must not incapacitate the consent-giver:

> *Incapacitated.* Physician gives Patient a sedative to relieve their anxiety. Known side effects are that people think less clearly and are less concerned about risks. These side effects cause Patient to agree to an operation that Physician proposes.

The Facilitative Duty Principle implies that Patient's consent does not justify Physician in performing the operation. This is because the consent results from Physician failing to discharge their duty not to worsen Patient's position for making their decision whether to consent.

[9] Elsewhere, I have defended this principle at greater length with respect to the ways in which valid consent must be informed (Dougherty 2020).

As you might expect, the Facilitative Duty Principle also applies to consent given under duress. By imposing a penalty on withholding consent, the consent-receiver would worsen the consent-giver's position to give consent. This would constitute a breach of the consent-receiver's facilitative duties when the consent-giver has a legitimate complaint against the imposition of this penalty. Therefore, if conditions (i), (iii), and (iv) of the Consent-Receiver Principle are met, then the consent-receiver has failed to discharge their facilitative duties toward the consent-giver. If condition (ii) of the Consent-Receiver Principle is also met, then the consent-giver is consenting because of this failure to discharge these duties. Since this consent is constituted by an expressed choice, the Facilitative Duty Principle implies that the consent-receiver cannot justify interfering with the consent-giver's domain by appealing to the consent. But if the consent were valid, then the consent-receiver would be able to justify interfering with the consent-giver's domain by appealing to the consent. Therefore, the consent is invalid. In this way, the Facilitative Duty Principle helps illuminate why the satisfaction of conditions (i)–(iv) of the Consent-Receiver Principle is jointly sufficient for invalid consent.

2.5 Summary

In this Chapter, I have defended and developed the Consent-Receiver Principle as a principle that states a sufficient condition for when someone's consent is undermined by duress from the consent-receiver:

> Consent-Receiver Principle (Draft). Under conditions of full information, X's consent to Y performing action A is not valid if:
>
> (i) Y will impose a penalty on X's withholding consent to A;
> (ii) the prospect of this penalty causes X to consent to A;
> (iii) X has a legitimate complaint against Y conditioning this penalty on X's withholding consent; and
> (iv) this complaint concerns the way that the penalty alters X's incentives for withholding consent.

This is a draft of the principle because in Chapter 6 it will require a small revision in light of our introduction of a distinction between fully valid and partially valid consent.

My defense of the principle had three parts. First, I considered the ways in which the consent-giver would retain legitimate complaints against certain behavior from the consent-receiver. Roughly, I argued that when the consent-giver has a certain complaint against the way that the consent-receiver has obtained consent, the consent-receiver cannot rebut a separate complaint against this behavior by appealing to the consent. Second, I argued that the principle has the correct implications for the cases that we have considered. In particular, it gets the right results for the *Threat*, *Slander*, *Boycott*, *Warning*, *Reputation*, and *Distant Bomb* cases. Third, I motivated the principle on the back of a more general view of the significance of choice. This view includes the following general principle:

> Facilitative Duty Principle. If Y's expressed choice is explained by X's failure to discharge their duties to put Y in a sufficiently good position for making and expressing this choice, then X cannot appeal to this expressed choice in order to justify interfering with Y's personal domain.

As well as providing a plausible rationale for why consent-receiver duress can invalidate consent, the Facilitative Duty Principle can also explain why consent is invalid because the consent-giver is uninformed or incapacitated.

Still, our discussion in this Chapter does not amount to a full defense of the Consent-Receiver Principle. This is because of an outstanding issue—minor duress. The Consent-Receiver Principle does not place any restrictions on the strength of the duress that invalidates consent. For example, there is no requirement that the consent-giver "could not reasonably resist" suffering the penalty for withholding consent. As a result, the principle implies that consent is invalidated by minor duress. For example, the principle implies that someone's sexual consent would be invalidated when given in order to avoid angry behavior from a partner. While many people will balk at this implication, I believe that it is basically correct. But to defend that implication, we will need to add complexity to our overall theory of consent under duress, and in doing so, we will revise the draft of the Consent-Receiver Principle into its final version. We will take up those tasks in Part 2. But before leaving the topic of duress from the consent-receiver, we should consider different forms that this duress can take.

Consent under Duress. Tom Dougherty, Oxford University Press. © Tom Dougherty 2024.
DOI: 10.1093/9780198922360.003.0004

3

Emotional Duress, Paradoxical Proposals, and Exploitation

In Chapters 1 and 2, we considered duress from the consent-receiver that involves the consent-receiver imposing a penalty on withholding consent. In this Chapter, we will look at three types of consent-receiver duress which at least in part do not fit this pattern.

I call the first type "emotional duress." It occurs when the consent-receiver causes the consent-giver to feel fear that overwhelms their ability to decide whether to give consent.

The second type of duress consists in the consent-receiver making what I call a "paradoxical proposal." This involves the consent-receiver proposing to perform a certain action if consent is withheld, but this proposal has a puzzling combination of features: the proposal wrongs the consent-giver even though the action would otherwise be permissible. For example, a cop would ordinarily be permitted to pass on incriminating evidence to the prosecuting authorities. But a cop would wrong the spouse of the criminal by proposing to do this if and only if the spouse refuses to have sex with the cop.

The third type of duress involves the consent-receiver exploiting the consent-giver: the consent-giver is in a vulnerable position, and the consent-receiver takes advantage of this in order to get them to consent. For example, if someone is economically desperate, then they may be willing to consent to activities, such as sex work, that they are otherwise strongly opposed to.

3.1 Emotional Duress

Let us start by returning to one of our introductory examples:

> *Threat.* Bully sincerely threatens to smash Victim's glasses unless Victim lets Bully pinch them.

By penalizing the withholding of consent, Bully's threat changes Victim's incentives. When Victim deliberates about what to do, they will take into account this new landscape of incentives. This is one way that the threat could affect their decision-making.

There is another way that this threat could affect Victim's decision-making: it could have an emotional effect on Victim that leaves them less able to deliberate. For example, it would not be unusual for Victim to experience fear. Indeed, if the threat were severe enough, then they might become terrified. An emotion like fear can impair someone's decision-making. They may find that they are unable to think clearly about the options that they are choosing between. They may rush their decision in a panic. And their ability to weigh their options may be compromised so that they fail to identify what they most prefer.

Let us suppose that a consent-receiver's threat overwhelms the consent-giver with fear, and the result is that they consent. Could this invalidate consent?

I think that it could, but the explanation leads us to a different topic.[1] For someone to give consent, several conditions must be met. As well as being free from certain types of duress, the consent-giver must have sufficient capacity to make decisions. The threshold for capacity varies with the relevant type of consent. For example, sexual consent requires more capacity than consent to a haircut. Typically, the higher stakes the consent, the greater the requisite amount of deliberative capacity. Thus, children lack the capacity to give sexual consent: any consent that they give is invalid. Similarly, intoxication can incapacitate someone from giving valid consent. Consider a case in which someone's drink is spiked with a strong hallucinogen. In their altered state, any consent that they gave would not be valid. In addition, it seems that strong emotions could also leave someone without sufficient capacity to make decisions. So, if a consent-receiver's threat causes someone terror, then they may lack sufficient capacity to give valid consent.

It is beyond the scope of this book to give an account of the capacity necessary for giving valid consent. Still, some of the resources from Chapter 2 may be of some (modest) help with handling issues concerning capacity. Some people hold that it makes a difference whether the consent-receiver is responsible for the consent-giver being incapacitated. For example, when discussing intoxicated consent to sex, Alan Wertheimer (2001, 379) argues

[1] Provoking emotions in people in ways that affect their deliberation can also be a form of manipulation. See, e.g., Gibert (2023).

that we are more inclined to think that someone's consent is invalid if the consent-receiver surreptitiously gave them alcohol than if the consent-giver chose to drink the alcohol. If this point holds for intoxication, then an analogous point may hold for fear: if the consent-receiver is responsible for the consent-giver's overwhelming fear, then we may be more inclined to view the fear as invalidating the consent. To make good on this idea, we would then need to know when a consent-receiver is responsible for the fear. A sufficient condition is suggested by the analysis of Chapter 2: if the consent-giver has a legitimate complaint against the way that the consent-receiver caused them to feel fear, then the consent-receiver would be responsible for the fear. On the assumption that the fear left them with inadequate capacity, the consent-giver may then be unable to give valid consent. If this sufficient condition is correct, then we would have one part of an account of capacity for consent. But this will be a small part, since the condition is not plausibly a necessary condition. A full account of capacity would need to consider much else besides.

3.2 Paradoxical Proposals

In Chapters 1 and 2, we considered cases in which the consent-receiver will behave in a way that is at least *pro tanto* wrongful if the consent-giver withholds consent. For example, it is *pro tanto* wrongful to smash someone's glasses (the *Threat* case) or detonate a bomb in a far-off city (the *Distant Bomb* case). In addition, we should be interested in a class of cases in which the consent-receiver is proposing to act in a way that would otherwise be entirely permissible. To illustrate this class, consider a case of Victor Tadros's (2016, 228):

> *Cop Threat.* Bobby, a police officer, has discovered compelling evidence that Han, Yolanda's husband, has committed armed robbery, for which he will serve several years in prison if he is convicted. Bobby tells Yolanda that he will bury the evidence if she has sex with him. To avoid him doing this, she has sex with him.

Tadros continues,

> Bobby is permitted, or even required, to do what he implicitly threatens Yolanda that he will do if she does not have sex with him—to give the

evidence to the prosecuting authorities. His doing this will make Yolanda very badly off. He gives her an option to avoid this outcome by having sex with him, and her having this option may seem to improve her situation.

With a nod to the literature on the so-called paradox of blackmail, I will call this a "paradoxical proposal."[2] I define such a proposal as follows:

X makes a paradoxical proposal to Y (or X accepts a paradoxical proposal initiated by Y) if and only if:

(i) X makes a proposal to Y (or X accepts a proposal initiated by Y);
(ii) a term of the proposal is that X will Φ if and only if Y does not consent to X Ψ-ing;
(iii) because of this term, X wrongs Y by making (or accepting) the proposal; and
(iv) X would otherwise not wrong Y by Φ-ing.

Can paradoxical proposals constitute duress that invalidates consent?

To answer this question, we have to consider whether a deliberator is made worse off by the paradoxical proposal itself. This depends on what the agent is otherwise going to do. The initial version of the *Cop Threat* case is under-described in this respect. Consider two ways to elaborate the case:

Lazy Cop. Bobby, a police officer, has discovered compelling evidence that Han, Yolanda's husband, has committed armed robbery, for which he will serve several years in prison if he is convicted. Bobby threatens to pass on the evidence unless Yolanda agrees to have sex with him. Bobby and Yolanda both know that because Bobby cares about being a person of his word, Bobby always follows through on threats. Bobby and Yolanda both know that Bobby is lazy and hence would not otherwise pass the evidence on to the prosecuting authorities. Yolanda is not attracted to Bobby and has no desire to have sex with him except insofar as doing so would protect Han. Yolanda has sex with Bobby because she wants Bobby to bury the evidence.

Proactive Cop. Bobby, a police officer, has discovered compelling evidence that Han, Yolanda's husband, has committed armed robbery, for

[2] For overviews of the literature on the paradox of blackmail, see Berman (2011) and Shaw (2012).

> which he will serve several years in prison if he is convicted. Bobby tells Yolanda that he will bury the evidence if she has sex with him. Bobby and Yolanda both know that because Bobby cares about being a person of his word, Bobby always keeps his agreements. Bobby and Yolanda both know that Bobby is proactive and hence otherwise would pass the evidence on to the prosecuting authorities. Yolanda is not attracted to Bobby and has no desire to have sex with him except insofar as doing so would protect Han. Yolanda has sex with Bobby because she wants Bobby to bury the evidence.

The key difference between the cases is that in the *Lazy Cop* case, Bobby does not independently plan to pass on the evidence to the authorities but in the *Proactive Cop* case he does.

To characterize the difference between these cases, let us introduce two distinctions. First, to cash out whether a proposal worsens or improves a deliberator's choice situation, let us distinguish the deliberator's incentives from their disincentives:

> Incentive. If a deliberator D has an option O with consequence C, then C is an incentive for D to choose O if and only if C makes D better off.
>
> Disincentive. If a deliberator D has an option O with consequence C, then C is a disincentive for D to choose O if and only if C makes D worse off.

Second, let us distinguish consequences according to whether they causally depend on a paradoxical proposal:

> Introduced Consequence. A consequence is introduced by an agent's paradoxical proposal to a deliberator if and only if the paradoxical proposal creates a causal connection between one of the deliberator's options and the consequence.
>
> Independent Consequence. A consequence is independent of an agent's paradoxical proposal to a deliberator if and only if before making the paradoxical proposal the agent is already poised to bring about this consequence.

As with most causal notions, these notions face the problem of deviant causal chains. Accordingly, phrases like "causal connection" would have to be charitably interpreted as "the right sort of causal connection."

Now we can analyze the difference between the cases as follows. In the *Lazy Cop* case, Bobby has no independent plan to pass on the evidence to the authorities. Instead, Bobby will pass on the evidence to the authorities as an execution of the threat that is contained within the paradoxical proposal. In this way, the consequence of passing on the evidence is introduced. It is a consequence that results from Yolanda withholding consent. Since it is a consequence that makes Yolanda worse off, it is a disincentive. So, Bobby is introducing a disincentive to withhold consent.

By contrast, in the *Proactive Cop* case, Bobby is already poised to pass on the evidence to the authorities, and so this is an independent consequence. Instead, the paradoxical proposal introduces a consequence of consenting: this is the consequence that Bobby does not pass on the evidence. Since this makes Yolanda better off, it is an incentive. So, Bobby is introducing an incentive to consent.

Because of these differences between the cases, we need to analyze them differently. Let's start with the *Lazy Cop* case and consider two choice situations that Yolanda could occupy:

(1) If Yolanda has sex with Bobby, then Bobby will not pass on the evidence; if Yolanda does not have sex with Bobby, then Bobby will not pass on the evidence.
(2) If Yolanda has sex with Bobby, then Bobby will not pass on the evidence; if Yolanda does not have sex with Bobby, then Bobby will pass on the evidence.

By introducing the disincentive of passing on the evidence in response to consent being withheld, the effect of Bobby's proposal is to move Yolanda from choice situation (1) to choice situation (2). Bobby lacks a justification for doing so. Bobby cannot justify his proposal by appealing to Yolanda's interests, since choice situation (2) is worse than choice situation (1). And Bobby cannot justify his action by appealing to considerations of justice: justice would require him to simply pass on the evidence to the authorities. Since Bobby has no justification for worsening Yolanda's choice situation, Yolanda has a legitimate complaint against Bobby for making the paradoxical proposal.

Because of this legitimate complaint, the Consent-Receiver Principle applies to the *Lazy Cop* case:

Consent-Receiver Principle (Draft). Under conditions of full information, X's consent to Y performing action A is not valid if:

(i) Y will impose a penalty on X's withholding consent to A;
(ii) the prospect of this penalty causes X to consent to A;
(iii) X has a legitimate complaint against Y conditioning this penalty on X's withholding consent; and
(iv) this complaint concerns the way that the penalty alters X's incentives for withholding consent.

Because Bobby is introducing a disincentive as a consequence of Yolanda's withholding consent, Bobby is imposing a penalty on her withholding consent. And Yolanda has a legitimate complaint against Bobby's imposing this penalty—a complaint that concerns how it has put her in a worse position for deciding whether to consent. Therefore, if Yolanda consents in response to Bobby's threat, then the Consent-Receiver Principle implies that Yolanda's consent is invalid.

Does the Consent-Receiver Principle apply to the *Proactive Cop* case? To answer this question, we need to consider whether Bobby is worsening Yolanda's choice situation. Bobby had already planned to pass on the evidence, and so this plan is independent of the paradoxical proposal. As such, the paradoxical proposal does not introduce this consequence as a new disincentive for withholding consent. Instead, the paradoxical proposal introduces a new incentive for consenting: this will lead to Bobby not passing on the evidence to the authorities. In this respect, the paradoxical proposal is not worsening Yolanda's choice situation. Instead, in this respect, the proposal is improving her choice situation. Moreover, Yolanda is not entitled to Bobby burying the evidence. So, it might seem that Bobby's paradoxical proposal puts Yolanda in a better position than she is entitled to be in. If that's right, then we should not say that a penalty is being imposed on Yolanda's withholding consent, and so the first condition (i) of the Consent-Receiver Principle is not satisfied.

But before we jump to that conclusion, we should consider other respects in which Bobby's paradoxical proposal is worsening Yolanda's choice situation. Consider Tadros's (2016, 228–9) analysis:

> First... it is distressing for Yolanda to have this choice. She can save her husband from a terrible fate, but only by doing something that she may well be disgusted by. Second, suppose that she does not have sex with Bobby in order to secure her sexual integrity, but in doing so seals her husband's fate. She may well find this distressing and difficult to live with. Third, if she decides not to have sex with Bobby, she will be involved in

> the trial and punishment of her husband, at least in the sense that she had an opportunity to avoid his suffering this fate.

Here Tadros is identifying respects in which Bobby's proposal worsens Yolanda's choice situation. Let us focus on the second and third respects. We may say that these are respects in which Bobby's proposal could make Yolanda entangled in Han's fate. In addition, Bobby's proposal is making this entanglement a consequence of Yolanda withholding consent. Moreover, it seems plausible that Yolanda has a legitimate complaint against Bobby for imposing this consequence on her withholding consent. So, after all, there may actually be grounds for applying the Consent-Receiver Principle to this case.

So does Bobby's proposal invalidate Yolanda's consent? I suggest that this depends on whether the proposal improves Yolanda's choice position or worsens it overall. The answer to this question depends on the relative strength of Yolanda's various interests. On the one hand, Tadros identifies interests that Yolanda has in avoiding a certain type of entanglement in Han's fate. In light of these interests, Bobby's proposal worsens Yolanda's choice situation in certain respects. The greater Yolanda's interest in avoiding this entanglement, the more that Bobby's proposal worsens Yolanda's choice situation in this respect. Meanwhile, Yolanda has an interest in saving Han from jail. This interest is served by Bobby's proposal. The greater that this interest is, the more that Yolanda's choice situation is improved by Bobby's proposal. But to determine the extent to which Yolanda's choice situation is made better off in this respect by acquiring the option of saving Han, we must also consider Yolanda's interest in avoiding sex with Bobby, given that this is the precondition of saving Han. The greater that Yolanda's interest is in avoiding sex with Bobby, the less that Yolanda's choice situation is improved by Bobby's proposal. Putting all these pieces together, we can see that our overall assessment of whether Bobby's proposal improves Yolanda's choice situation depends on the strength of various interests of Yolanda. The strength of these interests will plausibly depend on Yolanda's psychology and other aspects of her life (e.g., the value of her relationship with Han, the social environment in which she lives, and so on). The cases are under-described in these respects, and we could imagine filling in the details in different ways that affect the strength of Yolanda's interests.

For our purposes, what matters is that there are some versions of the *Proactive Cop* case in which it is true that Bobby's proposal improves Yolanda's choice situation overall. Let us focus on these versions of the case. Because Bobby's proposal is improving Yolanda's choice situation overall, it is plausible that Yolanda lacks a legitimate complaint against this proposal. And without a legitimate complaint, the Consent-Receiver Principle would not imply that Yolanda's consent is invalid. Therefore, there are some cases involving paradoxical proposals that are not covered by the Consent-Receiver Principle.

Even if the Consent-Receiver Principle does not imply that Yolanda's consent is invalid in these cases, it does not follow that Yolanda's consent is valid.[3] This is because the principle states only a sufficient condition for invalidity; it does not state a necessary condition. Thus, there remains the possibility that the consent is invalid on different grounds. There could be an alternative principle that implies Yolanda's consent is invalid. I have not found such a principle, but I leave open the possibility that there is one to be found.

Even if an alternative principle is not forthcoming, it is worth recalling that there is no need for us to rely on consent to do all the work in our theory of sexual ethics. It is open to us to hold that there are sexual wrongs that do not obtain in virtue of someone's consent being invalidated. Accordingly, we could say that in the *Proactive Cop* case Bobby commits a wrong, but this wrong does not obtain in virtue of Yolanda's consent being invalid. Along these lines, consider Tadros's (2016, 228–32) analysis of the original *Cop Threat* case:

> Bobby is permitted to render Yolanda worse off by giving evidence of Han's crime to the prosecuting authorities. Yolanda's interest against Bobby harming her in this way is outweighed by the importance of bringing Han to justice. It does not follow that Bobby may act in any way that harms Yolanda, where he does not bring Han to justice. That is so even if the harm that he inflicts on Yolanda is less than the harm that he could permissibly inflict on her were he to bring Han to Justice. In other words, if Bobby is going to bring Han to justice, he may render Yolanda worse off. But Yolanda retains a right against him rendering her worse off if he does not bring Han to justice.

Tadros continues:

> When [Bobby] threatens Yolanda, he uses the fact that he can make Yolanda worse off than she is to secure unwanted sex with her. Suppose

[3] I give some reasons for thinking that the consent is valid in cases like this in Dougherty (2024).

> that when he has sex with her, he makes her worse off than she would be were he neither to have sex with her nor to bring Han to justice, but better off than she would be were he not to have sex with her but to bring Han to justice. He cannot justify making her worse off than she would be were he neither to have sex with her nor bring Han to justice by appealing to the value that would be secured by bringing Han to justice. He has not achieved this goal, so he cannot use it to justify making her worse off... when Bobby makes Yolanda worse off without achieving the relevant justifying goal, he violates her rights—specifically, her right that he makes her worse off only if he does so with justification. This explains why Bobby not only violates his professional duty, but also wrongs Yolanda.

Tadros's account provides us with resources with which to explain why Bobby acts wrongly. It is stipulated that Yolanda is not attracted to Bobby and has no desire to have sex with him except in order to protect Han. So by having sex with Yolanda, Bobby sets back her interest in sexual integrity. This is a weighty interest, and so Bobby would need compelling reasons to justify his behavior. However, Bobby lacks these reasons. The only relevant powerful considerations are those of justice. But these considerations would only justify Bobby in passing on the evidence about Han. These considerations do not justify Bobby in having sex with Yolanda. As such, Bobby lacks an adequate justification for setting back Yolanda's interest and hence wrongs her.

While Tadros does not discuss whether Bobby's threat invalidates Yolanda's consent, it seems to me that his account identifies a wrong that is separate from the wrong of non-consensual sex. This is because the wrong of unjustifiably setting back someone's interests is a distinct wrong from the wrong of mistreating them in a non-consensual way. After all, it is possible to unjustifiably set back someone's interests in situations where no issues of consent arise. For example, Bobby could have said that he will pass on the evidence unless Yolanda destroys some of her own clothes. If Yolanda destroys these clothes, then Bobby will have unjustifiably set back her interests and thereby wronged her. But Bobby has not wronged Yolanda by performing an action of his own, for which he needs, but lacks, her valid consent. Thus, I conclude that Tadros's account offers us resources with which to explain why Bobby's conduct is seriously wrong without appealing to considerations of consent.

3.3 Exploitation

Another possibility is to say that Bobby wrongs Yolanda by sexually exploiting her. It is striking that Yolanda is in a vulnerable position: her husband, Han, faces losing his liberty for several years. Meanwhile, Bobby is not vulnerable in any such way, and so there is an asymmetry between Bobby and Yolanda with respect to vulnerability. This is likely to strike many of us as a particular type of power asymmetry, which is additional to the general power asymmetry between a law enforcement official and a citizen. Bobby is benefiting from these asymmetries, and so it is tempting to describe Bobby as taking advantage of the asymmetries. As such, we may be inclined to describe Bobby as exploiting Yolanda.[4] On the grounds that sexual exploitation is a serious wrong, we could say that Bobby seriously wrongs Yolanda.

Here is another case that involves consent and exploitation:

> *Sex Tourism*. In a developing country, Indigent has no other employment options apart from engaging in sex work with tourists. Sex work is against Indigent's religious principles, and Indigent experiences shame when engaging in it. Out of economic desperation, Indigent offers Tourist sex in return for money, and Tourist accepts.

It is controversial how to analyze a case like *Sex Tourism*. Some will say that Tourist does not wrong Indigent because Indigent is voluntarily taking part in a free market exchange. But many of us will be inclined to say that Tourist wrongs Indigent by having sex with them.

Should we characterize sexual exploitation as a wrong of nonconsensual sex? One way to do so would be to invoke a principle like the following:

> Vulnerability Principle. Y gives invalid consent to X if Y consents because X is taking advantage of Y's vulnerability.

[4] I will not enter the debate about how to define exploitation. But a representative view is that exploitation involves unfairly taking advantage of someone's vulnerability (Berman 2002, 85). On the assumption that Bobby is behaving unfairly, this view would imply Bobby sexually exploits Yolanda.

But a principle like this has implausible implications. Consider:

> *Lodger.* In a developing country, Homeowner struggles to make ends meet, and so they rent out their spare room to tourists who are attending a local language school. Homeowner rents out the room to Tenant at a very low price.

Perhaps, because the amount of rent is so low, Tenant wrongs Homeowner. But such a wronging should be characterized as Tenant's failing to meet a moral claim of Homeowner's to be paid more. We should not say that Tenant fails to meet a moral claim of Homeowner's that Tenant does not spend time in their home. That is, Tenant does not wrong Homeowner in the way that someone would wrong Homeowner by trespassing in their home without their valid consent. But the Vulnerability Principle implies that Homeowner gives invalid consent to Tenant's presence in their home. Therefore, we should reject the Vulnerability Principle.

There is another way to argue that Indigent gives invalid consent in *Sex Tourism*. To explain this, let us note that Indigent is a person in desperate economic need, and plausibly Tourist has a duty of beneficence to help people in need. However, before Indigent and Tourist meet, they are strangers, and so Indigent has no special claim to Tourist's beneficence: other needy strangers would stand in a similar moral relation to Tourist. However, it may be that Indigent's and Tourist's moral relationship changes as a result of them becoming involved in a sexual interaction. Along these lines, Hallie Liberto (2022, 261) argues that:

> sometimes when we enter sexual trysts or employment contracts with another person, the new relationship grounds moral responsibilities that did not previously exist. As such, it might be the case that once someone is our employee, or is our sexual partner, they are entitled to wellbeing-enhancing help from us that would not have otherwise been their right.

Liberto (2022, 263) argues that this provides a rationale for holding that in some cases of exploitation, consent is invalidated:

> If I am correct, then an agreement that looks consensual (even if exploitative) at the outset might not be an arrangement that can proceed consensually. Sexual exploitation of adults, low-wage labor contracts involving extensive and intimate physical or emotional services (e.g. elder care or

childcare), low-wage commercial surrogacy contracts, risky medical research, and exploitative pricing for healthcare are all arenas where the phenomenon I just described is rampant. Maybe you owe a poor stranger nothing before she is your patient, your child's nanny, your elderly parent's caregiver, or the birthmother using her uterus to gestate your child. After she stands in one of these relations to you, you probably owe her more just in virtue of the special relationship. For instance, you owe a patient a considerable duty of care. This duty does not just arise from her payment. The duty arises from her becoming your patient.

We could apply this reasoning to the *Sex Tourism* case. Let us suppose that before Tourist and Indigent meet, Indigent is merely one of very many strangers that Tourist could give money to. As a result, prior to their meeting, we may assume that Tourist did not previously have a special duty to provide Indigent with money. However, Tourist may come to have a duty to give Indigent money unconditionally as a result of engaging in a sexual interaction with them. If this duty extended to the provision of a certain amount of money, then Tourist would wrong Indigent by withholding this money if Indigent refused to consent. If this were the case, then we could view Tourist as imposing a penalty on withholding consent. The imposed penalty would be the withholding of a financial benefit that Tourist owes to Indigent.

In this respect, the case would be morally analogous to a case we encountered in Chapter 1:

Return. Bully has already stolen Victim's sunglasses. Bully proposes to return the sunglasses if and only if Victim lets them use their phone. Victim agrees.

In *Return*, Bully is proposing to withhold a benefit unless Victim consents. Since Victim is entitled to this benefit, we should view Bully as imposing a penalty on Victim's withholding consent. Since Bully has the right sort of complaint against the imposition of this penalty (namely, a legitimate complaint that concerns the way that the penalty alters Victim's incentives for withholding consent), the Consent-Receiver Principle implies that Victim's consent is not valid. Analogously, we might argue that Indigent also has the right sort of complaint against Tourist withholding the financial benefit unless Indigent consents. And if Indigent has this complaint, then the Consent-Receiver Principle would also imply that Indigent's consent is not valid.

There is a difficulty for this analysis. It seems that Tourist acquires the duty to provide assistance by engaging in sex with Indigent. But if that is right, then we could not appeal to that duty to explain why Indigent's prior sexual consent is invalid. Perhaps this difficulty can be overcome, and this is the right way to analyze the *Sex Tourism* case. Even if that is correct, this approach will not generalize to cover all cases of exploitation. For example, in the *Cop Threat* case, it may well be that Bobby owes Yolanda special duties as a law enforcement official handling a case to which Yolanda is connected. And it may also be that Bobby owes Yolanda special duties as her potential sexual partner. But it does not seem plausible that these duties extend to burying the evidence that implicates Han.

There is much more to say about the ethics of exploitative offers, but I take the foregoing to illustrate some of the difficulties of finding a suitably general principle that covers all cases of exploitation. A key reason why it is hard to find such a principle is that some exploitative offers improve someone's position for deciding whether to consent, and this improvement makes it puzzling why the offer would invalidate this consent. I have not been able to solve this puzzle by discovering a general principle that covers all cases of exploitation, and others have not been able to do so as well (Liberto 2022). Admittedly, there remains the possibility that future research will discover an additional principle here. But if an additional principle is not forthcoming, then we would need to appeal to other theoretical resources besides consent in order to explain the wrongs that occur in these cases. One possibility is to simply appeal to the idea that exploitation is itself wrong.

Still, some people will have the intuition that there is something especially problematic about sexual exploitation that still needs to be accounted for. One way to do so is to appeal to the idea of subordination (Kolodny 2017). We can illustrate this with the *Proactive Cop* case. Everyone has a general interest in standing in equal social relations with others. Sometimes, there can be a justification for limited forms of subordination that set back this interest. For example, law enforcement considerations justify Bobby having the asymmetric power to arrest Yolanda. But these law enforcement considerations do not justify Bobby in making use of this power relation to subordinate Yolanda in other ways. By making unwanted sex a condition of keeping Han out of jail, Bobby takes advantage of the power relation to get Yolanda to serve Bobby's sexual interests. This is an especially problematic form of subordination insofar as it is an affront to Yolanda's dignity.[5] Yolanda's interest in avoiding subordination is not merely a matter of her personal preferences: even if an individual does not care about subordination or willingly takes part in it, there can still be a setback to their interest in standing in equal social relations with others. Thus, even if Yolanda gives valid consent to Bobby, Bobby still wrongs Yolanda by sexually subordinating her. On the grounds that sexual subordination is a grave wrong, and that sexual exploitation involves sexual subordination, we could conclude that sexual exploitation is gravely wrong.

3.4 Summary

Let us take stock. In this Chapter, we looked at three types of duress from the consent-receiver.

First, there was emotional duress that arises from the consent-receiver making a threat that terrifies the consent-giver, with the consequence that they are less able to deliberate about whether to consent. I argued that these cases are best thought of as involving incapacitation: the consent-giver ends up with reduced capacity to give consent. It is standard to hold that valid consent requires that the consent-giver has sufficient capacity to give consent. It is also standard to distinguish this capacity condition from a separate condition that the consent-giver be sufficiently free from duress. Providing an account of capacity for consent lies outside the scope of this book. Still, our argument for the Consent-Receiver Principle in Chapter 2 suggests that capacity may be invalidated by certain incapacitations on the grounds that the consent-giver has a legitimate complaint against being incapacitated in these ways.

Second, there were paradoxical proposals. In our running example, a cop has discovered incriminating evidence that will send a criminal to jail. But the cop proposes a deal to the criminal's spouse: the cop will not pass the evidence on to the prosecuting authorities if and only if the spouse has sex with the cop. This is a paradoxical proposal because the cop wrongs the

[5] There remain hard questions concerning what explains the magnitude of this affront to someone's dignity. For example, we might like to know why this affront is greater than, e.g., the affront of humiliation. One answer might concern the cultural norms around sex. Another might be that there is something inherent to sex itself. And there may be other possibilities besides.

spouse with the proposal, and yet the cop would ordinarily be permitted to pass on the evidence to the prosecuting authorities. With respect to invalidating consent, these paradoxical proposals form a heterogeneous class. They can be distinguished according to whether, e.g., the cop independently plans to hand over the evidence. I argued that if the cop has no such independent plan, then the paradoxical proposal would be introducing a disincentive: now withholding consent causes the criminal to go to jail. Since the spouse would have a legitimate complaint against the cop putting her in a worse position to decide whether to consent, the Consent-Receiver Principle implies that her consent is invalid. But the Consent-Receiver Principle would not apply to some cases in which the cop does have an independent plan to pass on the evidence to the authorities. I did not reach a settled conclusion about this type of scenario. But I pointed out that even if we do not conclude that the relevant consent is invalid, we can still find other reasons for holding that the consent-receiver wrongs the consent-giver by acting on the consent. For example, we can follow Tadros in saying that the cop wrongs the spouse by unjustifiably setting back her interest in sexual integrity.

Third, there were cases of exploitation. In these cases, the consent-receiver takes advantage of the fact that the consent-receiver is in a vulnerable position. For some exploitation cases, the consent-receiver may have a duty to improve the position that the consent-giver is in. If the consent-receiver will only make this improvement on the condition that they receive consent, then they are in effect imposing a penalty on withholding consent. Since the consent-giver has a complaint against the consent-receiver doing so, the Consent-Receiver Principle implies that the consent is invalid if it is given to avoid this penalty. However, in other exploitation cases, the consent-receiver lacks a duty to improve the consent-giver's position in these ways. I have not been able to discover a principle that implies that consent is invalidated by exploitation in these cases. It may turn out that future research leads to the discovery of such a principle. But even if it does not, we can appeal to other moral considerations to explain why sexual exploitation is wrong. For example, we can hold that exploitation is wrong in general, and sexual exploitation is especially wrong in virtue of constituting sexual subordination.

Consent under Duress. Tom Dougherty, Oxford University Press. © Tom Dougherty 2024.
DOI: 10.1093/9780198922360.003.0005

PART 2
DEGREES OF DURESS

In Part 2, we consider the moral significance of the fact that duress comes in degrees of severity. The draft of the Consent-Receiver Principle from Part 1 is not sensitive to these degrees. Roughly, the draft states that someone's consent is not valid when they are subject to illegitimate duress. Since this duress could be minor, the principle allows that minor duress can invalidate consent.

This means that the principle faces a challenge, which I discuss in Chapter 4. It seems that when consent is given under minor duress, it still has some sort of moral effect. We can illustrate this by comparing two cases:

> *Anger.* Cameron attempts to initiate sex, implicitly threatening to behave angrily if Morgan refuses. To avoid an angry outburst from Cameron, Morgan agrees, and they have sex.
>
> *Refusal.* Cameron attempts to initiate sex once more, and again Morgan declines. Frustrated, Cameron concludes that by this point they are entitled to sex and Morgan would enjoy sex once begun. Cameron uses physical force to have sex with Morgan.

In the *Refusal* case, Morgan's consent is absent, and so Cameron gravely wrongs them by raping them. However, in the *Anger* case, Morgan's consent is present but given under minor duress. While Cameron wrongs Morgan in the *Anger* case, this is not a wronging of the same magnitude as the one Cameron commits in the *Refusal* case. Therefore, it seems that Morgan's consent is having a moral effect. I call the problem of explaining what this effect is the "Problem of Minor Duress." I argue that we must take the problem seriously and that we cannot provide a satisfactorily general explanation of why the relevant misconduct is less gravely wrong by appealing to phenomena besides consent. In addition, I argue that we should not try to solve the problem by placing a threshold restriction on the Consent-Receiver Principle—a restriction that would have the consequence that the principle would imply that consent is invalidated by duress that meets or exceeds a threshold of severity.

In Chapter 5, I present my solution to the Problem of Minor Duress. I distinguish two ways that an agent can fail to be guided by consent that an individual gives in a sufficiently good position to give consent. First, the agent can act without the individual's consent. This is a very grave wronging in the case of sexual consent. When the individual's consent is given under minor duress, the consent's presence at least means that the agent does not wrong the individual in this way. Second, the agent can act on the basis of consent that the individual has given in response to illegitimate duress from the consent-receiver. The fact that the duress is minor does not prevent the agent from wronging the individual in this way. However, the minor nature of the duress does reduce the gravity of the wronging. Thus, the presence of consent under minor duress reduces the overall gravity of the consent-receiver's misconduct, even though it does not imply that the consent-receiver avoids misconduct altogether. I call this an "ameliorative effect" of the consent.

Once we recognize that consent can have an ameliorative effect, we should accept what I call the "Ameliorative View" of consent, which I develop in Chapter 6. This view posits three categories of consent. First, there is fully valid consent to an action, which releases the consent-receiver from their duty not to perform the action. Second, there is fully invalid consent to an action, which has no effect at all: it remains just as gravely wrong for the consent-receiver to perform the action. Third, there is partially valid consent to an action, which has an ameliorative effect: it is now less gravely wrongful for the consent-receiver to perform the action. Partial validity comes in degrees, which determine the size of the ameliorative effect. And the degree of partial validity is also explained by scalar phenomena: in the case of duress, it is explained by the severity of the duress. I argue that the Ameliorative View is helpful for theorizing sexual misconduct, as it provides us with a tool to recognize a spectrum of misconduct that varies in its gravity. Finally, I argue that once we accept the Ameliorative View, we should revise our earlier draft of the Consent-Receiver Principle, so that it states a sufficient condition for consent that is not fully valid.

4
The Problem of Minor Duress

In Part 1, I defended a draft of a principle concerning how consent is undermined by duress from the consent-receiver. Roughly, the Consent-Receiver Principle states that someone's consent is invalid when they consent in order to avoid a penalty and they have a legitimate complaint against the consent-receiver imposing this penalty.

When we apply the Consent-Receiver Principle to sexual consent, it leads to an expansive view of sexual misconduct. This is because the principle is not restricted to complaints against egregious forms of coercion like violent threats. It also applies to complaints against less severe coercion, such as someone's threat to behave angrily toward their partner for refusing sex.

This implication leads to a problem, which I will illustrate by considering a pair of cases that continue the following narrative:

> *Background.* Cameron and Morgan have been dating. They have not had sex because Morgan has reservations about Cameron. However, Morgan also second-guesses themselves, wondering whether they should be more accepting of Cameron's flaws. On several occasions, Cameron has attempted to initiate sex. At first, Cameron was disappointed but took Morgan's refusal with fairly good grace. But in response to each subsequent refusal, Cameron has become increasingly angry with Morgan.

The first case continues the *Background* narrative as follows:

> *Anger.* Cameron attempts to initiate sex, implicitly threatening to behave angrily if Morgan refuses. To avoid an angry outburst from Cameron, Morgan agrees, and they have sex.

In this continuation, I am assuming that an angry reprisal would have only a moderate effect on Morgan, noting that in certain contexts, expressions of anger can constitute emotional abuse comparable to physical violence (Walker 1979, xv). Plausibly, Morgan has a complaint against Cameron imposing an angry reprisal on their withholding consent. Because Morgan has sex to avoid this reprisal, the Consent-Receiver Principle implies that Cameron has wronged Morgan by having sex without their valid consent.

Now it is typically thought that someone commits a very grave wrong by having sex without someone's valid consent. Roughly, it is thought that this is in the same moral ballpark as forcible rape—i.e., rape in which there is no issue of consent because the perpetrator simply overpowers their victim with brute force. But most people's intuitions will be that in the *Anger* case, Cameron does not commit a wrong that is in the same moral ballpark as forcible rape. To see this, let us compare *Anger* with the following continuation of the *Background* narrative:

> *Refusal.* Cameron attempts to initiate sex once more, and again Morgan declines. Frustrated, Cameron concludes that by this point they are entitled to sex and Morgan would enjoy sex once begun. Cameron uses physical force to have sex with Morgan.

By committing rape, Cameron wrongs Morgan more gravely in the *Refusal* case than they do in the *Anger* case. This is explained by the fact that Morgan does not consent in the *Refusal* case but does consent in the *Anger* case. Consequently, Morgan's consent is having a moral effect in the *Anger* case.

This creates a theoretical problem, which I will call the "Problem of Minor Duress." This is the problem of explaining how consent has a moral effect when obtained via minor duress. While all theories of consent have to provide a solution, the problem is particularly acute for our draft of the Consent-Receiver Principle, since it implies that Cameron does not give valid consent in the *Anger* case.

I will discuss this problem in this Chapter and in Chapter 5. In this Chapter, I will explain why we should not just bite the bullet and accept that consent is morally inefficacious when obtained via minor duress (Section 4.1). Then I will motivate and critique a potential solution to the problem—the Threshold Solution (Section 4.2). This solution holds that duress invalidates consent only when it reaches a threshold of severity.

4.1 Why We Should Take Seriously the Problem of Minor Duress

Before we consider solutions to the Problem of Minor Duress, let us see why an advocate of the Consent-Receiver Principle should not bite the bullet and concede that Morgan's consent is morally inefficacious in the *Anger* case. Insofar as we have the intuition that Morgan's consent makes a moral difference, this bullet-biting response means that the Consent-Receiver Principle comes with a theoretical cost that would have to be weighed against the principle's benefits. To mitigate the size of this cost, an advocate of the Consent-Receiver Principle might argue that our theory can at least recognize another important moral difference between these cases. For example, on natural assumptions, Morgan would suffer more harm in the *Refusal* case than in the *Anger* case. On the grounds that harm aggravates sexual misconduct, this would explain why Cameron wrongs Morgan more gravely in the *Refusal* case than in the *Anger* case.

This argument relies on a true premise: harm does aggravate sexual misconduct (Gardner and Shute 2000; Archard 2007; Dougherty 2013, 727; Tadros 2016, 255–6). Indeed, there are many types of harm that can aggravate it (Archard 2007; Whisnant 2017). These include experiential harm, psychological harm (Brison 2002), and social harm (Foa 1998, 586). These points make a theory containing the Consent-Receiver Principle more attractive, as we now have extra resources with which to draw moral distinctions within the principle's expansive class of sexual misconduct.

However, these resources will not help with the Problem of Minor Duress because even in the absence of aggravating harms, sex without any consent is gravely wrong. This can be exemplified by misconduct against an unconscious victim (Gardner and Shute 2000, 198). Consider a third continuation of the *Background* narrative:

> *Drug*. Cameron attempts to initiate sex once more, and again Morgan declines. Frustrated, Cameron puts a drug in Morgan's drink that leaves Morgan unconscious. While Morgan is unconscious, Cameron engages in sexual activity with Morgan. Morgan never discovers the sexual activity, and it causes no other effects.

In the *Drug* case, Cameron rapes Morgan and hence wrongs Morgan more gravely than in the *Anger* case. The difference in the gravity of the wronging cannot be explained by harm. Instead, the most plausible explanation concerns the fact that Morgan consents in the *Anger* case but does not consent in the *Drug* case.

Could we explain the difference between the cases by adopting a moralized conception of harm, such that someone is harmed simply in virtue of being mistreated? Along these lines, Jean Hampton (2001, 135) argues that a rape victim suffers a "moral injury." Hampton's idea is that an action causes a moral injury when the action is an affront to the victim's value or dignity. Similarly, Marilyn Frye and Carolyn Shafer (1977, 341–2) claim that the victim suffers an "expressive harm" in virtue of being subject to sexual misconduct: the victim is treated in a degrading way that expresses that their interests and claims do not matter. If we adopt these conceptions of harm, then we should allow that the *Anger* case and the *Refusal* case differ in this respect: Morgan suffers more moralized harm in the *Refusal* case than the *Anger* case.

But this difference cannot explain why Cameron's misconduct is worse in the *Refusal* case than the *Anger* case. Since a moral injury or expressive harm arises only in the context of conduct that is independently wrong, it would be circular to posit this harm as the ground of the independent wrongfulness of this conduct (Berkich 2009, 388). Consequently, moral injury or expressive harm could not be the fundamental explanation of the difference between the *Refusal* case and the *Anger* case.

Just as we make little progress toward mitigating the intuitive cost of the bullet-biting response by appealing to harm as an aggravating factor, we also make little progress by appealing to a victim's desires (Tadros 2016, 259; Brown 2020). On a natural reading of the cases, we might expect that Morgan has a stronger desire to avoid the encounter in the *Refusal* case than the encounter in the *Anger* case. But even if we hold fixed the strength of Morgan's desires across both cases, Cameron would still wrong Morgan more gravely in the *Refusal* case than the *Anger* case.

Similarly, we do not make progress by claiming that the use of force or drugging is an aggravating factor for sexual misconduct. This claim is advanced by Jed Rubenfeld (2013), who proposes that we theorize sexual offenses in terms of force rather than the absence of valid consent.[1] We can see both why Rubenfeld's approach will not provide a viable alternative to a consent-based approach and why an appeal to force cannot help with the Problem of Minor Duress by considering sexual offenses against passive victims. We can imagine a version of the *Refusal* case in which Morgan does not consent and remains immobile and a version of the *Anger* case in which Morgan remains immobile while consenting because of Cameron's threat.

[1] The response that I offer to Rubenfeld also applies to Scott Anderson's (2016) proposal that rape should not be defined by either the presence of force or the absence of valid consent but instead should be defined as "coerced sex." Anderson's (2017, 77) proposal is premised on a non-standard definition of coercion as involving "certain ways of using a kind of relative power generated and deployable by some agents, namely, the ability to overpower another or broadly inhibit her actions."

In both cases, we can imagine that Cameron's physical behavior is the same and hence equally forceful. With those assumptions, Cameron still wrongs Morgan more gravely in the *Refusal* case than in the *Anger* case, and this must be explained by the presence of Morgan's consent in the latter case.

4.2 The Threshold Solution

Since the bullet-biting response to the Problem of Minor Duress comes with an intuitive cost, it should be the option of last resort for an advocate of the Consent-Receiver Principle. In this Section and the next Chapter, I will consider potential solutions to the problem. Each aims to explain why Morgan's consent has a moral effect in the *Anger* case.

In this Section, I will discuss a solution that introduces a "Threshold Restriction" to the application of the Consent-Receiver Principle as follows: someone gives invalid consent in response to duress from the consent-receiver only if the duress has reached a threshold of severity. Assuming that threats of violence exceed this threshold, the resulting view allows that a perpetrator commits rape by threatening someone with a knife. But if this threshold is not reached by threats of angry reprisals, then the Threshold Restriction prevents the Consent-Receiver Principle from implying that Morgan's consent is invalid in the *Anger* case. If Morgan's consent is valid, then it would have a moral effect. I call this the "Threshold Solution."

While the Threshold Solution implies that in the *Anger* case Cameron does not commit sexual misconduct in virtue of failing to receive valid consent from Morgan, a proponent of the solution can say that Cameron wrongs Morgan in another respect. For example, they can say that Cameron wrongs Morgan in virtue of setting back Morgan's interest in avoiding unwanted sex. Similarly, they can say that Cameron is "barred from profiting from [their] own wrongs" and that by having sex with Morgan, Cameron would be profiting from their previous wrong of issuing a threat to react angrily (Ferzan 2018, 981–8).

The Threshold Restriction has been supported by two arguments that scholars have made in service of their goal of demarcating rape as an especially grave form of sexual misconduct. The first argument has been offered by Heidi Hurd and Kimberly Ferzan. For brevity, I focus primarily on Hurd's presentation of the argument. Hurd (1996, 138–45) argues that the conditions for morally transformative consent mirror the conditions for culpability for wrongdoing. For consent to possess the moral "magic that transforms the moral obligations of others," Hurd (1996, 138–40)

> requires the [consent-giver] to be free of those constraints on autonomy that, if present in the case of the defendant, would legitimately result in an excuse. According to [this] thesis, the conditions under which a [consent-giver's] exercise of will alters the morality of another's actions are identical to the conditions under which a defendant is fully responsible for bad actions.

Hurd's thought is that underlying both morally efficacious consent and culpability is a unitary conception of responsible agency.[2] Now, with respect to wrongdoing, minor coercion does not exculpate. For example, you are not exculpated from shoplifting on the grounds that a bully was otherwise threatening to pinch you. Since coercion must reach a threshold of severity to exculpate someone from wrongdoing, Hurd concludes that coercion must meet the same threshold to prevent consent from being morally transformative. Arguing along parallel lines, Ferzan (2018, 974) reaches the conclusion that someone's consent is not vitiated by a threat that would be resisted by a "person of ordinary firmness."

The second argument is Conly's (2004, 106), who claims that a threat is coercive only when it is a threat to impose harm that is sufficiently great that the victim has no reasonable option other than to comply:

> For a choice to be coerced…it is necessary that the person doing the choosing has no reasonable choice between doing what the coercer wants and the bad option which the coercer has introduced. Not every threat constitutes coercion, because some threats don't introduce harms great enough to affect my decision procedure. My neighbor can't say he was coerced into supporting my bid for election because I told him I would make terribly unfriendly faces at him if he didn't do so; while I shouldn't be making faces at people who don't support me, it's not so bad that he can claim that he had no other option than to vote my way.

For example, Conly (2004, 106–7) claims that a threat of a pinch "would probably not count as coercive, because being pinched is a reasonable option to choose over having sex with someone you don't want to have sex

[2] This thought is shared by H. L. A. Hart (1968).

with." To flesh this out, we need to know what makes an option "reasonable." Conly does not give us an explicit account of this, but their discussion does rule out one possible interpretation. For Conly's purposes, a threat cannot make the option of non-compliance unreasonable simply in virtue of the victim having a moral objection to the threat. Otherwise, we have not fended off the results that Conly aims to avoid—namely, that someone can be coerced by a threat of an unfriendly face or a pinch.

Hurd and Conly are right to claim that a perpetrator's coercion must reach a degree of severity in order for them to commit rape. In Chapter 5, I will put forward a solution that accommodates this point. But while I agree with Hurd's and Conly's theoretical goal, I disagree with the arguments that they offer as means to this goal. These arguments are overly broad.

Let us start with Conly's argument. Conly runs together two claims that we should distinguish. First, Conly (2004, 106) claims that consent would not be invalidated by a threat that does not "affect [a consent-giver's] decision-procedure." I agree with this claim, and it is consistent with the Consent-Receiver Principle, which states that consent is not valid when the consent is *caused* by a certain type of duress. But requiring this causal connection does not impose any necessary constraint on the severity of duress that invalidates consent. This constraint comes from Conly's second claim, which is that a threat is coercive only when it is unreasonable for the victim to choose non-compliance. I deny this claim. Consider:

> *Windows*. Thug threatens to paint graffiti on Shopkeeper's window unless they let the thug take a television. The cost of removing graffiti is the same as the cost of the television. Consequently, the Shopkeeper is indifferent about whether to let Thug take the television. Shopkeeper arbitrarily breaks the tie in favor of letting Thug take the television.

Since Shopkeeper is indifferent between complying with the threat and resisting it, it would be reasonable for them to refuse to comply. Still, their consent is not valid because the consent is given in response to the threat. Thug is presenting Shopkeeper with a choice between being wronged in one way or another. Shopkeeper's choice of one wronging over the other does not prevent them from being wronged by the option that they choose.

This case also helps us see why we should reject Hurd's view that a unitary conception of responsible agency underlies both culpability for wrongdoing and the validity of consent. Suppose that Thug's behavior is explained by the fact that a bigger menace threatened to paint graffiti on Thug's windows. The menace's threat does not exculpate Thug from wrongdoing. All the same, Shopkeeper does not give valid consent to Thug taking the television. Therefore, it is a mistake to claim that a threat prevents consent from being valid only if the threat would also exculpate someone for wrongdoing. Thus, we should not hold that "the conditions under which a [consent-giver's] exercise of will alters the morality of another's actions are identical to the conditions under which a defendant is fully responsible for bad actions" (Hurd 1996, 140).

Moreover, in the *Windows* case, Thug's threat does not need to reach a threshold of severity to invalidate Shopkeeper's consent to letting Thug take the television. It is sufficient that the threat is wrongful.[3] Any unacceptable threat will invalidate the consent, regardless of how severe the threat is. In this key respect, consent differs from excuses. This is because the excusatory force of duress does depend partly on what is being excused. Let us assume for the sake of argument that someone has an excuse when they are subject to duress.[4] For example, if a villain threatens to punch you in the face unless you steal a pen, then this duress would plausibly provide you with an excuse if you stole the pen. But if the villain threatens to punch you in the face unless you steal a retiree's life savings, then this duress would not plausibly provide you with an excuse for doing so. Thus, excuses and consent operate in dissimilar ways, and so we should deny that there is a unitary notion of responsibility underlying both consent and exculpation.

Finally, the *Windows* case also undermines the strategy of solving the Problem of Minor Duress by imposing the Threshold Restriction on the application of the Consent-Receiver Principle. Shopkeeper gives consent because they are subject to a relatively minor form of duress: vandalized windows. Yet the ensuing consent is not valid in the sense that it does not preclude Thug from wronging Shopkeeper by taking the television. The Consent-Receiver Principle explains this: because the threat of vandalism constitutes mistreatment, Shopkeeper's consent is not valid. However, the Consent-Receiver Principle cannot provide this explanation if the Threshold Restriction limits the application of the principle.

[3] Or to put the point more precisely, and in the language of the Consent-Receiver Principle, it is sufficient that Shopkeeper has a legitimate complaint against Thug making the threat, in light of how the threat changes Shopkeeper's incentives.

[4] I have challenged this assumption in Chapter 1.

4.3 Summary

In this Chapter, I have introduced the Problem of Minor Duress. This is the problem of identifying the difference made by consent given under minor duress. The problem can be illustrated by comparing two versions of a case. In the first version, an agent has sex with another person while entirely lacking their consent. In the second version, the agent has obtained the other person's consent by subjecting them to minor duress by threatening to behave angrily in response to sexual refusal. Since there is a clear difference concerning how we should evaluate the agent's conduct, it seems that the consent is making a moral difference. The problem is to explain this difference—an especially pressing task for adherents of the Consent-Receiver Principle, which implies that consent is invalidated by all types of illegitimate duress.

There are ways to sidestep the problem: rather than appealing to the difference made by the consent, we could instead appeal to other moral considerations, such as harm to the victim, the frustration of the victim's desires, or the use of force against the victim. I argued that we cannot get a sufficiently general explanation by appealing to these considerations, and so I concluded that we should take the Problem of Minor Duress seriously.

Then I argued against the "Threshold Solution." According to this solution, we should place a restriction on the Consent-Receiver Principle by further requiring that the duress invalidates consent only when it exceeds a certain threshold of severity. On the assumption that the minor duress of a threat of angry behavior falls below this threshold, we would have a straightforward explanation of why the consent has a moral effect: the consent is morally valid and hence releases the consent-receiver from their duty not to have sex. I argued that this solution has the wrong implications for nonsexual cases and that it comes with an unwanted cost: it stops the Consent-Receiver Principle from explaining why certain instances of consent are invalid when given under duress.

Consent under Duress. Tom Dougherty, Oxford University Press. © Tom Dougherty 2024.
DOI: 10.1093/9780198922360.003.0006

5

The Constraint Solution to the Problem of Minor Duress

In Chapter 4, we introduced the Problem of Minor Duress—the problem of identifying the difference made by consent given under minor duress. In this Chapter and in Chapter 6, I will argue that under minor duress consent can have an ameliorative effect: the consent turns an action of the consent-receiver into a less grave wronging than it would otherwise be. This idea allows us to distinguish the following cases from Chapter 4:

> *Anger.* Cameron attempts to initiate sex again, implicitly threatening to behave angrily again if Morgan refuses. To avoid an angry outburst from Cameron, Morgan agrees, and they have sex.
>
> *Refusal.* Cameron attempts to initiate sex once more, and again Morgan declines. Frustrated, Cameron concludes that by this point they are entitled to sex and Morgan would enjoy sex once begun. Cameron uses physical force to have sex with Morgan.

On the grounds that Morgan's consent has an ameliorative effect in the *Anger* case, we can say that Cameron does not wrong Morgan as gravely in the *Anger* case as they do in the *Refusal* case.

It is easy to set out that key idea in simple terms. What is difficult—or at least what I have found difficult—is getting the details of that idea right and independently motivating it. To motivate this idea, I will defend the Constraint Solution to the Problem of Minor Duress in this Chapter. This solution involves pinpointing what Cameron must do to avoid wronging Morgan: Cameron must be guided by the choice that Morgan gives in a sufficiently good position to give consent. There are two ways that Cameron can fail to do so. First, Cameron can act without Morgan's consent. Second, Cameron can act on consent that Morgan gives because they are in an insufficiently favorable position to give consent. I will argue that when consent is given in response to minor duress, the consent precludes Cameron from wronging Morgan in the first way, which is an especially grave wronging. But the consent does not preclude Cameron from wronging Morgan in the second way.

This Chapter is organized as follows. In Section 5.1, I motivate and critique another potential solution—the Stance Solution. This holds that consent under minor duress is morally effective in virtue of changing the consent-giver's stance on how much they mind the consent-receiver's action. In Section 5.2, I argue for the Constraint Solution.

5.1 The Stance Solution to the Problem of Minor Duress

In Chapter 4, we considered the Threshold Solution. This solution came unstuck because it implies that if consent is given under minor duress, then it precludes an agent from wronging the consent-giver in virtue of acting within their personal domain. This is the normative effect of eliminating a wronging. Our two remaining solutions employ the claim that the consent has a different moral effect: the consent makes it the case that the agent *less gravely* wrongs the victim by acting within the consent-giver's domain. I call this an "ameliorative effect." The claim that consent can have an ameliorative effect is novel, but we cannot help ourselves to this claim for free. Instead, we need to develop explanatory foundations for this claim.

The first foundation starts by focusing on what an individual says about how much they mind certain mistreatment. This can be prospectively significant for an agent who is choosing between various options, one of which involves mistreating that individual. Suppose that you tell your friend that you will be late to meet them. If they do not mind, then you could relax and take your time. If they mind a little, then you should hurry; if they mind a great deal, then you better hurry even more. Alternatively, suppose that you ask a friend whether they mind if you go on a date with their ex. In the absence of their blessing, how much they mind would bear on the strength of the countervailing considerations that would justify you in pursuing the romantic interest. Minding is also retrospectively significant: it can determine the size of a victim's grievance and hence what atonement is needed from the agent.

I assume that minding is a so-called reactive attitude toward another person's action (Strawson 1962). Since this makes minding a mental phenomenon, we cannot directly appeal to minding to solve the Problem of Minor Duress. We encountered the reason why in Chapter 4 when considering whether the difference between the *Anger* case and the *Refusal* case could be explained by appealing to Morgan's desires: even if we stipulate that Morgan has the same mental states in these cases, there is still a moral difference in the gravity of Cameron's misconduct. However, a separate moral difference is made by the stance that people take in virtue of communicating how much they mind another person's action. This stance can come apart from their mental states. For example, your friend might judge that they are being unreasonably jealous and so tell you that they mind you dating their ex only a little. This stance would be normatively significant insofar as you can appeal to this stance when attempting to justify your behavior to your friend.

How is someone's stance related to consent? If your friend says that they do not mind you dating their ex, then it is tempting to say that your friend thereby gives you consent. However, consent is traditionally conceived of as a *binary* normative power to determine whether an agent wrongs the consent-giver by acting in their personal domain. By contrast, minding is *scalar*—one minds actions to varying degrees. Since someone's stance represents their minding, this stance can consequently be thought of as a scalar phenomenon. What should we conclude from the fact that minding is scalar while the traditional conception of consent is binary? Well, we may just conclude that the traditional binary conception is overly narrow and that consent can also determine one's stance concerning how much one minds mistreatment. Consider the *Anger* case. We might think that in virtue of consenting, Morgan is taking the stance that they mind the sex less than the anger. If this limits how gravely Cameron wrongs Morgan, then Morgan's consent is having an ameliorative effect. I call this the "Stance Solution."

I find it plausible that sometimes a victim's stance affects the gravity of the mistreatment that they suffer. In particular, this is plausible in the case of minor mistreatment, such as being made to wait for a friend. However, there are two reasons why we should be unsatisfied with appealing to a victim's stance to solve the Problem of Minor Duress. The first reason is that for serious sexual misconduct, there is a limit to how much of an ameliorative effect, if any, can be made by a victim's stance. Consider the *Refusal* case. If Morgan takes no stance, then Cameron wrongs Morgan especially gravely. To express this point, let us say that in the *Refusal* case Cameron's misconduct is "stance-independently" especially grave. Because Cameron's misconduct is stance-independently especially grave, Morgan's stance would not significantly affect how gravely Cameron wrongs Morgan: in the logically possible scenario that Morgan takes the stance that they do not mind the mistreatment, Cameron still wrongs Morgan especially gravely. Therefore, Morgan's stance would have a significant ameliorative effect only on misconduct that is not stance-independently especially grave. However, we would now need an explanation of why Cameron's misconduct in the *Anger* case is not stance-independently especially grave. This explanation would amount to an independent solution to the Problem of Minor Duress—a solution that is not provided by appealing to Morgan's stance.

The second reason why we should be dissatisfied with the Stance Solution is that there are scenarios in which a victim's stance is morally insignificant. For example, a victim might take the stance that they do not mind mistreatment as part of a coping mechanism for surviving an abusive relationship or coerced employment in sex work. Alternatively, a victim's stance could result from false normative beliefs. For example, they could be gaslit by a perpetrator into thinking that they have not been mistreated; they might believe that their marriage vows ceded all their sexual rights; or they might believe that sexual misconduct is less grave when committed by an intimate partner. These false beliefs could be individual errors or part of a more systematic ideology that normalizes sexual domination (Haslanger 2012, 406–28, 446–77; Hänel 2018; Manne 2018, 78–132). If these factors explain why a victim takes a lenient stance, then these factors disable the ameliorative effect of the stance. Therefore, we cannot appeal to Morgan's stance to explain the moral difference between versions of the *Anger* case and the *Refusal* case in which these disabling factors are present. But even if these disabling conditions are present in versions of both cases, Cameron would still wrong Morgan more gravely in the *Refusal* case than in the *Anger* case. Since this difference cannot be explained by Morgan's stance, appealing to this stance cannot provide us with a sufficiently general solution to the Problem of Minor Duress.

5.2 The Constraint Solution

This brings us to what I take to be the correct solution to the Problem of Minor Duress. Like the Stance Solution, this appeals to the idea that in the *Anger* case Morgan's consent has an ameliorative effect: the consent makes it the case that Cameron wrongs Morgan less gravely. The solution explains this effect in terms of the threat of anger wrongfully constraining Morgan's freedom only to a minor degree. I call this the "Constraint Solution."

The Constraint Solution focuses on how the constraints on a victim's freedom bear on the ways that a perpetrator wrongs them. To develop this solution, let us review why another person's choice is morally significant. Often, when an agent interacts with another individual, the agent must consider the choices that the individual makes and expresses. This includes the agent's need to obtain the individual's permissive consent—the consent that licenses the agent to act in the individual's personal domain. As we noted in Chapter 2, the moral significance of an individual's expressed choice for an agent depends on whether the agent has discharged their duties to put the individual in a sufficiently good position for making the choice. In Chapter 2, we introduced the following principle:

> Facilitative Duty Principle. If Y's expressed choice is explained by X's failure to discharge their duties to put Y in a sufficiently good position for making and expressing this choice, then X cannot appeal to this expressed choice in order to justify interfering with Y's personal domain.

When introducing this principle, I noted that there are two ways that an agent can breach a facilitative duty to put an individual in a sufficiently good position for making and expressing a choice: either the agent breaches a duty to improve the individual's position, or the agent breaches a duty not to worsen the individual's position. And we noted that there are various ways that a consent-receiver may fail to put the consent-giver in a sufficiently good position for making and expressing their choice. The consent-receiver might incapacitate the consent-giver. The consent-receiver might fail to disclose pertinent information to the consent-giver. And the consent-receiver may subject the consent-giver to illegitimate duress. Thus, if an agent needs to appeal to an individual's expressed choice to justify their behavior, then the agent must be guided by a choice that the individual makes and expresses in a sufficiently good position. Here, a "sufficiently good" position should be understood as the position that the individual would be in as a result of the agent discharging their facilitative duties. Since it will quickly become cumbersome to talk in those fully explicit terms, I will simply talk of a "sufficiently good" position.

How gravely would the agent wrong the individual by failing to be guided by a choice that the individual makes and expresses in a sufficiently good position? This depends on what the failure consists in. Suppose that the failure consists in the fact that the individual did not discharge their duties to put the individual in a sufficiently good position for making their choice. These duties include a duty not to subject the individual to illegitimate duress. Now, duress comes in degrees, and so the agent can fall short of discharging this duty to varying degrees, according to the severity of the duress to which the agent subjects the individual. To the extent that the agent has subjected the individual to illegitimate duress, and the agent acts on the basis of the individual's choice, the agent falls further short of satisfying the individual's claim that the agent be guided by the choice that they make and express in a sufficiently good position.

To the extent that the agent falls short of satisfying the claim, the agent more gravely wrongs the individual. We see this pattern elsewhere in ethics. If a friend has a claim on you that you meet them for lunch at noon, then you fall further short of satisfying this claim and hence wrong them more gravely by arriving an hour late than by arriving fifteen minutes late. If a wedding invite specifies that men must wear black tie, then a man falls further short of satisfying the claim of the bride and groom by attending wearing an open-collared shirt than he would by wearing a dark gray suit and tie. Of course, there are differences between those cases and cases in which an individual's claim is that the agent be guided by a choice that they make and express in a position that is suitably improved by the agent's discharge of their facilitative duties. But the cases are alike in the respect that coming closer to satisfying someone's claim mitigates the grievance that they have. As such, all else equal, coming close to satisfying this claim is a less grave wronging than falling short of satisfying the claim by a considerable distance.

Applying this reasoning to an individual's claim that an agent is guided by the choices that they make and express in a sufficiently good position, the agent can come closer to or move further from satisfying this claim according to how far the agent has fallen short of putting the individual in a sufficiently good position for making their choice. To the extent that the agent has fallen short in this respect, the agent more gravely wrongs the individual by acting on their choice. Consider the following case:

> *Violence*. Cameron attempts to initiate sex once more, and again Morgan declines. Frustrated, Cameron threatens Morgan with physical violence unless Morgan agrees. Morgan agrees.

In the *Violence* case, Morgan is significantly more constrained by Cameron's duress than in the *Anger* case:

Anger. Cameron attempts to initiate sex again, implicitly threatening to behave angrily again if Morgan refuses. To avoid an angry outburst from Cameron, Morgan agrees, and they have sex.

Therefore, Morgan consents in *Violence* because they are in a significantly worse position than in the *Anger* case. Because this position is significantly worse, Cameron falls further short of satisfying Morgan's claim that Cameron be guided by the choices that Morgan makes and expresses in a sufficiently good position. In light of this, Cameron wrongs Morgan significantly more gravely in the *Violence* case than in the *Anger* case.

Now consider the *Refusal* case:

Refusal. Cameron attempts to initiate sex once more, and again Morgan declines. Frustrated, Cameron concludes that by this point they are entitled to sex and Morgan would enjoy sex once begun. Cameron uses physical force to have sex with Morgan.

In the *Refusal* case, Cameron fails to be guided by a choice that Morgan makes and expresses in a sufficiently good position. But this is not because Cameron has failed to put Morgan in a sufficiently good position for making and expressing this choice. Instead, it is because Morgan has paid no regard to what choice, if any, Cameron makes and expresses. Since this causally insulates Cameron's behavior from Morgan's decision-making, it means that Cameron has fallen an extremely long way short of satisfying Morgan's claim that Cameron be guided by the choice that Morgan makes and expresses in a sufficiently good position. Because Cameron falls so short, Cameron wrongs Morgan especially gravely. Indeed, this wronging is approximately as grave as the wronging in the *Violence* case. I say "approximately as grave" because the wrongings differ in morally relevant respects. In the *Violence* case, Cameron makes Morgan's capacity for choice an instrument in Morgan's own violation, and fear of physical violence can have a distinctive damaging effect. Meanwhile, in the *Refusal* case, Cameron treats Morgan like a physical object in the respect that Cameron lays hands on Morgan while ignoring the choices that Morgan makes. For our purposes, we need not determine how these differences compare. It is enough to say that the wrongings are approximately as grave as each other.

Putting these points together, we end up with the following comparison of the gravity of Cameron's misconduct in the *Refusal* case and the *Anger* case. Disregarding whether the individual makes a choice is an especially grave way to wrong them. Meanwhile, the gravity of an agent's acting on a choice that the individual makes and expresses in an insufficiently good position depends on how bad the individual's position is. There is a point at which the individual is in such a bad position that following this choice is comparably grave to disregarding whether the individual made a choice. That is what is going on in the *Violence* case, where Cameron's misconduct is comparably grave as Cameron's misconduct is in the *Refusal* case. Since Cameron wrongs Morgan significantly less gravely in the *Anger* case than in the *Violence* case, it follows that Cameron wrongs Morgan significantly less gravely in the *Anger* case than in the *Refusal* case.

So, what normative effect does Morgan's consent have in the *Anger* case? Morgan's consent makes it the case that Cameron does not disregard what choice, if any, Morgan makes and expresses. By contrast, in the *Refusal* case Cameron wrongs Morgan in this respect. However, in the *Anger* case Cameron does still wrong Morgan by failing to be guided by a choice that Morgan makes and expresses in a sufficiently good position for making this choice. But the gravity of this wronging is limited by the fact that Cameron constrains Morgan's freedom to only a minor degree. Because Cameron subjects Morgan to minor duress, Cameron comes closer to satisfying Morgan's claim that Cameron respects the choice that Morgan makes and expresses in a sufficiently good position than if Cameron subjected Morgan to severe duress. Therefore, the net result is that in the *Anger* case Morgan's consent does not prevent Cameron from wronging Morgan, but the consent's presence does have the normative effect of decreasing the gravity of this wronging. In other words, Morgan's consent has an ameliorative effect.

If a view implies that Morgan's choice is normatively efficacious during sexual misconduct, then it potentially faces the objection that the view amounts to victim-blaming, in the sense that the view makes a more lenient assessment of sexual misconduct because the victim is complicit in, or partly responsible for, what happens to them. Whether a view is undermined by this objection depends on the reason why the view says that a victim's choice is morally efficacious. The objection does not get a grip on the Constraint Solution because this solution makes no appeal to the idea that a victim is complicit in, or responsible for, what happens to them. Instead, the solution explains the normative efficacy of the choice by distinguishing two ways that a perpetrator can wrong a victim, one of which consists in disregarding altogether whether the victim consents. To say that a victim's choice precludes this wronging is not to say that the victim is in any way responsible for being wronged in another respect.

Similarly, the Constraint Solution does not imply that a victim's compliance with a minor threat constitutes a valuable expression of their autonomy. This contrasts with a view of Victor Tadros's (2016, 260–1). Tadros argues that a deliberator can value having extra options "because then the choice that she makes will be an expression of her autonomy. The act of selecting between options may, in itself, enhance the value of the option selected." For example, if one chooses an academic career from a range of career options, as opposed to being externally assigned an academic career, then one's pursuit of academia would be a valuable expression of one's autonomy. On the grounds that "in the case of serious threats, the alternative options are typically valueless," Tadros concludes that compliance with egregious coercion, such as that involved in the *Violence* case, is not a valuable expression of autonomy. However, Tadros (2016, 261) suggests that this

> may make a more significant difference in cases where the threat is much less grave. A person who has sex to prevent a much more trivial threat being executed might be more inclined to see the sex that she has as an expression of her autonomy than one who has sex to prevent a much more serious threat being executed.

I am unmoved by Tadros's assumption that an academic's career choice is sufficiently analogous to a victim's choice to suffer one wronging rather than another wronging. With the career choice, the academic is choosing between valuable options. It is plausible that extra value is added by their expressing their individuality over a range of valuable options. But it is not plausible that any value is created when a victim chooses to suffer one wronging rather than another. For example, consider two scenarios in which a wrongdoer will break either a victim's right leg or left leg. In the first scenario, the wrongdoer acts of their own accord and breaks the victim's right leg. In the second scenario, the wrongdoer gives the victim the choice of which leg will be broken, and the victim chooses their right leg. If we assume that every other detail of the cases is the same, then we should view the scenarios as morally equivalent, and we should deny that the latter case contains a valuable form of autonomy that the former case lacks. Similarly, when a victim chooses to comply because they are subject to a perpetrator's illegitimate duress, this compliance does not constitute a valuable form of autonomy.

5.3 Summary

In this Chapter, I have defended the Consent-Receiver Principle against the objection that the principle mistakenly implies that someone suffers a wrong comparable to forcible rape when they consent to sex under minor duress. My defense has been comprised of developing a solution to the Problem of Minor Duress—the problem of explaining how consent has a moral effect when obtained under minor duress.

To solve the Problem of Minor Duress, I have defended the Constraint Solution. This involved distinguishing different ways that an agent can fail to meet a victim's claim to be guided by consent that the victim gives in a sufficiently good position. First, an agent can act without the victim's consent. Second, an agent can act on consent that a victim gives because they are not in a sufficiently good position to decide whether to consent. (By this, I mean that the agent has failed to discharge either their duties to improve the victim's position or their duties not to worsen the victim's position.) I have argued that when consent is given because of minor duress, the consent precludes the agent from failing to meet the victim's claim in the first way. This is an especially grave wronging. However, the consent does not preclude the agent from failing to meet the victim's claim in the second way. I have further argued that the gravity of this wronging is limited by the fact that the duress is minor.

This solution allows us to offer the following analysis of the *Anger* case in which Morgan consents in response to Cameron's threat to behave angrily. We should say that Morgan's consent means that Cameron does not disregard whether Morgan has chosen to have sex. But the consent does not prevent Cameron from wronging Morgan in virtue of being guided by a choice that Morgan makes and expresses because Morgan is not in a sufficiently good position to give consent. Since the gravity of this wronging depends on the extent to which Cameron has failed to improve Morgan's position, the minor nature of the duress limits the gravity of the wronging—so much so that the wronging is less grave than the wronging Cameron commits in the *Refusal* case, in which they forcibly rape Morgan.

Consent under Duress. Tom Dougherty, Oxford University Press. © Tom Dougherty 2024.
DOI: 10.1093/9780198922360.003.0007

6
The Ameliorative View of Consent

In Chapter 5, I defended the Constraint Solution to the Problem of Minor Duress—the problem of explaining how consent has a moral effect when obtained under minor duress. The Constraint Solution combines two ideas. First, when consent is given because of minor duress, the consent precludes the agent from wronging the victim by acting without their consent, which is an especially grave wronging. Second, when given under minor duress, the consent does not preclude the agent from wronging the victim by acting on the consent that they give because they are not in a sufficiently good position to give consent. When the duress is minor, this is a less grave wronging than acting without the victim's consent. Consequently, the presence of the consent under minor duress has the effect that the agent wrongs the victim less gravely than they would in the absence of the consent.

The Constraint Solution leaves us with the following novel idea. When an individual gives consent to an agent's action, this consent can have two normative effects. The first is familiar. When all goes well, the consent can have the effect that the agent does not wrong the individual by performing the action. This is the effect of *eliminating* a wronging. The second effect is novel. Under certain conditions, such as minor duress, the individual's consent does not have the effect of eliminating the wronging, but it does have the effect that the agent would wrong the individual less gravely by performing the action than the agent would wrong the individual in the absence of the consent. This is the effect of *ameliorating* a wronging.[1]

In this Chapter, I will develop what I will call the "Ameliorative View of Consent." This recognizes three categories of consent: fully valid consent, partially valid consent, and fully invalid consent. With this new taxonomy, we should re-cast the Consent-Receiver Principle as stating a sufficient condition for when someone's consent is not fully valid, in the sense that the

[1] For completeness, I note the theoretical possibility that consent has an aggravating effect by increasing the gravity of the wronging. It is beyond the scope of this book to determine whether consent can have an aggravating effect. But if consent can have an aggravating effect, then we should generalize the Ameliorative View by adding a fourth category of consent defined in terms of this effect.

consent does not release the consent-receiver from a duty. As such, the principle leaves open whether the consent is partially valid or fully invalid. In other words, the principle leaves open whether the consent has an ameliorative effect or no normative effect at all.

6.1 The Details of the Ameliorative View

Accordingly, we arrive at an innovative tripartite view of consent's possible effects. Previously, the orthodoxy has been to categorize consent in terms of a binary of valid and invalid consent—categories that are defined in terms of consent's effects. I propose that we generalize this into the "Ameliorative View." This view posits three categories of consent, also defined in terms of what effects, if any, the consent has. Let us say that "fully valid consent" has the familiar effect of eliminating a wronging. Meanwhile, "fully invalid consent" has no normative effect: it neither eliminates a wronging nor ameliorates a wronging. Between the poles of fully valid and fully invalid consent, "partially valid consent" has an ameliorative effect. The category of partially valid consent is spectral in the respect that consent can be more or less partially valid: the degree to which the consent is partially valid consists in the size of the ameliorative effect. For example, below the threshold of severe duress that leads to fully invalid consent, there will be threats that vary with respect to how coercive they are. The degree of the severity of the duress would determine the degree to which the consent is partially valid, or equivalently, the size of the consent's ameliorative effect.

A brief terminological aside. I just stated the Ameliorative View using "consent" in such a way that it is possible that consent is not normatively efficacious. Other people prefer to use "consent" as a success term so that consent is necessarily normatively efficacious (Alexander 1996; Hurd 1996; Ferzan and Westen 2017). On that usage, we can formulate the Ameliorative View as positing three categories of "full consent," "partial consent," or "no consent," and we can describe the view as positing "degrees of consent" (Ferzan 2018, 1002–4). Nothing substantive turns on which terminology we use. From now on, I will continue to use "consent" in such a way that it is coherent to talk of normatively inefficacious consent. Consequently, I will frame the Ameliorative View as positing the categories of fully valid, partially valid, and fully invalid consent.

By adopting the Ameliorative View, we are not rejecting the binary framework as fundamentally misguided but instead embracing a generalization of that framework. To see why it is a generalization, note that we can translate claims made within the binary framework into the Ameliorative View without any loss of substance. Within the binary framework, "valid consent" is defined as the consent that has the effect that an agent does not wrong the consent-giver by acting in their personal domain. Since "fully valid consent" is also defined as having this effect, any substantive claim about valid consent can straightforwardly be translated into a claim about fully valid consent. The translation is more nuanced with respect to claims that have been made about "invalid consent." For this translation, we must work on a case-by-case basis. Sometimes, by talking of "invalid consent" a scholar may have substantively committed themselves to a claim about consent that is not fully valid. In this scenario, a claim about invalid consent should be translated as a claim about consent that is either partially valid or fully invalid. At other times, by talking of "invalid consent" a scholar may have substantively committed themselves to a claim about consent that has no moral effect at all. In this scenario, a claim about invalid consent should be translated as a claim about fully invalid consent. Finally, there may be occasions on which by talking of "invalid consent" a scholar has not substantively committed themselves either way. This scenario creates indeterminacy in translating between the binary framework and the Ameliorative View. But nothing hangs on this indeterminacy, given the absence of a substantive commitment. Therefore, by adopting the Ameliorative View, we can retain any substantive claim that a scholar has made within the binary framework. As such, replacing the binary framework with the Ameliorative View is incremental theoretical reform rather than revolution.

6.2 The Ameliorative View as a Resource for Theorizing Sexual Misconduct

Still, it is important reform, as the Ameliorative View provides us with a richer framework for drawing moral distinctions between instances of sexual misconduct.

For understandable reasons, theorists and (e.g., legal) practitioners have made it a priority to characterize rape and comparably serious sexual misconduct. But this should not be our only focus. A comprehensive treatment of sexual misconduct means taking seriously its less grave forms as well. In that spirit, Sarah Conly (2004, 210) makes the following call to arms:

> We need to expand our conceptual framework and our terminology so that we can capture greater differences than we typically do. There is a cultural tradition which has divided sexual intercourse into either morally unacceptable rape or morally acceptable nonrape. The truth is that there are many finer distinctions which we need to recognize and to which we need to develop a sensitivity.

Adequately developing this framework and terminology will require much more than any single innovation. Not least, this is because there are many ethical concepts that bear on misconduct—consent, harm, respect, and so on. Still, while the Ameliorative View is only one tool among many, I hope that it can help us understand some of the myriad ways that people exploit various dimensions of social power to influence and control others' sexual choices.

The main (though not exclusive) focus of this book is on duress that fits the model of threatening someone with illegitimate penalties for withholding consent. For this, the Ameliorative View allows us to draw distinctions between sexual encounters that arise from a wide range of coercive pressures that vary in their intensity. As well as the various forms of violent and nonviolent coercion in relationships, these pressures include improper solicitation of sex within institutional environments, particularly in the context of unequal relations of power and authority. One such paradigm is *quid pro quo* harassment in the workplace (Schulhofer 1998). This comes in multiple forms, and the Ameliorative View allows us to draw moral differences according to the severity of the duress that is used.

The Ameliorative View is also useful for understanding misconduct that lies beyond the scope of this book. For example, the Ameliorative View can help with theorizing sexual consent that is obtained either by deception or from people who fall below the threshold for the competence that is necessary for giving fully valid consent. Misinformation and incompetence come in degrees. The categories of partially valid consent and fully invalid consent are resources with which we can track the moral differences made by these degrees, while allowing that some ways of wrongfully obtaining consent are so egregious that the consent has no normative effect.

In addition, the Ameliorative View is helpful for theorizing illegitimate control that does not neatly fit the model of a threat to impose a penalty on someone for withholding consent. For example, a characteristic feature of domestic abuse is that perpetrators establish controlling relationships over their victims (Stark 2007; Johnson 2010, 13; Salzberger 2020). This control will commonly be established by abusive retaliation to noncompliance with a perpetrator's demands. However, once the controlling relationship is established, the control may not be reducible to threats of retaliation. Separately to disincentivizing noncompliance with a demand, a perpetrator may control their victim by undermining their agency and sense of self. The perpetrator would wrong their victim by exploiting these aspects of the controlling relationship, even when the victim complies with a command as such rather than as a result of instrumental reasoning aimed at avoiding retaliation. Plausibly, someone's agency can be undermined to varying degrees—from a minuscule amount to a debilitating amount—and it is possible for these degrees to vary across times. We should welcome a theoretical framework that allows us to acknowledge the moral significance of these degrees.

In promoting the Ameliorative View as a resource with which to understand sexual misconduct, I am not advocating for a lenient treatment of any particular instance of misconduct. Rather, I hope to be offering a theoretical tool for people who are confronted with sexual misconduct that they already recognize is not as grave as rape. There is a variety of reasons why it can be valuable to understand this type of misconduct. We should welcome resources that enable victims to understand their own experiences of misconduct and communicate these experiences to others—remedying the "hermeneutical injustice" that consists in lacking concepts for doing so (Fricker 2007). In addition, designers of institutional codes and laws need to know which concepts to use when defining offenses, and bystanders need to understand how to react to perpetrators of misconduct. The Ameliorative View widens our ability to gain this understanding while working with the tool of consent.

6.3 The Many Roads to the Ameliorative View

To investigate how the Ameliorative View can fit with different views, let us pinpoint the motivation for it.

The strongest argument for the Ameliorative View is taking seriously the Problem of Minor Duress while endorsing the Consent-Receiver Principle. The Problem of Minor Duress is the problem of explaining how consent has a moral effect when obtained via minor duress. Our running example involved Morgan consenting to sex to avoid angry behavior from their partner Cameron. We noted that Morgan's consent has some moral effect by comparing that sexual encounter with an encounter in which Morgan does not consent at all: the latter encounter involves a much more gravely wrong instance of sexual misconduct. The question then is: what effect does Morgan's consent have?

One answer is that the consent releases Cameron from their duty not to engage in sex. But that answer is foreclosed by accepting the Consent-Receiver Principle. Roughly, that principle implies that Morgan's consent does not release Cameron from their duty when Morgan consents to avoid a penalty and Morgan has a legitimate complaint against Cameron imposing this penalty on Morgan's withholding consent. Since Morgan does have a legitimate complaint against Cameron making an angry reprisal conditional on Morgan's refusing sex, this principle implies Morgan's consent does not release Cameron from their duty.

Putting the pieces together, the Problem of Minor Duress implies that Morgan's consent has some moral effect, while the Consent-Receiver Principle implies that this is not the effect of releasing Cameron from their duty not to have sex with them. This leaves us with the hypothesis that the consent has an ameliorative effect: the presence of Morgan's consent under minor duress means that Cameron wrongs Morgan less gravely than they would in the absence of the consent. And once we allow that consent can have an ameliorative effect, we will end up accepting the Ameliorative View.

I think that we should not be fully satisfied with the foregoing until we can explain why Morgan's consent has an ameliorative effect. As an explanation, I defended the Constraint Solution to the Problem of Minor Duress. At its heart is a distinction between two ways that an agent can wrong a victim. First, an agent can act without the victim's consent. When consent is given because of minor duress, the agent does not wrong the victim in this way, which would be an especially grave wronging. But there is a second way that an agent can wrong a victim: the agent can act on consent that a victim gives because they are not in a sufficiently good position to give consent. (They are not in a sufficiently good position because the agent has breached either a duty to improve this position or a duty not to worsen this position.) When consent is given because of minor duress, it does not preclude the agent from wronging the victim in this second way. I have further argued that the gravity of this wronging is limited by the fact that the duress is minor. Thus, when consent is given under minor duress, the consent's presence means that the agent wrongs the victim less gravely than they would in the absence of the consent. In other words, the consent has an ameliorative effect.

But while the Constraint Solution provides support for the Ameliorative View, it is not essential to it. This is because there are other roads to the Ameliorative View. Let us consider two.

First, in Chapter 5, we considered the idea that a victim's consent under minor duress could constitute their stance concerning how much they mind certain mistreatment. Specifically, we discussed the idea that a victim's stance could reduce the gravity of the mistreatment that they suffer. I argued that this idea had limited purchase in the case of sexual consent, and so we should not appeal to a victim's stance to solve the Problem of Minor Duress. However, I am sympathetic to this idea in other contexts, particularly when we are not dealing with sexual consent. This is significant because the Ameliorative View can be motivated by the existentially qualified claim that there are some cases in which a victim's consent constitutes their stance and this stance reduces the gravity of the mistreatment that they suffer. Since the reduction of this gravity would be an ameliorative effect, accepting the existentially qualified claim would lead us to the Ameliorative View.

Second, consider the view that duress diminishes someone's responsibility for their behavior.[2] We can develop the view so that it endorses the following:

> The severity of the duress bears on the degree to which the responsibility is diminished. In the case of severe duress, someone has such little responsibility for their behavior that they are unable to give fully valid consent. But under minor duress, someone's responsibility is only diminished in such a way that they give partially valid consent. That is, their consent has an ameliorative effect. The strength of this ameliorative effect varies with the severity of the duress. Which is to say, the severity of the duress determines how partially valid the consent is.

Similar points could be added to the nearby view that duress diminishes someone's voluntariness or the nearby view that duress diminishes someone's autonomy for giving consent. If we developed these views in this way, then they would provide a different way of arriving at the Ameliorative View of consent.[3]

[2] I owe this idea to David Owens, whose workshop commentary on this Chapter pointed out that this view could provide support for the Ameliorative View.

[3] I personally do not endorse these views as providing the underlying explanations of the relevant moral phenomena. As well as the criticisms that I have developed in Chapters 1 and 5,

I would not be surprised if there turned out to be other ways of motivating the Ameliorative View besides appealing to a victim's stance or a victim's responsibility. The Ameliorative View is in its infancy, and there is ample opportunity for future research to uncover additional support for it. But for now, I point to these two alternative motivations to clarify that if someone wishes to reject the Constraint Solution that I endorsed in Chapter 5, then this does not mean that they also have to reject the Ameliorative View. There are many roads to amelioration.

6.4 Revising the Consent-Receiver Principle

Once we accept the Ameliorative View, we need to make a small revision to our earlier draft of the Consent-Receiver Principle. This is because the draft specified a sufficient condition for consent being invalid as opposed to valid. However, once we replace the valid/invalid dichotomy with the tripartite taxonomy of fully valid/partially valid/fully invalid consent, we need to reformulate the principle in those terms. Fortunately, the revision is straightforward. We simply replace "not valid" with "not fully valid" and thereby arrive at the final draft of the principle:

> Consent-Receiver Principle. Under conditions of full information, X's consent to Y performing action A is not fully valid if:
>
> (i) Y will impose a penalty on X's withholding consent to A;
> (ii) the prospect of this penalty causes X to consent to A;
> (iii) X has a legitimate complaint against Y conditioning this penalty on X's withholding consent; and
> (iv) this complaint concerns the way that the penalty alters X's incentives for withholding consent.

This is the final version of the principle that I endorse. Since this principle states a sufficient condition for consent lacking full validity, it leaves open how gravely wrong it is to act on this consent. As a result, the principle does not have the untenable implication that Cameron wrongs Morgan in the *Anger* case as gravely as they do in the *Refusal* case.

they also face a significant challenge in the form of Liberto's objection to Moral Debilitation views, which I discuss in Chapter 7.

6.5 Summary

To sum up, in this Chapter, I have developed the Ameliorative View of consent. It contrasts with the binary orthodox view that posits a twofold taxonomy of valid and invalid consent. The Ameliorative View generalizes this into a threefold taxonomy of fully valid consent, partially valid consent, and fully invalid consent. When someone gives fully invalid consent to an action, the consent has no effect, and so the consent-receiver's duty remains in place in full force. When someone gives fully valid consent to an action, they release the consent-receiver from their duty not to perform this action. When someone gives partially valid consent to an action, the consent does not release the consent-receiver from their duty, but the consent does have an ameliorative effect: the consent makes it the case that, by performing the action to which consent is given, the consent-receiver wrongs the consent-giver less gravely than they would in the absence of the consent.

The Ameliorative View is a helpful additional resource for theorizing sexual misconduct because it allows us to account for a spectrum of misconduct that varies in its gravity. Not only is this resource helpful for understanding consent under duress of greater or lesser degrees, it is plausibly also helpful for understanding consent that has been fully or partially invalidated on other grounds besides duress.

My argument for the Ameliorative View was based on Chapter 5's Constraint Solution to the Problem of Minor Duress. But the Ameliorative View need not be tied to this solution. Instead, there are other rationales that one might offer for holding that consent can be partially but not fully invalidated. For example, one might hold that duress's invalidating effect on consent is to be understood in terms of the duress undermining the consent-giver's responsibility for giving consent. On the grounds that this responsibility can be undermined to a lesser or greater degree, one could hold that the resulting consent is more or less partially valid.

Finally, I revised our initial draft of the Consent-Receiver Principle in light of the Ameliorative View. Working within the traditional binary framework of valid and invalid consent, that initial draft had specified a sufficient condition for invalid consent. The revised and final draft instead specifies a sufficient condition for consent that is not fully valid.

Consent under Duress. Tom Dougherty, Oxford University Press. © Tom Dougherty 2024.
DOI: 10.1093/9780198922360.003.0008

PART 3

DURESS FROM THIRD PARTIES, NATURAL CAUSES, AND SOCIAL NORMS

In Parts 1 and 2, we discussed duress that comes from the consent-receiver. In Part 3, we will broaden our inquiry to include other types of duress. We will focus on three types in particular: duress from third parties, duress from natural causes, and duress from social norms.

In Chapter 7, we will look at duress that comes from an agent who is a "third party," in the sense that they are neither the consent-giver nor the consent-receiver. Third-party duress is theoretically puzzling because sometimes it invalidates consent and sometimes it does not. To illustrate when third-party duress does not prevent consent from being fully valid, consider:

> *Crockery Dilemma—Request.* Bully threatens to smash Victim's vase unless Bystander smashes Victim's teapot. Bystander is aware of the conditional threat but cannot prevent Bully from smashing the vase. Victim asks Bystander to smash the teapot.

To handle this type of case, I introduce the Authorization Principle. Roughly, this principle states that someone's consent to an action is fully valid when they are authorizing the consent-receiver to perform the action as an extension of their own agency. To make room for the Authorization Principle, we have to leave exceptions when developing a principle that governs third-party duress. For this, I defend the Third Party Principle. Its rough idea is that, unless someone is suitably authorizing an action, their consent to the action is not fully valid when it is given in response to third-party duress against which they have a legitimate complaint. Similarly,

I leave room for the Authorization Principle when developing a more fundamental principle that provides a rationale for the Third Party Principle. This more fundamental principle is the Adequate Position Principle. Roughly, it states that unless an individual is suitably authorizing an action, an agent cannot justify the action to the individual by appealing to the individual's expressed choice when the individual is not in a sufficiently good position to give consent.

In Chapter 8, we will look at duress that comes from natural causes. I argue against the Standard View that consent is not fully invalidated by this type of duress. The Standard View may seem appealing insofar as it can explain why consent is valid in cases like:

> *Disease*. Patient has a malignant tumor. If the tumor is not removed, then the disease will spread, and Patient will lose a limb. Patient consents to Surgeon removing the tumor.

But I argue that we do not need the Standard View to explain the full validity of Patient's consent. It is already explained by the Authorization Principle given that Patient is authorizing Surgeon to perform the surgery as an extension of their agency. Moreover, I consider a case in which someone's consent is invalidated by duress from a human agent. I then construct an analogous case that is similar in the respect that the consent-giver is under exactly the same duress. But in the analogous case, the duress comes from natural causes. I argue that the source of the duress makes no difference to whether the consent is fully invalidated: all that matters are the options open to the consent-giver and the consequences of these options. Consequently, I conclude that duress can be fully invalidated by natural causes.

In Chapter 9, we will look at duress from social norms. In particular, we will focus on social norms that imply that it is rude for someone to decline sex. These social norms can be sources of duress in two ways. First, these norms can indirectly shape the consent-receiver's behavior. For example, if social norms dictate that declining sex is rude, then this could explain why a consent-receiver imposes a penalty on withholding consent. Second, social norms can be direct sources of duress. For example, when social norms mark withholding consent as rude, someone may thereby consent because they are intrinsically motivated to avoid behaving rudely. For this type of scenario, I defend the Social Norm Principle. Roughly, its key idea is that consent may not be fully valid when the consent-giver is entitled to withhold consent without this instantiating an adverse property like rudeness.

7
Third-Party Duress

To illustrate third-party duress, consider a real-life case:

> *Burnham.* In the context of an abusive relationship, Victor Burnham threatened Rebecca Burnham with violence unless she attempted to stop passing motorists and solicit sex from them. (Westen 2004, 139–40)

Since Victor Burnham was neither the consent-giver nor the consent-receiver, he was a third-party source of duress. In the real-world version of the case, the motorists may be ignorant of Victor Burnham's threat. We will discuss this type of ignorance in Part 4. For now, to avoid ignorance being a confounding factor, let us make an assumption of full information and suppose that the motorists are aware of Victor Burnham's threat. On that assumption, I take it to be clear that Rebecca Burnham's consent was fully invalid.[1]

This example brings out that third-party duress can render consent fully invalid. But even if that is easily established, it is difficult to develop a principle that explains why third-party duress undermines consent. As we shall see, this difficulty partly stems from the fact that there are some types of third-party duress that do not prevent consent from being fully valid. Consider:

> *Crockery Dilemma—Request.* Bully threatens to smash Victim's vase unless Bystander smashes Victim's teapot. Bystander is aware of the conditional threat but cannot prevent Bully from smashing the vase. Victim asks Bystander to smash the teapot.

Bystander would not wrong Victim by smashing the teapot. The most straightforward explanation is that Victim has given fully valid consent. If we endorse this explanation, then we must allow that sometimes third-party

[1] I am assuming that Rebecca Burnham escapes the violence if the motorists decline sex. If this assumption does not hold, then the case is analogous to *Crockery Dilemma-Request* and the other cases in which third-party duress does not fully invalidate consent.

duress does not fully invalidate consent. This creates a challenge to fashion a principle that identifies when third-party duress fully invalidates consent and when it does not.

This Chapter is organized as follows. In Section 7.1, I introduce a draft of a principle governing third-party duress, the "Third Party Principle," and a draft of a more fundamental principle that provides a rationale for it, the "Adequate Position Principle." In Section 7.2, I show how these draft principles come unstuck in light of an important pair of cases of Hallie Liberto. In Section 7.3, I argue that these cases can be handled by introducing the "Authorization Principle," which allows that consent can sometimes be fully valid even when given under third-party duress. To leave room for the Authorization Principle, I revise the drafts of the Adequate Position Principle and the Third Party Principle.

7.1 The Adequate Position Principle and Third-Party Duress

Third-party duress can prevent consent from being fully valid. For example, consider the following case:

> *Third Party Acquiescence.* Bully proposes to smash Victim's glasses if and only if Victim does not ask Stranger to pinch them. In other words, Bully is allowing that Victim saves their glasses by making the request, even if Stranger has no desire to pinch Victim and so refuses the request. Stranger knows the terms of Bully's threat but is powerless to prevent Bully from enforcing the threat. Victim asks Stranger to pinch them.[2]

[2] This case causes trouble for Mollie Gerver's (2021) "relational autonomy" account of third-party coercion. Gerver's idea is that someone gives valid consent if the consent-receiver has given them all the options to which they are entitled (and has not provided any options that they are under a duty not to provide). Given that Stranger is unable to improve Victim's options, Stranger has done all they could to improve Victim's options. Therefore, Gerver's account implies that Victim's consent is valid. Gerver attempts to avoid this result by arguing that Stranger has a duty to provide Victim with the option of not pinching them. But this attempt is unconvincing for two reasons. First, the option of not pinching is an option for Stranger, not for Victim. Second, it is circular to appeal to a duty of Stranger's not to pinch Victim. The reason why Stranger has this duty is that Victim's consent is not valid. Thus, we cannot appeal to the duty in order to explain why the consent is invalid.

For similar reasons, the case also causes trouble for Maximilian Kiener's (2022, 372) "Recipient-Focus-View," according to which "the validity of consent depends on the conduct of the person receiving consent rather than on the third party's coercion alone." To handle a case

Since Victim makes the offer to avoid having their glasses smashed by Bully, and Victim is not voicing any genuine desire for Stranger to pinch them, Stranger would wrong Victim by pinching them. I assume that the best explanation for this fact is that Victim's consent is not fully valid. This datum needs to be explained.

This datum cannot be explained by the Consent-Receiver Principle from Chapter 2. That principle concerns duress that comes from the consent-receiver. But Stranger is the consent-receiver, and Stranger is not subjecting Victim to any duress. Similarly, we cannot explain the case by appealing to the Facilitative Duty Principle from Chapter 2:

> Facilitative Duty Principle. If Y's expressed choice is explained by X's failure to discharge their duties to put Y in a sufficiently good position for making and expressing this choice, then X cannot appeal to this expressed choice in order to justify interfering with Y's personal domain.

This principle fails to find purchase with the Third Party Acquiescence case because Stranger cannot do anything to prevent Bully from enforcing the threat. As such, there is nothing that Stranger can do to put Victim in a better position to give consent. So, Stranger has not failed to discharge their facilitative duties to improve (and not to worsen) Victim's position for making and expressing their choice.

There are independent reasons for thinking that a deliberator's choice may lack moral significance for an agent, even though the agent cannot put the deliberator in a better position to make a choice. For example, the deliberator may lack certain decision-making capacities when they make the choice:

> *Drinking*. At a dinner party, Guest is close to the point at which they will become excessively inebriated. Guest asks Host for another drink. To prevent Guest become excessively inebriated, Host refuses the request.

like this, Kiener (2022, 383) argues that "that consent is invalid when [Stranger] 'facilitates coercive success,' i.e. when [Stranger] denies Victim an alternative to acting on consent, which would also allow Victim to avoid the threatened harm and not impose an unreasonable cost." This is a circular explanation. In this case, "facilitating coercive success" is equivalent to acting on the consent that is received by Bully's coercion. We need an explanation of why it is wrong to act on the consent that is received by Bully's coercion. We do not get this explanation by claiming that Victim's consent is invalidated by Stranger's "facilitating coercive success." That simply states what we need to explain.

Normally, we let individuals decide for themselves how to trade off the pros and cons of certain amounts of drinking. But because Guest is significantly inebriated, their decision to continue drinking does not have its usual significance for Host. As such, it is reasonable for Host to cut them off. With certain background assumptions, this lack of significance of Guest's choice would not be explained by Host breaching a duty to Guest to put them in a better position to decide whether to continue drinking. For example, let us assume that at the moment when Guest makes their request, there is nothing that Host can do to sober them up. And let us also assume that Host has not breached any duties toward Guest by serving them alcohol thus far in the evening.

The *Drinking* case does not involve consent. But we see the same point emerging in cases that do involve consent:

> *Underage*. Fan is fifteen years old. They have a crush on their favorite musician, Singer, who is twenty-five years old. By chance, Fan's and Singer's paths cross. Fan sexually propositions Singer.

Singer cannot justify having sex with Fan by appealing to their decision to sexually proposition them. This is because Fan is too young for their choice to have this justificatory force. Yet, since Singer cannot accelerate Fan's aging, there is nothing that Singer can do to put Fan in a better position to make this choice.

Both the *Drinking* and *Underage* cases involve a decision-maker who lacks sufficient capacity to make a choice. The same point also arises for cases in which a decision-maker lacks sufficient information. Consider:

> *No Shared Language*. Mortar fire has partially destroyed a shelter and Refugee is trapped. Medic has three options. First, Medic can rescue Refugee from the rubble, but this will impose a 50% risk of paralysis from spinal damage. Second, Medic can wait for Engineers to arrive, who could rescue Refugee safely. But if Medic waits, then there is a 10% chance that meanwhile the shelter collapses, killing Refugee. Third, Medic could buttress the remaining structure with a beam. But this would increase the load on Refugee's foot, crushing it. Because Refugee and Medic do not share a language, Medic can communicate neither the risk of paralysis nor the nature, risks, and benefits of the other options. But through gestures, Medic does communicate the option of moving Refugee. With a thumbs-up gesture, Refugee communicates their consent to Medic moving them.[3]

[3] This is a case that I introduced when discussing informed consent (Dougherty 2020, 139).

Given the communicative limitations, Medic fully discharges their facilitative duties to put Refugee in a better position to make a choice: given what Medic is able to do, Medic takes all reasonable steps to help Refugee decide how to proceed. However, this attempt fails to make Refugee understand the alternative options and their risks. All the same, Refugee's ignorance means that they are insufficiently informed to give fully valid consent to being moved, and Refugee's thumbs-up is not enough to justify Medic in moving them.[4]

To govern cases like *Drinking*, *Underage*, and *No Shared Language*, we need a principle that will cover cases in which the consent-giver is simply in an insufficiently good position to make a choice, even though the consent-receiver cannot improve this position. I propose the following:

> Adequate Position Principle (Draft). If Y's expressed choice is explained by the fact that Y is not in a sufficiently favorable position to make and express this choice, then X cannot appeal to this expressed choice in order to justify interfering with Y's personal domain.

I call this the "Adequate Position Principle" since the principle focuses on whether Y is in an adequately good position for making and expressing their choice. This is merely a draft of the principle, as we will shortly see that it needs revision to handle certain cases, such as those of third-party duress. But that revision need not detain us now.

One reason to accept this principle is that it explains the moral insignificance of the choices made in the *Drinking*, *Underage*, and *No Shared Language* cases. Since these include cases that involve consent and cases that do not involve consent, the Adequate Position Principle is thus motivated by its ability to explain a wide variety of phenomena concerning the significance of people's expressed choices.

A second source of support for the Adequate Position Principle is that it coheres with the Facilitative Duty Principle that we independently motivated earlier. Indeed, it is plausible to think of the Adequate Position Principle as the more fundamental principle from which the Facilitative Duty Principle can be derived. The derivation would appeal to a claim along the following lines:

[4] Plausibly, Refugee's consent is partially valid. For example, a thumbs-down may make it harder for Medic to justify moving them.

Facilitation Claim. Part of what it is for Y to be in a sufficiently favorable position to make and express a choice for how X interferes in Y's personal domain is for X to have discharged their duties to improve and not to worsen Y's position for making and expressing this choice.

In light of this derivation, the Adequate Position Principle attractively allows for a unified explanation of cases in which the consent-receiver can improve the consent-giver's position to make a choice and cases in which the consent-receiver cannot.

If we accept the draft of the Adequate Position Principle, then we can derive a specific principle for third-party duress. It seems independently plausible that a consent-giver is not in a sufficiently good position to give consent if they are subject to a certain type of duress from a third party: namely, the third party is imposing a penalty on their withholding consent, and the consent-giver has a legitimate complaint against the way that the third party is doing this. That assumption, in conjunction with the Adequate Position Principle, allows us to derive the following principle:

Third Party Principle (Draft). Under conditions of full information, X's consent to Y performing action A is not fully valid if:

(i) a third party Z will impose a penalty on X's withholding consent to A;
(ii) the prospect of this penalty causes X to consent to A;
(iii) X has a legitimate complaint against the way that Z has conditioned this penalty on X's withholding consent; and
(iv) this complaint concerns the way that the penalty alters X's incentives for withholding consent.

This principle would allow us to reach the right results concerning the *Third Party Acquiescence* case. That is a further source of motivation for the principle in addition to the argument from the Adequate Position Principle. Also, the principle neatly coheres with the Consent-Receiver Principle, which adds unity to our overall account of consent under duress.

But as we will shortly see, the above formulation of the principle fails to handle the full array of cases involving third-party duress. For that reason, this formulation is merely the principle's "draft." We will revise this draft in Section 7.4.

7.2 Liberto's Objection to Moral Debilitation Views

Both the draft of the Adequate Position Principle and the draft of the Third Party Principle need to be revised in light of an objection that Hallie Liberto (2021, 2022) makes to a family of views on why coercion invalidates consent. These views can be understood as implying conditions under which the consent-giver is "morally debilitated" from exercising a normative power to give consent. Here are some examples of these views:

> Coercion invalidates consent because the coercion prevents the consent-giver from acting autonomously.
>
> Coercion invalidates consent because the coercion prevents the consent-giver from acting voluntarily.
>
> Coercion invalidates consent because the coercion restricts the consent-giver's freedom.
>
> Coercion invalidates consent because the coercion removes an option to which the consent-giver is entitled. (Pallikkathayil 2011)

Let us call Liberto's targets "Moral Debilitation Views."

Liberto has shown that Moral Debilitation Views cannot give an adequate account of third-party duress. Liberto's (2022, 219), critique centers around a certain case involving third-party duress:

> *Third Party, Gunpoint.* Wanting to cause his victims pain and trauma, Ajay coerces Bea and Carlos into having sex with each other. Ajay knows that Bea and Carlos would never want to have sex with each other, perhaps because both Bea and Carlos are only attracted to members of their own sex, or Bea and Carlos are close colleagues or platonic friends. Whatever the reason, Ajay knows that it would cause Bea and Carlos great distress to have sex with each other. Ajay takes out a gun and tells Bea and Carlos that he will shoot them if they do not have sex. They both agree to comply and then have sex with each other.

Liberto argues that Bea's and Carlos's agreement to comply has a moral effect on each other's range of permissions. To show that the agreement is making a moral difference, Liberto (2022, 219–20) compares a nearby case:

> *Third Party, Gunpoint**: Bea wants to comply with Ajay's demands, but Carlos would prefer to die than to have sex with Bea under these conditions. Bea is physically stronger than Carlos, which he knows, and proceeds to have sex with him despite his unwillingness to comply with Ajay's demands. He is unable to physically resist, given Bea's strength, but internally maintains and verbally communicates to Bea that he would rather be shot than for her to continue to have sex with him.

Liberto argues that "there is an important difference between" the *Third Party, Gunpoint* case and the *Third Party, Gunpoint** case.[5] Liberto argues that the moral difference consists in Carlos exercising his normative power to grant Bea a permission in the *Third Party, Gunpoint* case. But this difference cannot be explained by Moral Debilitation Views. Because of Ajay's coercion, the Moral Debilitation Views must see Carlos as morally debilitated and hence unable to exercise a normative power to grant Bea a permission in the *Third Party, Gunpoint* case.

Liberto's central insight is extremely important for understanding third-party duress. However, Liberto's pair of cases is not ideal for mining this insight, for a variety of reasons. First, these are emotive cases, and we may feel particularly unsure about what to say about sexual consent in this regard. In particular, we will be struck by the fact that Carlos suffers a sexual violation in the *Third Party, Gunpoint** case, and some people will be inclined to explain this in terms of Carlos's not giving fully valid consent to Bea.[6] In addition, both cases are additionally complicated by the fact that Bea herself will suffer death unless she has sex with Carlos. Some people may believe that this fact implies that Bea has a justification for having sex with Carlos in the *Third Party, Gunpoint** case. Because of these confounding features of the cases, it is likely that people will lack clear intuitions and that people's intuitions will vary. I suspect that this may be why Liberto hesitates to draw what I take to be the correct conclusion about the cases, which is that Carlos gives valid consent in the *Third Party, Gunpoint* case but not in the *Third Party, Gunpoint** case.

[5] Liberto maintains that one should acknowledge this difference "even if one thinks that there is no consent rendered in either case, and even if one thinks that Bea's actions are justified or exculpated in *Third Party, Gunpoint**."

[6] This is not the only candidate explanation though. Drawing on ideas of Liberto's (2021, 2022), I propose that we see Ajay as violating Carlos, using Bea as an instrument in the violation.

We can see that this is the right conclusion by turning to simpler cases that avoid the confounding features. For a start, there are analogous cases involving medical consent:

> *Mafia Surgery—Request.* Mafioso has a benign tumor that protrudes. Godfather does not like its appearance and threatens to cut off one of Mafioso's limbs if Godfather sees the tumor again. Surgeon knows of the threat. Mafioso asks Surgeon to remove the tumor.
>
> *Mafia Surgery—Refusal.* Mafioso has a benign tumor that protrudes. Godfather does not like its appearance and threatens to cut off one of Mafioso's limbs if Godfather sees the tumor again. Surgeon knows of the threat. Mafioso refuses to let Surgeon remove the tumor.

I take it to be clear that Surgeon is permitted to remove the tumor in the *Mafia Surgery—Request* case but not in the *Mafia Surgery—Refusal* case. The explanation is that Mafioso has given fully valid consent to Surgeon in the former case but not in the latter. The difference between the cases is that in one case Mafioso requests treatment, and this type of request is standardly understood as giving medical consent.

In addition, there are mundane pairs of cases involving low-stakes consent:

> *Crockery Dilemma—Request.* Bully threatens to smash Victim's vase unless Bystander smashes Victim's teapot. Bystander is aware of the conditional threat but cannot prevent Bully from smashing the vase. Victim asks Bystander to smash the teapot.
>
> *Crockery Dilemma—Refusal.* Bully threatens to smash Victim's vase unless Bystander smashes Victim's teapot. Bystander is aware of the conditional threat but cannot prevent Bully from smashing the vase. Victim asks Bystander not to smash the teapot.

In the *Crockery Dilemma—Request* case, Bystander would not wrong Victim by smashing the teapot, but Bystander would wrong Victim by doing so in the *Crockery Dilemma—Refusal* case. The straightforward explanation is that Victim has given fully valid consent in the former case but not the latter.[7] We standardly take people's requests for how we use their property to be instances of consent.

[7] A less plausible possibility is that Bystander acts permissibly even though Victim does not give fully valid consent. To reach this conclusion, we would have to view the case as one of the

Once we see that this pattern plays out in other cases, we should be comfortable with concluding that it also obtains in Liberto's cases. That is, we should say that Bea is permitted to have sex with Carlos in the *Third Party, Gunpoint* case but not in the *Third Party, Gunpoint** case, and this difference is explained by the fact that Carlos gives valid consent in the former but not the latter.[8] But since these are complicated cases, I will pass over discussing them further. For our purposes, we can focus on the simpler *Crockery Dilemma* cases.

These cases cause trouble for our drafts of the Third Party Principle and the Adequate Position Principle. The problem for the Third Party Principle is straightforward. Since Victim has a legitimate complaint against Bully's threat in the *Crockery Dilemma—Request* case, the principle would mistakenly imply that Victim does not give valid consent in that case. The problem for the Adequate Position Principle requires a little more teasing out. In the *Crockery Dilemma—Request* case, Bully's threat puts Victim in a bad position to give consent. Indeed, this is the type of wrongful threat that standardly invalidates consent. Consider a variant of the *Third Party Acquiescence* case:

> *Crockery Acquiescence.* Bully proposes to smash Victim's vase if and only if Victim does not ask Stranger to smash Victim's teapot. In other words, Bully is allowing that Victim saves their vase by making the request, even if Stranger has no desire to smash the teapot and so refuses the request. Stranger knows the terms of Bully's threat but is powerless to prevent Bully from enforcing the threat. Victim asks Stranger to smash their teapot.

exceptional cases in which an agent acts permissibly in another person's domain despite lacking that person's fully valid consent. One example would be a case in which a patient is highly intoxicated and in need of urgent medical treatment. The intoxication makes it impossible for the patient to give fully valid consent. Still, even though the patient does not give fully valid consent, it is permissible for the physician to act in the patient's best interests, guided by any available information concerning the patient's beliefs, desires, and intentions about how they would like to be treated in the circumstances that are beyond the physician's control. We could appeal to a similar rationale to say that in the *Crockery Dilemma—Request* case, Bystander acts permissibly, given that it is impossible for Victim to validly consent, and given that Bystander acts in Victim's best interests, guided by how Victim would like them to act. Victim's request would end up with evidential significance: it would reveal what Victim sees as the lesser of two evils and hence how Bystander ought to behave in order to serve Victim's interests according to how Victim sees their interests.

[8] Some people say that Bea is permitted to have sex with Carlos only if she acts with the intention to save their lives, and that she is not permitted to do so for the sake of her own gratification. Along these lines, Victor Tadros (2021) develops a view according to which intentions can make a difference in cases involving consent given under unjust conditions.

Victim's consent is fully invalid, and Stranger could not justify smashing Victim's teapot. We introduced the Adequate Position Principle as a rationale for, e.g., why Stranger cannot justify smashing Victim's teapot by appealing to their expressed choice in this type of case. Since Victim is under the same threat of a smashed vase in the *Crockery Dilemma—Request* case, the Adequate Position Principle would presumably also imply that in this case Bystander cannot justify smashing Victim's teapot by appealing to Victim's request that Bystander do so. But this is the incorrect implication: Victim's request is part of the explanation of why Bystander can justify smashing the teapot in the *Crockery Dilemma—Request* case. This is what we learn by comparing the two versions of the *Crockery Dilemma* case.

In light of these problems, we need to revise our earlier draft of the Third Party Principle so that it avoids implying that consent is not fully valid in the *Mafia Surgery—Request*, *Crockery Dilemma—Request*, and *Third Party, Gunpoint* cases. Similarly, we need to revise our earlier draft of the Adequate Position Principle so that it avoids implying that the consent-receiver cannot justify acting on the consent. Of course, we still want these principles to have the correct implications for the *Third Party Acquiescence* and *Crockery Acquiescence* cases. That is, we want the Third Party Principle to imply that the consent is invalid in these cases, and we want the Adequate Position Principle to imply that the consent-giver cannot justify acting on the consent. The challenge is to revise these principles in such a way that they have these implications without having mistaken implications for the other cases.

7.3 The Authorization Principle

Liberto's objection shows that we need to revise the drafts of the Adequate Position Principle and the Third Party Principle. To do so, I will draw on a substantive view of what consent is. According to this view, consent requires engaging in external behavior that conveys that the consent-giver is changing their relationship with the consent-receiver (Dougherty 2015, 2021d). At this level of abstraction, it is safe to construe this as a speech-act, simply on the grounds that it is meaningful behavior. But in saying this, I require neither that the speech-act be correctly interpreted by the audience nor that the communicative behavior be verbal. For consent-giving, a paradigmatic speech-act is the explicit granting of a permission, as when a speaker says (stiltedly), "I hereby permit you to walk across my lawn." In addition, consent can be given by a range of other speech-acts, such as requests, offers, and invitations (Dougherty 2021d; Liberto 2022, 136).

Once we conceive of consent as granted by speech-acts like requests, we can make use of this conception in our inquiry into when third-party duress prevents consent from being fully valid. I will focus on the *Crockery Dilemma—Request* case, and I will assume that Victim gives fully valid consent to Bystander. To analyze this case, we should start by distinguishing sincere requests from insincere requests, according to whether the requestor genuinely, all things considered, wants the relevant action to be performed, given the options that are open to and not excessively costly for the agent. Now when someone sincerely requests another person to perform an action, we can think of them as enlisting that person as their proxy agent to act on their behalf. We can put this point by saying that they *authorize* the proxy agent to perform that action.

This analysis naturally fits the *Crockery Dilemma—Request* case. Victim requests that Bystander smashes the teapot, and this request expresses what Victim most prefers that Bystander does, given the options that are open to Bystander and not excessively costly for them. If Victim were directly able to control Bystander's behavior, then Victim would choose Bystander smashing the teapot. Of course, Victim would ideally prefer that none of their crockery is smashed. But neither Victim nor Bystander can ensure that Victim's ideal outcome obtains. In that sense, Bystander can do no better to respect Victim's agency than by choosing to smash the teapot. By smashing the teapot, Bystander would follow Victim's sincere request in the unfortunate circumstances that are beyond Bystander's control. In those respects, Bystander would be acting as Victim's proxy agent, and Victim would be authorizing Bystander's behavior.

We need to develop this analysis to take into account the costs that the consent-receiver would face when choosing certain options.[9] Consider the following modification of an earlier case:

> *Crockery Trilemma.* Bully threatens to smash Victim's vase unless Bystander smashes Victim's teapot or Bystander smashes Bystander's own window. Bystander is aware of the conditional threat but cannot prevent Bully from smashing the vase. Victim says to Bystander, "I'd most

[9] Thanks to Joe Horton for mentioning this point and to Horton and Mollie Gerver for suggesting ways to develop my view.

prefer that you smash your own window. But if you aren't willing to do that, then please smash my teapot."

Victim would most prefer that Bystander smash their own window. But this action is excessively costly for Bystander: Bystander is not required to smash their own window in order to save Victim's vase. As such, we should ignore this option when determining what Victim is sincerely authorizing. For determining this, we should restrict ourselves to the options that meet two conditions. First, the options are available to Bystander in the sense that Bystander can actually choose these options. Second, the options are not excessively costly to Bystander. Here a cost would be excessive if Bystander is not required to bear the cost for Victim's sake. Once we have restricted ourselves to the options that meet both these conditions, we should consider what Bystander most prefers. In the *Crockery Trilemma* case, when we restrict Bystander's options to the options that meet both conditions, we will view Bystander as choosing whether to smash Victim's vase or to do nothing. Given that Victim sincerely says, "if you are not willing to [smash your own window], then please destroy my teapot," Victim is sincerely authorizing Bystander to perform this action.

The same analysis would apply to the *Mafia Surgery* and *Third Party Gunpoint* cases. Not only does this analysis yield the right result about these cases, but the analysis also has the following, intuitively attractive rationale. The ethics of consent are structured by two aspects of our moral lives. First, we need protection from the ways that others might treat us, and this protection comes in the form of a default perimeter of rights against their interfering with our persons or property. Second, we need to be able to relax this protection in order to interact with others in valuable ways. Since fully valid consent is the means by which we toggle this protection on or off, it must strike a balance between these twin goals of protecting us and enabling us to engage in valuable interactions. Set the bar too low for what counts as fully valid consent, and we have insufficient protection. Set the bar too high, and we miss out on valuable interactions with others. We avoid setting the bar too low by positing a default requirement for fully valid consent that the consent-giver be in a sufficiently good position to give consent. But we avoid setting the bar too high by leaving room for sincere authorizations to constitute fully valid consent, even when the consent-giver is not in a sufficiently good position to give consent.

For these reasons, I endorse the following principle:

Authorization Principle. X gives fully valid consent to Y performing A if:

(i) X sincerely performs a speech-act that communicates that, out of the options that are available to Y and are not excessively costly for Y, X authorizes Y to perform A as an extension of X's own agency; and
(ii) all other validity conditions are met.

Here the "other validity conditions" are the conditions that do not pertain to duress. Examples include the condition that the consent-giver is suitably informed and the condition that the consent-giver has sufficient capacity.

In passing, let us note that the Authorization Principle will not apply to cases of duress from the consent-receiver. In these cases, the consent-receiver has the option of removing the duress that they are imposing on the consent-giver. The consent-giver would most prefer that the consent-receiver remove this duress. So, it is not the case that, of the options that are open to and not excessively costly for the consent-receiver, the consent-giver sincerely expresses that they most prefer that the consent-receiver perform the action to which the consent has been given. If the consent-giver were able to control the consent-receiver's behavior as their proxy agent, then the consent-giver would simply choose to remove the duress.

7.4 Revising the Adequate Position Principle and Third Party Principle

To leave room for the Authorization Principle to kick in, we should revise our drafts of the Adequate Position Principle and the Third Party Principle. We should revise the Adequate Position Principle as follows:

Adequate Position Principle (Final Draft). If Y's expressed choice is explained by the fact that Y is not in a sufficiently favorable position to make or express this choice, then X cannot appeal to this expressed choice to justify interfering with Y's personal domain, unless this expressed choice constitutes Y's sincere expression that, out of the options that are available to X and are not excessively costly for X, Y most prefers X to engage in this interference in the circumstances.

By calling this the final draft, I mean that this is the version of the principle that we should ultimately accept. The final draft differs from the first draft in the respect that it adds the "unless" clause for the exceptions created by the Authorization Principle.

To revise the Third Party Principle, we should add a fifth condition (v) as follows:

> Third Party Principle (Final Draft). Under conditions of full information, X's consent to Y performing action A is not fully valid if:
>
> (i) a third party Z will impose a penalty on X's withholding consent to A;
> (ii) the prospect of this penalty causes X to consent to A;
> (iii) X has a legitimate complaint against the way that Z has conditioned this penalty on X's withholding consent;
> (iv) this complaint concerns the way that the penalty alters X's incentives for withholding consent; and
> (v) it is not the case that X has sincerely expressed that, out of the options that are available to Y and are not excessively costly for Y, X most prefers Y to perform A in the circumstances.

In light of condition (v), this principle accommodates the Authorization Principle and hence avoids implying that Victim's consent is not fully valid in the *Crockery Dilemma—Request* case. Similarly, the principle avoids implying that Mafioso's consent is not fully valid in the *Mafia Surgery* case. In that case, Surgeon's two available options are to operate or not to operate. Since Mafioso has sincerely expressed that, of these two options, they prefer Surgeon to operate in the circumstances, condition (v) of the Third Party Principle is not met, and so the principle does not imply that Mafioso's consent is not fully valid. Likewise, in the *Third Party, Gunpoint* case, Bea's available options are to have sex with Carlos or not to have sex with him. Since Carlos has sincerely expressed that, of these two options, he prefers Bea to have sex with him, condition (v) of the principle is not met, and so the principle does not imply that Carlos's consent is not fully valid.

Meanwhile, the final draft of the Third Party Principle still entails that Victim does not give fully valid consent in the *Third Party Acquiescence* case:

> *Third Party Acquiescence*. Bully proposes to smash Victim's glasses if and only if Victim does not ask Stranger to pinch them. In other words, Bully

> is allowing that Victim saves their glasses by making the request, even if Stranger has no desire to pinch Victim and so refuses the request. Stranger knows the terms of Bully's threat but is powerless to prevent Bully from enforcing the threat. Victim asks Stranger to pinch them.

It is straightforward to see that the Third Party Principle's conditions (i)–(iv) are met. In addition, condition (v) is met for the following reason: Victim is not sincerely authorizing Stranger to pinch them. Stranger has the options of pinching Victim or not pinching them. Since Bully will impose no penalty on Victim if Stranger does not pinch them, Victim does not most prefer that Stranger pinch them. Put another way, if Victim were able to control Stranger's behavior as their proxy agent, then Victim would choose that Stranger not pinch them.

Since the final versions of the Adequate Position Principle and the Third Party Principle leave room for exceptions in which the Authorization Principle operates, these versions are inelegant. That is a shame, but it is more important for principles to be accurate than elegant. And we have already encountered two types of motivation for adding an exception for the Authorization Principle. First, the revised principles have the correct implications for the *Mafia Surgery*, *Crockery Dilemma*, and *Third Party, Gunpoint* cases. Second, the revisions are motivated by the fact that the standards for fully valid consent must strike a balance between protecting us from interference and allowing us to relax this protection.

In addition, we can add a third motivation for the exceptions that we are building into the Adequate Position Principle and the Third Party Principle. These exceptions are also motivated by the bigger-picture view of complaints from Chapter 2. This view gives interpersonal justification a central role in ethics. The idea is that we avoid mistreating someone if we can justify our behavior to them. However, we fail to justify our behavior if they have a legitimate complaint against the way that we have acted. We developed this view by considering how putative complaints can be made or rebutted as the result of our interactions with each other. For cases like *Mafia Surgery*, *Crockery Dilemma*, and *Third Party, Gunpoint*, the exception for the Authorization Principle makes room for the consent-receiver to offer a rebuttal to any putative complaint. The nature of the rebuttal is that the consent-receiver has tried their best to act exactly as the consent-giver has indicated that they would like the consent-receiver to act, given the circumstances that are beyond the consent-receiver's control. Since the consent-receiver cannot prevent the duress, there is nothing more that the consent-receiver could do to give the consent-giver more control over the course of affairs.[10] This provides the consent-receiver with a rebuttal of putative complaints about how the consent-giver has been treated. Therefore, the exceptions in the final versions of the Adequate Position Principle and the Third Party Principle are also motivated by the idea that we can appeal to the fact that another person has authorized us to act in a certain way by making a sincere request, in order to rebut any complaints that they might make about our conduct.

7.5 Merging the Consent-Receiver Principle and the Third Party Principle into the Constraint Principle

Anticipating that some—perhaps many—readers will not accept all of my principles, I have presented them separately and tried to argue for them as independently as possible. My aim has been that if someone is unpersuaded that they should accept, e.g., the Third Party Principle, then that need not prevent them from accepting the Consent-Receiver Principle. But I also want to discuss how far these principles can be merged into an overarching principle. For this overarching principle to be explanatory, it would have to have the status of being a more fundamental principle from which the aforementioned specific principles are derived.

It is possible to merge the Consent-Receiver Principle with the Third Party Principle so that both are derivative principles implied by a more fundamental principle. We can state the overarching principle as follows:

Constraint Principle. X's consent to Y performing action A is not fully valid if:

(i) X will face a penalty if they do not consent to A;
(ii) the prospect of this penalty causes X to consent to A;
(iii) X has a legitimate complaint against the way that someone has conditioned this penalty on X's withholding consent;
(iv) this complaint concerns the way that the penalty alters X's incentives for withholding consent; and
(v) it is not the case that X has sincerely expressed that, out of the options that are available to and not excessively costly for Y, X most prefers Y to perform A in the circumstances.

[10] Thanks to Niko Kolodny for this point.

This principle is identical to the Third Party Principle except for condition (iii). While the Third Party Principle states that the complaint must be against a third party, the Constraint Principle simply states that the complaint must be against someone. As a result, the Constraint Principle is more general than the Third Party Principle. In this respect, the Constraint Principle is also more general than the Consent-Receiver Principle, whose condition (iii) states that the complaint must be against the consent-receiver. In addition, the Constraint Principle includes condition (v), which the Consent-Receiver Principle lacks. But as we have noted, condition (v) is satisfied whenever someone consents under duress from the consent-receiver: in those circumstances, what the consent-giver wants most from the consent-receiver is for them to remove the duress.

The main reason to accept the Constraint Principle is theoretical: it adds greater unity to our account by tying together two principles. The alternative would be to have disparate principles that have similarities but hold independently of each other. For this reason, I propose that we aim to unify the Consent-Receiver Principle and the Third Party Principle by positing the more fundamental Constraint Principle.

But in saying this, we need not assume that the Constraint Principle is the most fundamental principle in the vicinity. Instead, we could see it as derived from the Adequate Position Principle. This principle states that, with one exception, an agent cannot justify interfering with a deliberator's personal domain by appealing to the deliberator's expressed choice when the following condition obtains: the expressed choice is explained by the fact that the deliberator is not in a sufficiently favorable position to make or express this choice. The exception is that this expressed choice constitutes the deliberator's sincere expression that, out of the options that are available to and not excessively costly for the agent, the deliberator most prefers that the agent engages in this interference in the circumstances.

7.6 Summary

In this Chapter, we have discussed third-party duress. This is duress that comes from an agent who is neither the consent-giver nor the consent-receiver.

We have wrestled with the difficulty of explaining why there are some cases in which third-party duress fully invalidates consent and some cases in which it does not. To explain when third-party duress does not fully invalidate consent, I have defended the Authorization Principle. The principle implies that someone gives fully valid consent to an action if they sincerely perform a speech-act that authorizes the consent-receiver to perform this action as an extension of their own agency in circumstances that are beyond the control of the consent-receiver.

I have made room for the Authorization Principle when formulating a principle that specifies when third-party duress prevents someone's consent from being fully valid. This is the Third Party Principle, which specifies several conditions that are jointly sufficient for consent not being fully valid. One of these conditions is that it is not the case that the consent-giver has sincerely expressed that, out of the options that are available to and not excessively costly for the consent-receiver, the consent-giver most prefers the consent-receiver to perform the relevant action in the circumstances. Other conditions imply that the consent-giver is consenting to avoid a penalty that a third party will in fact impose on consent being withheld. The remaining conditions are that the consent-giver has a legitimate complaint against the way that the third party has imposed this penalty, and that this complaint concerns the way that the penalty alters the consent-giver's incentives for withholding consent.

I have also made room for the Authorization Principle when developing a deeper rationale for the Third Party Principle. This rationale is the Adequate Position Principle. Its main idea is that the consent-giver cannot appeal to an expressed choice of the consent-giver to justify acting in a certain way if the consent-giver makes or expresses this choice because they are not in a sufficiently favorable position to do so. This main idea is supplemented by a qualification that makes room for an exception: the foregoing does not hold if this expressed choice constitutes the consent-giver's sincere expression that, out of the options that are available to and not excessively costly for consent-receiver, the consent-giver most prefers the consent-receiver to act in this way in the circumstances.

Finally, I have argued that the Third Party Principle can be merged with the Consent-Receiver Principle into the more general Constraint Principle.

Consent under Duress. Tom Dougherty, Oxford University Press. © Tom Dougherty 2024.
DOI: 10.1093/9780198922360.003.0009

8
Duress from Natural Causes

Can consent be fully invalidated by duress that does not come from a specific agent? Our answer to this question matters for whether we think consent could be fully invalidated by social norms—the topic of Chapter 9. While these norms are the products of many people's collective agency, they are not attributable to any particular agent.

To make progress on this question, let us consider first whether consent could be fully invalidated by duress that arises from natural causes. Insofar as this issue has been discussed, the consensus has been that consent is not invalidated by natural causes (Feinberg 1986, 149–50, 196–7; Alexander 1996, 171; Hurd 1996, 144–5; Millum 2014). I will call this the "Standard View." In my terminology, I interpret holders of the Standard View as making a claim about fully valid consent. That is, duress from natural causes does not prevent consent from being fully valid.

Since the Standard View has received less defense than you might expect, I am forced to speculate about why people are drawn to it. My hunch is that people adopt the view because they hold that consent is fully valid even when it is given in dire circumstances that result from forces of nature. This scenario is illustrated by the following case:

> *Disease*. Patient has a malignant tumor. If the tumor is not removed, then the disease will spread and Patient will lose a limb. Patient consents to Surgeon removing the tumor.

Patient consents to avoid a bad consequence—the spread of the disease. Nonetheless, Patient gives fully valid consent to Surgeon removing the tumor. If consent is not invalidated by natural forces like disease, then this would explain why Surgeon may operate. In this way, the Standard View implies that people can give fully valid consent to improve their lot when their lot has been worsened by nature.

However, in this Chapter, I will argue that the Standard View is wrong. To undercut the motivation for the Standard View, I will argue in Section 8.1

that there is a better way to explain why consent is fully valid in cases like *Disease* by appealing to the Authorization Principle that we developed in Chapter 7. In addition, I will argue in Section 8.2 that there are cases in which natural causes prevent consent from being fully valid. These cases bring out that what matters is whether an agent faces certain disincentives for withholding consent. What does not matter is the source of these disincentives. Specifically, it does not matter whether this source is an agent or natural causes. In Section 8.3, I will argue that the Adequate Position Principle can provide a deeper explanation of why natural causes invalidate consent. For a more proximate explanation, I will develop the Natural Causes Principle.

8.1 The Authorization Principle and Natural Duress

Insofar as the Standard View is motivated on the basis of a case like *Disease*, its appeal arises from conflating two features of the case. First, a non-agent is the source of the undesirable consequence (e.g., the loss of a limb). Second, the consent-receiver has no available alternative action of reasonable cost that the consent-giver prefers that the consent-receiver performs. It is the second feature that partly explains why Surgeon may operate in the *Disease* case: Surgeon has no available reasonable alternative that Patient prefers. This fact is enough to explain why Patient's consent is fully valid.

Indeed, that explanation of why Surgeon may operate in *Disease* is analogous to the explanation of why Surgeon may operate in the *Mafia Surgery—Request* case from Chapter 7:

> *Mafia Surgery—Request.* Mafioso has a benign tumor that protrudes. Godfather does not like its appearance and threatens to cut off one of Mafioso's limbs if Godfather sees the tumor again. Surgeon knows of the threat. Mafioso asks Surgeon to remove the tumor.

Mafioso is subject to duress when they give consent to Surgeon: Mafioso consents because Godfather is threatening to otherwise remove Mafioso's limb. But Mafioso's consent is fully valid because Surgeon has no available alternative of reasonable cost that Mafioso prefers.

In Chapter 7, I argued that the full validity of Mafioso's consent is explained by the Authorization Principle:

Authorization Principle. X gives fully valid consent to Y performing A if:

(i) X sincerely performs a speech-act that communicates that, out of the options that are available to Y and are not excessively costly for Y, X authorizes Y to perform A as an extension of X's own agency; and
(ii) all other validity conditions are met.

To apply this principle to the case, there are two options available to Surgeon which are not excessively costly: operating on Mafioso and not operating. Mafioso authorizes Surgeon to pursue the former option by sincerely requesting that Surgeon operates. This sincere request constitutes Mafioso's fully valid consent to the surgery.

The Authorization Principle also applies to the *Disease* case because it is similar to *Mafia Surgery—Request* case in the morally relevant respects. First, the options open to Surgeon are the same: operating or not operating. Second, the consent-giver is authorizing the same action: Patient sincerely requests that Surgeon operate on them. Therefore, the Authorization Principle explains why Patient's consent is fully valid in *Disease*. Thus, we can explain the full validity of consent in common-garden medical cases without appealing to the Standard View that natural forces do not invalidate consent.

Here is the moral that we should draw. To know why the consent is fully valid in the *Disease* and *Mafia Surgery—Request* cases, we should not look to the source of the incentives and disincentives that the relevant consent-giver faces. In particular, we should not pay attention to whether this source is a human threat or natural causes. Instead, we should simply consider which action the consent-giver is sincerely authorizing the consent-receiver to perform out of the options that are available to them and that are not excessively costly to them. What matters is the scenario consisting in the consent-giver's decisions, the various options that the consent-giver and the consent-receiver have, and the consequences of these options. What does not matter is how this scenario has come about—whether by natural forces or human agency.

8.2 Why We Should Reject the Standard View

Similar reasoning explains why we should reject the Standard View that duress from natural causes does not prevent consent from being fully valid. To know whether duress prevents someone's consent from being fully valid, we should not pay attention to the source of the duress. Instead, we should consider the incentives and the disincentives that the consent-giver faces.

To argue for rejecting the Standard View, I will discuss a pair of cases that have two key features. First, someone consents to an action because they will suffer a harm if they do not consent. Second, whether they suffer this harm does not depend on whether this action is performed. In one member of the pair, another agent has brought about this scenario, and in the other member of the pair, natural causes have brought about this scenario. I aim to show that both members of the pair are similar in the morally significant respects and that both cases involve consent that is not fully valid.

Unfortunately, I have not found it possible to construct a suitable pair of realistic cases. As a result, my pair will be outlandish. But even if you do not have a taste for outlandish cases, I hope that you will still see the force of the argument that I am making. The case simply illustrates a deeper philosophical point: holding fixed the consent-giver's and consent-receiver's options, as well as the consequences of these options, the lack of full validity of the consent is the same, regardless of whether these consequences have resulted from natural forces or human agency.

Let us start with the case involving duress from an agent:

> *Hacker*. Hacker has accessed Victim's computer, where Victim stores personal photos and their contact list. Hacker sends Victim a threat, "Send Neighbor an email in which you give Neighbor your social media password and invite them to log on to your account. And b-cc me in this email. Otherwise, I will share your photos with your contacts." Unbeknownst to Victim, Hacker bcc's Neighbor into the threatening email and Neighbor reads the email. So Neighbor is aware of the threat. Since some photos are embarrassing, Victim sends Neighbor the email with their social media password.

Victim consents to avoid suffering a harm—the harm that Victim's photos are shared with their contacts. Whether Victim suffers this harm depends on whether Victim gives consent to Neighbor logging on to their social media accounts. However, whether Victim suffers this harm does not depend on whether Neighbor logs on. Since Victim consents because of the threat of this harm, Victim's consent is not fully valid. Since Neighbor knows that Victim consents under duress, and since Neighbor has the alternative option of not logging on, Neighbor cannot appeal to Victim's consent to justify logging on.

Crucially, no part of that explanation appeals to the fact that Hacker is an agent. As such, analogous reasoning would apply to a case that has a similar causal structure, except for the fact that the source of the relevant duress is not an agent:

> *Lightning.* In a freak accident, lightning strikes Victim's building, causing a power surge that fries Victim's computer's circuits. An error message indicates that the computer will share Victim's personal photos with all of Victim's contacts unless Victim immediately sends Neighbor an email with Victim's social media password and invites Neighbor to log on to Victim's account. The malfunction also notifies Neighbor that Victim received this message, and so Neighbor is aware of what is going on. Victim tries disconnecting the computer but suffers a shock. Since some photos are embarrassing and time is running out, Victim sends Neighbor the email.

Because the malfunction notifies Neighbor, Neighbor knows that Victim consents to avoid suffering a harm—the harm that Victim's photos are shared with their contacts. Neighbor cannot appeal to Victim's consent to justify logging on. This is because of three facts: Victim consents under duress, Neighbor has the alternative option of not logging on to Victim's account, and Victim prefers that Neighbor choose this option. Note though that Victim's consent is not fully valid, even though Victim's decision-matrix has not been shaped by an agent but by lightning. Thus, natural forces can prevent someone's consent from being fully valid.[1]

I suspect that the Standard View is such an entrenched part of orthodoxy that the view will not go down easily. So, to bring out the strength of my argument against the view, let me put the argument in its most general form. I constructed the *Lightning* case as a counterpart to the *Hacker* case by using the following recipe:

> Take any case in which someone's consent is not fully valid because they consent in response to duress from a human agent—specifically, duress that takes the form of the agent imposing a negative consequence on withholding consent. Consider the consent-receiver's options and the causal consequences of giving or withholding consent. There are logically

[1] Indeed, I take this case to show that natural forces can make someone's consent fully invalid, but for the purposes of arguing against the Standard View, I restrict myself to discussion of preventing consent from being fully valid.

> possible counterpart cases, such that (i) the consent-receiver has the same options open to them, (ii) giving or withholding consent has the same causal consequences, and (iii) the fact that giving or withholding has these causal consequences is explained not by human action but by natural causes. In these counterpart cases, if someone consents to avoid the negative consequence of withholding consent, then their consent also is not fully valid.

If we follow this recipe, then the counterpart cases will typically be outlandish. But that outlandishness should not distract us from the underlying philosophical point of this argument: the relevant moral feature in these cases is the duress that the consent-giver faces rather than the source of the duress.

Similarly, there is a recipe that works in the other direction. This recipe allows us to construct the *Mafia Surgery—Request* case as a counterpart to the *Disease* case. Here is the recipe:

> Take any case in which natural duress does not prevent consent from being fully valid. As before, there are logically possible counterpart cases in which the consent-receiver has the same options open to them, and giving or withholding consent has the same causal consequences, but human action explains why giving or withholding has these causal consequences. In those counterpart cases, the duress also does not prevent the consent from being fully valid.

Together, these recipes show that generally it makes no moral difference to the validity of consent whether duress comes from a human agent or natural causes.

8.3 The Natural Causes Principle

How should we explain why Victim does not give fully valid consent in the *Lightning* case?

We cannot use the Third Party Principle to explain this. This is because that principle concerns duress against which a consent-giver has a legitimate complaint. Such a complaint is interpersonal: one person addresses a complaint to another person (Darwall 2006). As such, it is impossible for Victim to have a complaint against the lightning or their smoldering computer. Therefore, we need other conceptual tools to explain why Victim's consent does not justify Neighbor logging on in the *Lightning* case.

We can use the Adequate Position Principle to explain why Victim does not give fully valid consent in the *Lightning* case:

> Adequate Position Principle. If Y's expressed choice is explained by the fact that Y is not in a sufficiently favorable position to make or express this choice, then X cannot appeal to this expressed choice to justify interfering with Y's personal domain, unless this expressed choice constitutes Y's sincere expression that, out of the options that are available to X and are not excessively costly for X, Y most prefers X to engage in this interference in the circumstances.

This principle applies to consent-giving on our assumption that consent consists in an expressed choice. We have been assuming that for someone to be in a sufficiently favorable position to give consent, they must have a certain amount of freedom from duress. In the case of Victim's consent to Neighbor's use of their social media accounts, this freedom would be compromised by the following constraint:

> Photo Constraint. Victim is constrained in the respect that their withholding consent will lead to their photos being shared with their contacts.

To use the Adequate Position Principle to explain why Neighbor cannot justify acting on Victim's consent, we would need to assume that the Photo Constraint means that Victim is in an insufficiently favorable position to give consent. That assumption is motivated by the *Hacker* case. In that case, Victim's consent is not fully valid, and this is explained by the fact that Victim is not free from the Photo Constraint. Since Victim faces the same constraint in the *Lightning* case, we should conclude that Victim is not in a sufficiently good position to give consent. In turn, we should conclude that the Adequate Position Principle implies that Neighbor cannot justify logging on to Victim's social media account by appealing to their consent.[2]

A crucial feature of the foregoing analysis is that whether Victim is in a sufficiently favorable position does not depend on the source of this

[2] Or rather, to be fully precise, the principle implies this on the assumption that it is not the case that Victim's consent constitutes their sincere expression that, out of the options that are available to and not excessively costly for Neighbor, Victim most prefers that Neighbor log onto the accounts.

constraint. That is, it does not matter whether the Photo Constraint comes from an agent like Hacker or natural causes like lightning. All that matters is that Victim faces the Photo Constraint and consequently is not in a sufficiently good position to give consent.

Is there a principle that states when duress from natural causes prevents someone's consent from being fully valid? To try to develop such a principle, we might start by noting that the foregoing arguments support the following bridge thesis:

> Nature/Agency Link. Someone's consent is not fully valid as a result of natural duress imposing a consequence on withholding consent if someone's consent would not be fully valid as a result of a human agent imposing the same consequence on withholding consent (and all other morally relevant features remain the same).

This thesis connects the *Hacker* and *Lightning* cases as follows. In the *Hacker* case, Victim's consent is not fully valid as a result of Hacker imposing photo-sharing on Victim's withholding consent. In light of this point, the Nature/Agency Link implies that Victim's consent is not fully valid in *Lightning*.

Then we could try to appeal to the Nature/Agency Principle to fashion a principle governing duress from natural causes:

> Counterfactual Principle. Under conditions of full information, X's consent to Y performing action A is not fully valid if:
>
> (i) natural causes will impose a penalty on X's withholding consent to A;
> (ii) the prospect of this penalty causes X to consent to A;
> (iii) if this penalty had been imposed by a third party Z, then X would have a legitimate complaint against the way that Z has conditioned this penalty on X's withholding consent;
> (iv) this complaint would concern the way that the penalty alters X's incentives for withholding consent; and
> (v) it is not the case that X has sincerely expressed that, out of the options that are available to Y and are not excessively costly for Y, X most prefers Y to perform A in the circumstances.

This candidate principle is based on the Third Party Principle. The Third Party Principle's third condition is "X has a legitimate complaint against the way that Z has conditioned this penalty on X's withholding consent." The Counterfactual Principle replaces this with "if this penalty had been imposed by a third party Z, then X would have a legitimate complaint against the way that Z has conditioned this penalty on X's withholding consent." In this way, the Third Party Principle and the Nature/Agency Principle support the Counterfactual Principle. In addition, the Counterfactual Principle has the correct implications for the cases that we have considered. So, the principle has two sources of support.

However, the principle also has a serious weakness. In our investigation into why different types of duress prevent consent from being fully valid, we are not just after principles that are extensionally correct in the sense that they imply the right results with respect to cases. In addition, we seek principles that are explanatory in the sense that they identify the grounds of why the consent is not fully valid. I am skeptical that the Counterfactual Principle is explanatory in this sense. Its third clause concerns a counterfactual state of affairs—whether the consent-giver would have a legitimate complaint against a penalty if the penalty issued from an agent. This counterfactual consideration strikes me as too recherché and distant to be the explanation of why consent is not fully valid as a result of duress from natural causes. In light of this explanatory shortcoming, I do not endorse the Counterfactual Principle.

To develop a better principle, let us start by noting that legitimate complaints are under-written by other moral phenomena. Plausibly, these phenomena include interests.[3] For example, an individual has a legitimate complaint against another person assaulting them in response to withholding consent partly because the individual has an interest in being free to withhold consent without being assaulted.

Now from the mere fact that an individual has an interest in avoiding a consequence of withholding consent, it does not follow that the individual has a legitimate complaint against this consequence. Recall one of our examples from Chapter 1:

> *Steroids*. Coach proposes that unless Player agrees to take a steroids test, Coach will drop Player from the team.

[3] Compare R. Jay Wallace's (2019) recent account, according to which the moral foundations of people's demands are their interests. If, like Thomas Scanlon (1998), you think that legitimate demands are underwritten by reasons rather than interests, then feel free to substitute "reason" for "interest" throughout. Wallace (2019, 176–89) argues that their account can be reconciled with Scanlon's view.

Player has an interest in playing for the team in the event that they withhold consent to the test. However, this interest is outweighed by other considerations that bear on the value of fair competition in sports. Consequently, Player cannot legitimately complain that Coach has made the threat.

Thus, to specify when interests underwrite legitimate complaints, we need to consider whether people's interests are outweighed by competing considerations. There are different principles that we could adopt in this regard. One possibility is to make pairwise comparisons of the interests of different individuals (Scanlon 1998). Along these lines, consider the following principle that specifies a sufficient condition for an individual's interest being "trumped" by another individual's interest:

> Individualist Principle. For any penalty p that an individual X faces as a result of withholding consent, X's morally-weighted interest in avoiding p is trumped if there is another individual Y who has a stronger morally-weighted interest in p being imposed on X's withholding consent.

Here, an interest would be morally weighted as follows: insofar as the interest is morally illegitimate, the interest is discounted. For example, if someone took great sadistic pleasure in hurting animals, then this would be a weak (or maybe nonexistent) morally weighted interest. To apply the Individualist Principle to the *Steroids* case, we need to make a pairwise comparison of the following two interests. First, there is the player's interest in playing for the team while withholding consent to the test. Second, there is a rival player's interest in there being an institution that ensures that no one enjoys an unfair competitive advantage as the result of performance-enhancing drugs. Since the rival player's interest is the stronger, the Individualist Principle implies that the threatened player's interest is trumped. Since that player's interest is trumped, the burden associated with the steroids test can be justified to this player.

In addition to principles like the Individualist Principle that make pairwise comparisons between individuals' interests, there are also principles that allow for the aggregation of the interests of different individuals.[4]

[4] For example, consider the following sufficient condition:

> Aggregative Principle. For any penalty p that an individual X faces as a result of withholding consent, X's morally-weighted interest in avoiding p is trumped if (i) there is another group of individuals, Y1, Y2,..., Yn, who each have a morally-weighted interest in p; and (ii) in the aggregate, the morally-weighted interests of Y1, Y2,..., Yn, outweigh X's morally-weighted interest.

For our purposes, we need not take a stance on which of these principles is correct. Instead, we can make progress by reasoning only about cases in which it is uncontroversial whether someone's interest is trumped by competing interests or values. For example, I take it to be clear that in *Lightning* and *Hacker*, Victim's interest in withholding consent to Neighbor while keeping their photos private is not trumped by any competing interest or value. To invoke this fact in an explanation of why Neighbor may not act on Victim's consent, we should endorse the following principle:

> Natural Causes Principle. Under conditions of full information, X's consent to Y performing action A is not fully valid if:
> (i) natural causes will impose a penalty on X's withholding consent to A;
> (ii) the prospect of this penalty causes X to consent to A;
> (iii) X has an untrumped interest in being free from consenting leading to this penalty;
> (iv) this interest concerns how the penalty alters X's incentives for withholding consent; and
> (v) it is not the case that X has sincerely expressed that, out of the options that are available to Y and are not excessively costly for Y, X most prefers Y to perform A in the circumstances.

This principle would explain why Neighbor cannot justify acting on Victim's consent in the *Hacker* and *Lightning* cases.

However, I have some remaining doubts about this principle. This is partly because it is unclear how its conceptual currency of interests and freedom would naturally feature in interpersonal justification. For example, it is unclear why these considerations would enable Victim to rebut an attempt by Neighbor to justify logging on by appealing to Victim's consent.

In addition, there are also principles that allow impersonal values to trump individual's interests. For example, consider the following sufficient condition:

> Impersonal Principle. For any penalty p that an individual X faces as a result of withholding consent, X's morally-weighted interest in avoiding p is trumped if (i) an impersonal value is a consequence of p being imposed on X's withholding consent, and (ii) this impersonal value outweighs X's morally-weighted interest.

An advocate of the Aggregative Principle owes us an account of how interests aggregate to outweigh other aggregates of interests, and the advocate of the Impersonal Principle owes us an account of how impersonal values can outweigh individuals' interests. On the assumption that these debts can be paid, these principles can make precise the idea that a consent-giver's interest in avoiding a burden can be trumped.

Since I have not been able to find a better principle than the Natural Causes Principle, I am inclined to tentatively endorse it. Still, it is the principle that I am least sure about in this book. If we reject the principle and cannot find a substitute, then the absence of a principle governing duress from natural causes would mean that my account of consent under duress is incomplete. It may turn out that future research discovers a suitable principle. But if no such principle turns out to be forthcoming in the future, then its continued absence would count against my claim that natural duress sometimes prevents consent from being fully valid. Still, even if the support for the claim is weakened in this way, I suggest that we should persist with this claim. This is because I take this to be the correct conclusion to draw from our analysis of the *Hacker* and *Lightning* cases.

8.4 Summary

The Adequate Position Principle places importance on whether someone is in an insufficiently good position to give consent. But the principle does not place any importance on what has caused someone to be in an insufficiently good position to give consent. As a result, the principle places no importance on whether they are in such a position as a result of other agents' behavior or natural causes.

In this Chapter, I have provided an independent defense of this implication by arguing, contra the Standard View, that natural causes can prevent someone's consent from being fully valid. My argument had two parts. First, I showed that we do not need the Standard View to explain the full validity of a patient's consent given in order to avoid illness. The full validity of their consent is already explained by the Authorization Principle that we encountered in Chapter 7. Second, I started with a case of third-party duress that prevents consent from being fully valid and constructed an analogous case in which the same type of duress issues from natural causes. I argued that this difference in the source of the consent does not affect whether the consent is fully valid. As a result, I concluded that there are some cases in which duress from natural causes prevents consent from being fully valid.

Finally, I developed a principle that would explain why someone's consent is not fully valid when given in response to duress from natural causes. This was the Natural Causes Principle. This principle focuses on whether the consent-giver has an untrumped interest in withholding consent without this resulting in a negative consequence. When they have such an untrumped interest, their consent may not be fully valid when given to avoid this consequence. While this principle is the most plausible candidate principle that I have been able to come up with, and it gets the right results for the cases that we have considered, I am somewhat hesitant in endorsing it.

DOI: 10.1093/9780198922360.003.0010

9

Duress from Social Norms

In Chapter 8, we saw that natural causes can invalidate consent. This shows that duress can invalidate consent even when the duress is not attributable to a specific agent. This paves the way for our inquiry into how consent can be invalidated by social norms. These norms cannot be attributed to a specific agent. But our conclusions from Chapter 8 show that this need be no impediment to these norms invalidating someone's consent.

To illustrate duress from social norms, consider the following testimony of Rachel, a college student from New York:

> *Rudeness.* I hate admitting how much sex I've had because it was "polite" to just let him finish. You read stories of rape and sexual assault but never about your own manners pressuring you into having sex. Sometimes you just don't want to have sex after all the buildup but there is no way to get out of it without coming off as rude or disappointing your partner, who is probably a good person, not some creepy dude in a club. (Bennett and Jones 2019, 82)

Rachel describes herself as not wanting to have sex "after all" but finding "there is no way to get out of it" given that she does not want to come off as rude. Since rudeness is a social phenomenon that is determined by a culture's social norms, Rachel's consent is influenced by her social environment.[1]

There are two ways that social norms could constrain Rachel's consent. On the one hand, Rachel may wish to avoid her partner thinking of her as rude and retaliating. These causal consequences would be directly constraining Rachel's consent and the social context would only be doing so indirectly—by influencing her partner's thoughts and actions. On the other hand, Rachel may also be intrinsically motivated to avoid behaving rudely.

[1] Here I am assuming that Rachel has accurately recognized her culture's norms. This fits with our investigation's framing assumption of full information, which will only be relaxed in Part 4.

Many of us internalize social norms, with the result that they guide our behavior independently of our calculations of the consequences of this behavior. Our internalization of a norm that marks an action as rude can inhibit us from choosing the action in much the same way we can be inhibited from choosing an action that internalized norms mark as shameful or disgusting. If Rachel were intrinsically motivated to avoid being rude, then Rachel would be directly subject to duress from a social norm.

In this Chapter, I will develop an account of how social norms can prevent consent from being fully valid. In Section 9.1, I consider how social norms can indirectly constrain consent. In Section 9.2, I argue for the claim that consent is invalidated by duress from social norms. In Section 9.3, I start to explain this claim by introducing the idea that people are entitled to be free from certain effects of social norms. In Section 9.4, I then turn to formulating a principle that specifies when consent is invalidated by duress from social norms—the Social Norm Principle.

9.1 Social Norms as Structuring Duress from the Consent-Receiver

We will shortly look at how social norms can be a direct source of duress. But before we get to this, let us consider how social norms can be an indirect source of duress—by making it more likely that the consent-receiver imposes a penalty on withholding consent.

In Part 1 of this book, we considered duress that consisted in a consent-receiver imposing a penalty on someone for refusing to consent. There, I argued for the Consent-Receiver Principle. Roughly, this principle implies that if a consent-giver has a legitimate complaint against the consent-receiver imposing a penalty on withholding consent, then this can lead to the consent not being fully valid. As well as severe penalties like physical violence, this principle covers less severe penalties, such as expressions of anger. Social norms can partly explain why people impose these penalties.

There are two ways that rudeness can be a cultural phenomenon. First, some social conventions designate certain behaviors as rude. Examples include offensive gestures like flipping the bird. There is often some arbitrariness as to why these gestures are rude rather than polite. Second, a culture can deem behavior rude in virtue of being objectionable on independent grounds. An example is cutting in line. Since there are independent reasons why people should wait their turn, it is not arbitrary to deem cutting in line as rude. I assume that the second model is the right way to understand people who are concerned that refusing sex would be rude. There are potentially many reasons why people might be concerned that refusing sex would mistreat their partner. For example, they may take themselves to have moral reasons to be socially cooperative or to care for their partner's feelings. But there is one reason that is common and deserves special attention: people judge that they have given their partners legitimate expectations of sex, and they consequently feel obligated to meet these expectations.

Why do their partners form these sexual expectations? The answer concerns the way that people's expectations are influenced by social scripts that determine the "normal" ways for certain interactions to go. A paradigmatic social script is that for a restaurant interaction (Schank and Abelson 1977). This script provides a server and a customer with a range of conversational options from which they can choose from when pursuing their goals. In addition, the scripts shape each party's expectations. When people perceive each other as engaging in scripted behavior, they expect each other's subsequent behavior to conform to the script (Bicchieri 2006, 94–6). The fact that our culture contains a restaurant social script explains both the similarity of interactions in different restaurants and people's confident abilities to order food at restaurants.

Insofar as sexual encounters are undergirded by social scripts, these scripts are key sources of people's sexual expectations. In societies like the contemporary United States, a common script for a heterosexual college hookup is that the encounter begins with flirting, kissing, and going back to someone's room, before progressively advancing to intimate sexual activity that ends with male orgasm (Freitas 2018, 73–9). This script also normalizes the idea that once sexual activity has begun, one participant will not ask for it to stop. This script guides people's expectations: if an individual believes that their partner is following a sexual script, then the individual will expect their partner to follow the script to its end.

In some cultures, there are norms that imply that people are entitled to hold each other to account for their sexual expectations. This is reflected by the common charge that an individual has "led on" their sexual partner by proving unwilling to have sex with them. The strength of this charge cannot be understood simply in terms of the fact that their partner has been surprised, as there are all sorts of surprises, inside and outside of the bedroom, which are no big deal. Instead, the charge is rationalized by a background assumption that the individual's prior behavior has given their partner a legitimate sexual expectation, and the latter person can hold the individual accountable for meeting this expectation.

When someone feels mistreated by their sexual partner leading them on, they may retaliate and impose a penalty on consent being withheld. The severity of this penalty can be sensitive to how large a grievance they take themselves to have. For example, people feel more aggrieved by intentional mistreatment that they interpret as motivated by selfishness and indifference to their interests than by mistreatment that was an innocent mistake. This interpretation can be shaped by stereotypes, such as the stereotype of a "tease." This is primarily a gendered stereotype of a woman who does not intend to have sex with a man but intentionally causes him both to desire having sex with her and to think that sex is probable. Part of the stereotype is that the woman is motivated by selfish reasons, e.g., she enjoys feeling desired, she enjoys feeling that she has power over him, or she enjoys feeling that there is a respect in which he is subordinated to her. If a man interprets his partner as a tease, then this may increase his sense of mistreatment and hence increase the severity of his retaliation.

Thus, someone's social environment can explain the fact that they face penalties for refusing to consent. In particular, this can be explained by the presence of social norms, along with other social phenomena like social scripts and stereotypes. In this way, social norms can be an indirect source of duress for a consent-giver. Sometimes, this duress will lead to their consent not being fully valid. But to explain why this consent is not fully valid, we do not yet need to introduce a new principle concerning social norms. This is because when social norms are an indirect source of duress, there is a separate, direct source of the duress, e.g., the consent-receiver's imposition of a penalty for refusing consent. It is this direct source that explains why the consent is not fully valid, and we already have principles that can govern duress from this direct source, such as the Consent-Receiver Principle from Chapter 2.

9.2 An Argument that Consent can be Invalidated by Duress from Social Norms

Besides influencing the duress that someone faces from a consent-receiver, someone can be directly subject to duress from social norms. For example, Rachel could be intrinsically motivated not to behave rudely, and she could be intrinsically motivated not to breach any obligations that she takes herself to have, such as an obligation not to lead on her partner. If she were thus motivated, then she may feel pressured into having sex. Can this type of pressure prevent her consent from being fully valid?

Since we are postponing discussing issues of ignorance and uncertainty until Part 4, let us assume that Rachel's partner knows that she is consenting to avoid being rude. On that assumption, it is independently plausible that Rachel's partner wrongs her by having sex with her. After all, it seems uncontroversial moral advice to say that if you know that someone is consenting to sex to avoid being rude, and they otherwise do not want to have sex with you, then you should not have sex with them.

This piece of advice focuses on someone's reasons for consenting to sex—it is advice to avoid sex with someone who consents to avoid being rude. Plausibly, this motivation of Rachel's is at the heart of why her partner wrongs her.[2] In this respect, the case is similar to other cases we have considered, such as the *Anger* case from Chapter 4. In that case, Morgan consents to sex to avoid an angry response from their partner Cameron. It is because Morgan consents with this motivation that Cameron wrongs Morgan by acting on the consent. As such, these cases are similar in the respect that the relevant agent wrongs a victim because of the victim's reasons for consenting. This similarity suggests (although does not definitively show) that we should explain the wrongs in the same way—in terms of the victim's consent being less than fully valid.

To see why this is the right way to go, consider an unrealistic case:

> *Etiquette Dictator (Consent-Receiver).* In a small community, Influencer is widely seen as the authority on what is rude or polite. Other community members place so much trust in Influencer's judgment that when Influencer proclaims that a behavior is rude or polite, these community members come to believe that this behavior is rude or polite, and this belief shapes their interactions with each other. In this way, Influencer's proclamations determine the community's conventions concerning what counts as rude or impolite. Influencer wants to have sex with Polite. Previously, it had not been rude for Polite to decline sex. But Influencer proclaims that this is rude in order to get Polite to have sex with them. Because the society's norms now dictate that refusing sex with Influencer is rude, Polite agrees to have sex with Influencer in order to avoid being rude.

[2] This is consistent with holding that Rachel's partner would also simultaneously wrong her in other ways, e.g., by subjecting her to an unpleasant sexual experience.

Since Influencer can causally influence their community's social norms, and these norms determine what is rude, Influencer can determine what behavior counts as rude. From a moral point of view, this proclamation undermines the validity of Polite's consent in the same way that consent is invalidated by the other forms of duress from the consent-receiver that we encountered in Part 1. There, we developed the Consent-Receiver Principle. On the plausible assumption that Polite has a legitimate complaint against Influencer proclaiming that it is rude to refuse sex, the Consent-Receiver Principle implies that Polite's consent is not fully valid in the *Etiquette Dictator (Consent-Receiver)* case.

Now consider a variant of this case, which features third-party duress:

> *Etiquette Dictator (Third Party).* In a small community, Influencer is widely seen as the authority on what is rude or polite. Other community members place so much trust in Influencer's judgment that when Influencer proclaims that a behavior is rude or polite, these community members come to believe that this behavior is rude or polite, and this belief shapes their interactions with each other. In this way, Influencer's proclamations determine the community's conventions concerning what counts as rude or impolite. Previously, it had not been rude for someone in the position of Rachel to decline sex with her partner (who is not Influencer). But Influencer proclaims that this is rude. Because the society's norms now dictate that refusing sex with her partner is rude, Rachel agrees to have sex to avoid being rude.

This is a case of third-party duress. To explain how this type of duress invalidates consent, we developed the Third Party Principle in Chapter 7. Roughly, this principle implies that unless an exceptional condition obtains, someone's consent is invalidated when they have a complaint against the third-party duress. The exceptional condition is that the consent-giver sincerely performs a speech-act that indicates that they most prefer the consent-receiver to perform the action in question. However, this exceptional condition does not obtain in the *Etiquette Dictator (Third Party)* as Rachel does not all things considered prefer having sex: if Rachel were able to control her partner's agency, then she would direct him to refrain from sex. (Her partner's refraining from sex would not mean that Rachel has been rude.) Thus, the Third Party Principle implies that Rachel's consent is not fully valid in the *Etiquette Dictator (Third Party)* case.

But now recall a line of reasoning that we encountered earlier in our discussion of natural causes in Chapter 8. When determining whether duress undermines someone's consent, it does not make a difference whether the duress is caused by an agent or a non-agent. Instead, what matters is the nature of the duress that they are under: i.e., what matters are the disincentives attached to withholding consent. To be precise, to determine whether the consent is fully valid, we need to consider the options open to the consent-giver and the consent-receiver, along with the consequences of these options. But we do not need to consider what explains why these options and consequences exist. Consequently, we should take the same stance about the validity of Rachel's consent in the realistic *Rudeness* case as we do in the unrealistic *Etiquette Dictator (Third Party)* case. Accordingly, since Rachel's consent is not fully valid in the *Etiquette Dictator (Third Party)* case, we should conclude that her consent is also not fully valid in the *Rudeness* case (assuming, of course, that Rachel consents because of the social norm and not for some other reason). Since Rachel's consent is invalidated by duress from a social norm, we should conclude that sometimes consent is invalidated by duress from social norms.

9.3 Entitlements to be Free from Duress from Social Norms

So why is Rachel's consent not fully valid? We can answer this question by appealing to the Adequate Position Principle:

> Adequate Position Principle. If Y's expressed choice is explained by the fact that Y is not in a sufficiently favorable position to make or express this choice, then X cannot appeal to this expressed choice to justify interfering with Y's personal domain, unless this expressed choice constitutes Y's sincere expression that, out of the options that are available to X and are not excessively costly for X, Y most prefers X to engage in this interference in the circumstances.

On the grounds that the norms in Rachel's culture make it rude for her to withhold consent, we can say that Rachel is not in a sufficiently good position to give consent. Moreover, Rachel is not authorizing the sex as what she most prefers in the circumstances, given the options that are available to and not excessively costly for her partner. Thus, the Adequate Position

Principle implies that Rachel's partner cannot appeal to her consent to justify having sex with her.

While this is helpful progress, it does not provide a full explanation unless we say more about the respects in which Rachel is not in a sufficiently favorable position to give consent. So, we should ask: why is Rachel not in such a position? I suggest that the key reason is that Rachel is in a double bind: she has to choose between consenting or behaving rudely. Moreover, Rachel is entitled to be free of this double bind. This is why she is not in a sufficiently good position to give consent.

This explanation rests on the assumption that people's entitlements are not limited to their claims against specific individuals but instead range over social norms. To defend that assumption, consider two examples. First, we can recognize that it is unjust and oppressive when a misogynist culture's social norms deem hedonistic sexual behavior from women as shameful. Part of the explanation of this fact is that everyone is entitled to engage in this sexual behavior without this behavior instantiating the property of being shameful according to local social conventions. Second, consider a set of norms according to which, on the basis of their caste, an individual is subordinated in a hierarchy of status. This state of affairs is objectionable because the individual is entitled to stand as the social equal of others in their community. By saying that someone has these entitlements, I mean that if their entitlement is not met, then they are a victim of injustice in that society. So to the extent that a society's members' entitlements are not met, that society is unjust. By analogy, consider the claim that a society manifests distributive justice only if its central institutions are arranged so as to maximally benefit the worst-off members in economic terms. Using the conception of an entitlement that I am currently employing, this can be understood as the claim that the worst-off members are entitled to their institutions maximally benefiting them.

I hope that these claims strike you as plausible and familiar: one way to diagnose social injustices is to invoke individuals' entitlements to be free from these injustices. But notice that these entitlements need not be claims that are held against specific individuals. This is because injustices can arise structurally, without there being specifiable individuals to blame. As a result, these entitlements need not be held against specifiable individuals. For example, in the misogynist culture, no specific individual can alter the culture's norms so that hedonistic sexual behavior by women is no longer deemed shameful. Since no specific individual can change these norms, there is no specific individual against whom these women have a claim that this individual changes these norms. Nonetheless, women in this culture are still entitled to engage in sexual behavior without thereby acting shamefully according to the culture's norms. Therefore, this entitlement does not consist in a claim against a specific individual. Similar points can be made about the caste-based society, as no specific agent can alter the norms that give rise to the social hierarchy.

These examples show that, independently of considerations of consent, we are familiar with the idea that people have entitlements that do not consist in claims against specific individuals. Applying this general idea to the case of Rachel, Rachel is entitled to be free from her double bind, in the respect that she should be able to decline sex without this counting as rude according to her society's norms. Suppose that this is one of the cases where the rudeness is explained by her culture attributing to Rachel a social obligation not to disappoint her partner's sexual expectations that he has formed as a result of her kissing and flirting with him. Rachel would be free from the double bind if her culture shifted its norms so that these norms deem that flirting and kissing do not give one's partner a legitimate sexual expectation that one is obliged to meet. By analogy, if an individual waits in line for a food truck, then the truck server may expect that the individual will eventually place an order. But our culture's accountability norms imply that the server is not entitled to demand that this expectation is met. These norms leave the individual free to postpone making their mind up until they place an order. These norms also leave the individual free to change their mind and walk away from the truck while waiting in line. Similarly, alternative sexual norms could leave an individual free to flirt or kiss without incurring a commitment to engage in more intimate activity.

Not only is it independently plausible to think that Rachel is entitled to be free from this double bind, this also follows from an approach that explains what entitlements people have by considering the morally-weighted interests of the relevant parties.[3] On the one hand, since sexual freedom is valuable to Rachel, she has an interest in there being no social norm according to which flirting or kissing makes her accountable to her partner for fulfilling an expectation of intimate sexual activity. The absence of this norm would leave her better able to avoid unwanted sex. Since Rachel has a particularly strong interest in avoiding unwanted sex, Rachel

[3] To repeat a point from Chapter 8: when calculating the weight of people's interests, these interests would be morally-weighted insofar as we discount, partially or wholly, people's morally illegitimate interests, e.g., in taking sadistic pleasure in another person's suffering.

also has a strong interest in being free to withhold sexual consent without thereby behaving rudely. On the other hand, there is no sufficiently weighty collection of interests that trumps Rachel's interest in escaping this double bind. It is true that her partner has an interest in being able to rely on his sexual expectations. One reason that reliance is valuable is to provide people with reassurance in the face of anxiety and uncertainty. But someone's interest in avoiding anxiety and uncertainty concerning whether another person will have sex with them is trivial compared to that person's interest in avoiding unwanted sex. So compared to Rachel's interest in avoiding unwanted sex, this interest in reassurance is a relatively weak interest. Another reason that reliance is valuable is that it enables people to choose wisely whether to forego other possible benefits. For example, in choosing to go home with Rachel, her partner may be foregoing other activities that he might prefer to making out without sex. But again, this is not as weighty an interest as Rachel's interest in avoiding unwanted sex, and in addition, there are alternative means by which he could pursue this interest in reliance. For example, if he is willing to go home with Rachel only if they are likely to have sex, then he could explicitly discuss this with her, rather than rely on, e.g., her flirting with and kissing him as an evidential guide. Consequently, the overall balance of interests supports an entitlement on the part of Rachel to withhold consent without thereby acting rudely.[4]

While I hope that this provides a framework for thinking about which entitlements people have, I am not able to offer a general account of these entitlements. The absence of this account means that the view that I am developing is of limited help for controversial cases about which it is hard to know what to say. Sometimes, we will be unsure whether a social norm prevents someone's consent from being fully valid. It is likely that we will similarly be unsure whether the consent-giver is entitled to be free from the duress caused by this norm. If so, then my view will offer us little help for resolving our uncertainty about whether the consent is fully valid.[5] While

[4] For this reason, the Social Norm Principle that I go on to defend would fit neatly alongside the Natural Causes Principle from Chapter 8. The latter principle explains a lack of full validity of consent partly in terms of an agent having an untrumped morally-weighted interest in being free from a certain constraint—the constraint constituted by withholding consent leading to a penalty. We could formulate a similar principle for duress from social norms. This principle would be more fundamental than the Social Norm Principle.

[5] This limitation is similar to a limitation from Chapter 2, where I did not provide an account of the legitimate complaints that people have against being subject to duress. Since the Consent-Receiver Principle concerns these complaints, further work is needed to determine how to apply the principle.

I accept that this is a genuine explanatory limitation of my overall view, my aim in developing this view is not to resolve controversies. Instead, I aim to show how, in principle, duress from social norms invalidates consent. That aim can be achieved without adjudicating contentious cases.

Of course, it would be a serious blow to my account if it had implausible implications. And some may be worried in this regard by the idea that rudeness could invalidate consent. In particular, they may be worried that this idea has implausible implications for other types of consent. For example, suppose that you do not particularly like your aunt: growing up, you found her bossy and domineering, and as an adult you have found little to enjoy in her company. Nonetheless, you agree to invite her to your wedding purely out of politeness. Does my view imply that your consent was not fully valid?

In response, I would clarify that I am not claiming that as a general rule someone does not give fully valid consent when they consent to avoid rudeness. Instead, I am making the specific claim that this is true of sexual consent (at least with respect to cases like *Rudeness*). My reason is that these sexual encounters have distinctive features. First, people have an especially weighty interest in avoiding unwanted sex and hence also a weighty interest in sexual freedom. By contrast, people's interests in avoiding unwanted wedding guests are typically less weighty. Second, in the case of sex, there is not a plausible story to tell about why there are countervailing social benefits attached to a social norm that implies that it is rude to refuse sex in situations like Rachel's. By contrast, in the case of weddings, there is a story to tell about the benefits that derive from a system of social expectations about weddings. Typically, the rudeness of not inviting a family member is explained by the expectation that relatives are invited to weddings. That expectation is embedded within the social meanings that are attached to weddings and family, and these meanings can be a source of value.

9.4 The Social Norm Principle

In light of the foregoing points, we can now formulate a principle that specifies when social norms prevent someone's consent from being fully valid. In the case of Rachel, withholding consent would not *cause* rudeness. Rather, withholding consent would itself be rude. That is, rudeness would be a property that is directly instantiated by Rachel's withholding consent. In addition, rudeness would be a property that is "adverse," in the sense that the instantiation of this property makes withholding consent less desirable to Rachel. Using this notion, I will formulate our new principle as follows:

> Social Norm Principle. Under conditions of full information, X's consent to Y performing A is not fully valid if:
>
> (i) a social norm makes it the case that X's withholding consent to A directly instantiates an adverse property;
> (ii) the prospect of this property causes X to consent to A;
> (iii) X is entitled to withhold consent to A without it being the case that withholding consent directly instantiates this property; and
> (iv) it is not the case that X has sincerely expressed that, out of the options that are available to and not excessively costly for Y, X most prefers that Y perform A in the circumstances.

This is the principle that I take to explain how social norms can prevent someone's consent from being fully valid.

Let me clarify the Social Norm Principle by noting four implications that the principle does not have. First, the principle does not entail that the mere existence of, e.g., rudeness norms makes it the case that someone cannot give fully valid consent. Because of condition (ii), the principle only applies to cases where the social norm is part of the causal explanation of why someone consents. The mere presence of a social norm, without any causal connection to the consent, would not lead to consent that is not fully valid.

Second, the Social Norm Principle does not entail that someone's consent is not fully valid simply because their social world has shaped their sexual behavior. For example, it may be that a culture's beauty standards have caused someone to consent to sex with another person because they are beautiful according to these standards. The consent would not be invalidated simply because it is given on the basis of this socially-influenced desire. And the Social Norm Principle does not imply that the consent would not be fully valid. In the beauty standards example, it is not the case that the person is consenting because withholding consent has an adverse feature like rudeness. Therefore, conditions (i) and (ii) of the Social Norm Principle are not satisfied, and so the principle does not imply that this person's consent is not fully valid.

Third, the Social Norm Principle does not necessarily kick in when someone consents because background social norms make withholding consent instantiate an adverse property and they are entitled to withhold consent without this instantiating this property. To see this, consider the following case:

> *Social Failure.* Robin and Parker have been on several dates. If they do not have sex tonight, then according to local social norms, Robin will count as a social failure. To avoid counting as a social failure, Robin agrees to have sex with Parker, and they have sex.

In this case, Parker has two options open to them. The first is that they have sex with Robin. This would mean that Robin does not count as a social failure according to local social norms. The second is that Parker does not have sex with Robin. This would mean that Robin does count as a social failure according to local social norms. Since Parker cannot influence the social norms, these are the only two options. Of these two options, Robin prefers the first option to the second option, and Robin sincerely expresses this preference by consenting to sex with Parker. Therefore, out of the options that are available to and not excessively costly for Parker, Robin has sincerely expressed that they most prefer Parker to have sex with them in the circumstances. Therefore, condition (iv) of the Social Norm Principle is not satisfied, and so the principle does not imply that Robin's consent is not fully valid.

Fourth, the principle does not apply to agreements besides those that constitute permissive consent. Permissive consent is consent that releases an agent from a duty not to perform a certain action. By contrast, other types of agreement have different normative effects. For example, a property sale involves the transfer of property rights from one party to another. This type of agreement is not covered by the Social Norm Principle. Nor, for that matter, is this type of agreement covered by the Adequate Position Principle, insofar as that principle applies only to how agents can justify interfering with another individual's personal domain, while property transfers re-shape the boundaries of each person's domain. That said, I do believe that the duress from social norms can be normatively relevant for property transfers. But property transfers are particularly complex and introduce orthogonal considerations (e.g., concerning the value of being able to rely on retaining property that one has acquired in good faith). Since the Social Norm Principle and Adequate Position Principle have not been formulated to handle these additional complexities, it would be a mistake to apply these principles (or very similar principles) to cases involving property transfers.

Finally, let us turn to the possibility of merging principles. In Chapter 7, I argued that the Consent-Receiver Principle and the Third Party Principle could be merged into the more general Constraint Principle. Now we should ask: is it possible to merge the Constraint Principle with the Social Norm Principle? I used to believe that something along these lines was possible (Dougherty 2022). However, now I think that there is an important difference between the two principles. I have formulated the Constraint Principle in such a way that it focuses on the *complaints* that the consent-receiver has against certain forms of duress from a third party. Meanwhile, I have formulated the Social Norm Principle in such a way that it focuses on certain *entitlements* that the consent-giver has to be free from social norm duress. These complaints and entitlements are similar but not the same: we have complaints against individual agents but not against social norms. In light of that difference, I no longer think that it is possible to merge the Constraint Principle and the Social Norm Principle. To merge the principles, we would have to formulate them in a common currency. Unfortunately, I have not seen a way to do so while at the same time providing the principles with the motivations that I take to be correct.

9.5 Summary

In this Chapter, I started by showing how a social context can indirectly explain why someone consents under duress: the social context leads their sexual partner to believe that the consent-giver has breached an obligation not to disappoint their sexual expectations, and this belief causes their sexual partner to punish them in retaliation.

In addition, I argued that social norms can directly prevent someone's consent from being fully valid by focusing on cases in which someone consents to avoid being rude (the *Rudeness* case and the *Etiquette Dictator* series of cases). This argument is supported by the Adequate Position Principle, as this principle does not place any importance on what has caused someone to be in a good or bad position to give consent. As a result, the principle places no importance on whether other agents' behavior or social norms have put someone in an insufficiently good position to give consent.

I introduced the notion of an entitlement to explain why social norms can put someone in an insufficiently good position to give consent. I then argued, roughly, that someone is in an insufficiently good position if they are in a double bind and they are entitled to be free from this double bind. For example, someone can be in a double bind if they have to choose between refusing unwanted sex and being polite. Given their interest in sexual freedom, they would be entitled to be free from this double bind.

Drawing on these points, I defended the Social Norm Principle. It specifies several conditions that are jointly sufficient for someone's consent not being fully valid. Among these are the condition that withholding consent would directly instantiate an adverse property, and the condition that the consent-giver is entitled to withhold consent without this directly instantiating this property. Since social norms determine what counts as rude, this principle can explain why someone's consent is not fully valid when they give consent in order to avoid being rude.

Consent under Duress. Tom Dougherty, Oxford University Press.
DOI: 10.1093/9780198922360.003.0011

PART 4
UNCERTAINTY ABOUT DURESS

Until this point in our inquiry, we have been proceeding under an assumption of full information. In particular, we have been assuming that consent-givers are accurately informed about what will happen if they do not consent, and we have been assuming that consent-receivers know why consent-givers are consenting. In Part 4, we relax these assumptions and consider consent that is given under conditions of partial information. This leads us to consider consent-givers who mistakenly believe they will face a penalty for refusing to consent and consent-givers who take there to be a risk that they will face such a penalty. And it leads us to consider the moral significance of a consent-receiver's ignorance of the duress that the consent-giver is under.

In Chapter 10, I defend principles that state when duress prevents consent from being fully valid under conditions of partial information. These "Subjective Principles" are counterparts to the principles that I have previously defended in this book. I offer a recipe for constructing these counterpart Subjective Principles. The recipe focuses on the fact that each objective principle includes a "triggering condition"—a condition that specifies duress that exists in the world. For example, the Consent-Receiver Principle's triggering condition is that the consent-receiver will impose a penalty on the consent-receiver if they withhold consent. The recipe converts this triggering condition into a "doxastic condition"—the condition that the consent-receiver believes or has a credence that the triggering condition obtains. For example, the Subjective Consent-Receiver Principle's doxastic condition is that the consent-giver believes or has a credence that the consent-receiver will impose a penalty on the consent-receiver if they withhold consent. By including these doxastic conditions, the Subjective Principles imply that the consent-giver's perception of duress can be sufficient for rendering their consent not fully valid, even if this perception does not reflect reality.

In Chapter 11, I defend the Subjective Principles against rival principles. These rival principles include further conditions among those that are jointly sufficient for the consent to be not fully valid. One set of rival principles adds the condition that the consent-receiver intends the consent-giver to have the relevant belief or credence that they are under duress, while another set of rival principles adds the condition that the consent-receiver causes the consent-giver to have this belief or credence. Meanwhile, other sets of rival principles add the condition that the consent-receiver has certain evidence. We can subdivide these sets of principles according to the type of evidence in question. On the one hand, there are the Generic Evidence Principles. These add the condition that the consent-receiver has the generic evidence that any consent-giver might have a belief or credence that they are under duress. On the other hand, there are the Specific Evidence Principles. These add the condition that the consent-receiver has specific evidence that the consent-giver has the relevant belief or credence. Finally, there are rival principles that add the condition that the consent-giver's belief or credence is appropriately based on the evidence that is available to them. I argue that my Subjective Principles are preferable to all these rivals.

10
In Defense of the Subjective Principles

So far, we have focused on duress that undermines the consent of someone who knows full well what will happen if they do not consent. It has been hard enough giving an account of consent under duress under conditions of full information. But in the wild, consent under duress is even more complex because people are often unsure or misled about what will happen if they do not consent. This can happen for many reasons. Others can be menacing and demanding while leaving room for doubt as to whether they are actually making threats or what exactly they are threatening. And even without being threatened, people can be fearful of how others would respond if they do not consent, without being sure of how exactly they would respond.

To speak to common experiences like these, a theory of consent has to address consent given when the future remains unknown. Accordingly, in Part 4, we will ask which normative principles explain how consent lacks full validity as a result of uncertainty about duress. The right principles will not only predict the correct results about when consent is not fully valid but will also be explanatory in the sense that they specify the *grounds* of the consent's lack of full validity.

Answering this question is philosophically challenging since there is a tension between two competing considerations. On the one hand, if someone consents to an encounter because they believe that they are under duress, then they may view the encounter as a violation. On the other hand, if the consent-receiver does not intend the consent-giver's belief, has not caused this belief, and is unaware of the belief, then the consent-receiver may resist being described as someone who has engaged in an interaction without someone's fully valid consent. Because of this tension, any answer to this question will be unappealing in one light.

This is true of the answer that I defend in this Chapter. Riding roughshod over the consent-receiver, I defend principles that are "subjective" in the sense that they give pride of place to the subjective epistemic position of the consent-giver. I call these "Subjective Principles." These Subjective Principles are counterparts to the principles that I have defended so far in this book. For example, in Chapter 2, I defended the Consent-Receiver Principle. In this Chapter, I defend its counterpart, the "Subjective Consent-Receiver Principle," in Section 10.1. I then construct a recipe for how to formulate subjective counterparts of other principles in Section 10.2. Then I discuss how the Subjective Principles and Objective Principles can be merged in Section 10.3.

10.1 The Subjective Consent-Receiver Principle

Let us start with duress that apparently comes from a consent-receiver. First, there are cases in which a consent-giver has a false belief that they will suffer a penalty if they do not consent. This can occur when the consent-receiver is making a threat, but the threat is a bluff:

> *Bluff.* Perpetrator threatens to assault Victim if Victim does not let Perpetrator enter their home. Perpetrator will not in fact execute the threat.

Alternatively, a consent-receiver may intend to follow through on a threat but be unable to execute this intention:

> *Intervention.* Perpetrator threatens to assault Victim if Victim does not let Perpetrator enter their home. Perpetrator and Victim are unaware that Third Party would appear and intervene to prevent the assault.

There are also cases in which the consent-receiver leaves the consent-giver unsure whether they will suffer a penalty from the consent-receiver if they do not consent:

> *Roulette.* Perpetrator threatens Victim that if Victim does not consent to Perpetrator entering their home, then Perpetrator will spin the chamber of a gun containing one bullet and fire at Victim. (Wertheimer 2003, 166)

Perpetrator's threat exposes Victim to a risk of being shot. But at the time at which Victim decides whether to consent, they do not know whether they would be shot.

On the grounds that someone's consent would be invalidated by a bluff of a shot or a risk of a shot as much as by an actual threat of a shot, these cases lead me to adopt the view that what matters for the validity of someone's consent is not the actual penalties that they face but rather their beliefs or credences about these penalties. Roughly, a credence is a degree of belief. So, if you estimate that, on the basis of your evidence, there is a 0.25 chance that a penalty will occur, then you have a credence of 0.25 in the proposition that the penalty will occur. I will group these beliefs and credences together as the consent-giver's "doxastic attitudes."

This view can be supported by the following argument that draws on our earlier arguments in Chapters 1 and 2. Each individual is sovereign over their personal domain. This domain includes their person and property, and it is surrounded by a protective perimeter of claim-rights—henceforth "rights" for brevity (Hohfeld 1923; Hart 1982, 183–4). To enable the individual to interact with others, the individual has the authority to relax this protection by giving consent. By expressing their will to others, they can give fully valid consent and thereby relax this protection. However, their protection is relaxed only if they consent in a sufficiently good position to give consent. The question we now face is whether their doxastic attitudes bear on whether they are in a sufficiently good position to give consent. My answer is that their doxastic attitudes do bear on this. Ultimately, we are interested in the character of the choice that someone makes. Because people make decisions on the basis of their doxastic attitudes and motivations, the character of someone's choice is determined partly by their doxastic attitudes. For example, suppose that someone is forced to dance because another person is pointing a gun at them. The character of their decision to dance is determined by their desire to avoid being shot and their credence that they will be shot if they do not dance. But their decision to dance has the same character whether the gun is loaded or not. Thus, to determine whether an individual is in a sufficiently good position to give consent, we should take into account their doxastic attitudes about their circumstances rather than the objective facts about these circumstances.

It is natural to express this point by using the locution "of someone's own free will." When someone dances because a gun is pointed at their head, it is natural to say that this person does not dance of "their own free will." It remains natural to say this if we stipulate that the gun is not loaded but they believe that it is. It is also natural to say this if we stipulate that the dancer knows that there is exactly one bullet in the gun but does not know if the bullet is in the firing chamber. I mention these points not to rely on any substantive theory of what it is for someone's will to be free, but rather to bring out that there is a stability in our view of the dancer's actions even when there is variation in the facts about what actual threats they face. And just as we should see the dancer's decision as compromised in all these cases, we should similarly see a consent-giver's decision as compromised when they consent because they believe or have a credence that they face a penalty for withholding consent.

Following this argument, we arrive at the following principle:

> Subjective Consent-Receiver Principle. Under conditions of partial ignorance, X's consent to Y performing action A is not fully valid if:
>
> (i) X either believes or has a credence that Y will impose a penalty on X's withholding consent to A;
> (ii) this belief or credence causes X to consent to A;
> (iii) if Y had imposed this penalty on X's withholding consent to A, then X would have a legitimate complaint against the way that Y has done so; and
> (iv) this complaint would concern the way that the penalty alters X's incentives for withholding consent.[1]

The Subjective Consent-Receiver Principle can explain why consent is invalid in the cases that we have considered so far. Because the Subjective Consent-Receiver Principle concerns a consent-giver's beliefs, it can explain why their consent is invalidated by a threat of harm that they falsely believe will arise (e.g., bluffs). Because the principle concerns the consent-giver's credences, it can explain why their consent is invalidated either by a perpetrator imposing a risk of harm of which the consent-giver is aware or by a perpetrator keeping the consent-giver uncertain whether the consent-giver will suffer the harm. Thus, the principle has two sources of support. First, it is motivated by its explanatory power to return intuitive verdicts about cases, and second, it is motivated by the foregoing argument, according to which whether someone consents of their own free will turns on their factual beliefs about the penalties that they face.

While I endorse that argument in the respect that I take it to provide the correct rationale for the principle that governs coerced consent with an unknown future, I acknowledge that it is not a knock-down argument by any means. In particular, let me flag upfront that it is controversial in the

[1] With respect to sexual consent, Alexander (1996, 172–3) endorses a similar view.

respect that it focuses on the consent-giver at the expense of the consent-receiver. To see why this is controversial, note that a consent-receiver has an interest in being morally free to act in various ways. When the consent-receiver needs consent to perform an action, the consent-receiver has less moral freedom if they receive invalid consent than they would have if they receive valid consent. If the consent-receiver is not responsible for the consent-giver's belief that they will be penalized for withholding consent, and the consent-receiver is unaware that the consent-giver has this belief, then the consent-receiver could act on the consent in good faith. So, the conclusion of the foregoing argument imposes moral constraints on consent-receivers who act in good faith, and in this respect, the view is insensitive to their interests in moral freedom. Given that there is potentially a clash of interests between the consent-giver and the consent-receiver, any normative principle will come with some cost. This is why finding the correct normative principle is philosophically difficult and why we are unlikely to find knock-down arguments in favor of any principle. Since the foregoing argument is not knock-down, it needs to be supplemented by criticism of rival principles and of the arguments that may be offered in defense of these rivals. This criticism will come in Chapter 11.

10.2 The General Recipe for Subjective Principles

The Subjective Consent-Receiver Principle is closely related to the Consent-Receiver Principle. The latter principle is "objective" in the sense that it concerns consent that is given under conditions of full information. The Third Party Principle, the Natural Causes Principle, and the Social Norm Principle are also objective principles. So is the Constraint Principle, which itself is the result of merging the Consent-Receiver Principle and the Third Party Principle. For each of these principles, we can follow a recipe for constructing analogous subjective principles.

To see how the recipe goes, let us consider how the Subjective Consent-Receiver Principle is based on the Consent-Receiver Principle. Here is our final formulation of it:

> Consent-Receiver Principle. Under conditions of full information, X's consent to Y performing action A is not fully valid if:
>
> (i) Y will impose a penalty on X's withholding consent to A;
> (ii) the prospect of this penalty causes X to consent to A;

(iii) X has a legitimate complaint against the way that Y has conditioned this penalty on X's withholding consent to A; and
(iv) this complaint concerns the way that the penalty alters X's incentives for withholding consent to A.

Let us call this principle's first condition its "triggering condition." It specifies a state of the world that is external to the consent-giver's psychology. This state of the world "triggers" the consent in the sense that the consent is a response to the state of the world. Meanwhile, the second condition is the "causation condition": it is the condition that this triggering state of the world causes the consent. Finally, the principle includes two "normative conditions"—conditions (iii) and (iv).

Here is the main idea in my recipe. The Subjective Consent-Receiver Principle does not include the Consent-Receiver Principle's triggering condition. Instead, the Subjective Consent-Receiver Principle includes the condition that the consent-giver has a doxastic attitude (i.e., a belief or credence) that this triggering condition is satisfied. I will call this the "doxastic condition."

Doxastic Condition. X either believes or has a credence that Y will impose a penalty on X's withholding consent to A.

This leads us to a general recipe for deriving subjective principles that are counterparts to objective principles. We start with the objective principle but replace its triggering condition with a corresponding doxastic condition. The doxastic condition is that the consent-receiver believes or has a credence that the triggering condition is met.

That is the major change. Once we have made this change, two further minor changes are needed to clean things up. First, we replace the objective principle's causation condition with the condition that the relevant belief or credence causes the consent. Second, we change the normative conditions (iii) and (iv) so that they concern the complaints that the consent-giver *would* have against the penalty. (This change makes room for the idea that the penalty might not materialize.)

Using this recipe, we can formulate subjective counterparts of the Third Party Principle, the Natural Causes Principle, the Social Norm Principle, and the Constraint Principle. For brevity, I will state the Subjective Third Party Principle here, leaving the other principles for the Glossary of Principles at the end of this book:

Subjective Third Party Principle. **Under conditions of partial ignorance,** X's consent to Y performing action A is not fully valid if:

(i) **X believes or has a credence that** a third party Z will impose a penalty on X's withholding consent to A;
(ii) **this belief or credence** causes X to consent to A;
(iii) X would have a legitimate complaint against the way that Z has conditioned this penalty on X's withholding consent;
(iv) this complaint would concern the way that the penalty alters X's incentives for withholding consent; and
(v) it is not the case that X has sincerely expressed that, out of the options that are available to Y, X most prefers Y to perform A in the circumstances.

In this formulation, the bold text indicates the difference between the principle and its objective counterpart. Together, I will use the term "Subjective Principles" to refer to the Subjective Consent-Receiver Principle, the Subjective Third Party Principle, the Subjective Natural Causes Principle, the Subjective Social Norm Principle, and the Subjective Constraint Principle.

10.3 Merging the Subjective and Objective Principles

Earlier, in Chapters 7 and 9, we discussed the possibility of merging principles to create additional unity in our account. Following this line of thought, we should now ask: can the Objective Principles and the Subjective Principles be merged?

I am optimistic that they can be. Consider duress that comes from the consent-receiver. I formulated the Subjective Consent-Receiver Principle so that it began with the qualification "Under conditions of partial ignorance...." If we remove this qualification, then we end up with a general principle from which both the Consent-Receiver Principle and Subjective Consent-Receiver Principle can be derived:

General Consent-Receiver Principle. X's consent to Y performing action A is not fully valid if:

(i) X either believes or has a credence that Y will impose a penalty on X's withholding consent to A;
(ii) this belief or credence causes X to consent to A;

(iii) X has a legitimate complaint against the way that Y has conditioned this penalty on X's withholding consent; and
(iv) this complaint concerns the way that the penalty alters X's incentives for withholding consent.

I call this the "General Consent-Receiver Principle" because it applies generally to both conditions of full information and conditions of partial ignorance. Why think that this principle implies the Subjective Consent-Receiver Principle? Well, this principle is identical to the Subjective Consent-Receiver Principle except for the fact that it omits the initial qualification, "Under conditions of partial information." As such, the General Consent-Receiver Principle is strictly stronger than the Subjective Consent-Receiver Principle and hence implies that principle. And why think that this principle implies the Consent-Receiver Principle? Well, that objective principle implies that consent is not fully valid when certain actual duress from the consent-receiver causes the consent. For it to be plausible that this duress undermines the consent, the causal route must go through the decision-making of the consent-giver. As a result, the actual duress must cause the consent-giver to have a belief or credence that they face this duress. Thus, when the first two conditions of the Consent-Receiver Principle are satisfied, so too are the first two conditions of the General Consent-Receiver Principle. Since the principles are otherwise identical, it follows that whenever all of the conditions of the Consent-Receiver Principle are satisfied, all of the conditions of the General Consent-Receiver Principle are also satisfied. Thus, the General Consent-Receiver Principle implies the Consent-Receiver Principle.

However, there is one wrinkle. If we take the General Consent-Receiver Principle to be explanatory in the sense that it states the grounds of the lack of full validity, then it is noteworthy that the actual imposition of a penalty is not among these grounds. Since the Consent-Receiver Principle implies that this imposition is among the grounds, we cannot simultaneously take the General Consent-Receiver Principle to be explanatory, take the Consent-Receiver Principle to be derived from the General Consent-Receiver Principle, and take the Consent-Receiver Principle to be explanatory. Instead, if we take the General Consent-Receiver Principle to be explanatory and take the Consent-Receiver Principle to be derived from the General Consent-Receiver Principle, then we should view the Consent-Receiver Principle as a true principle that identifies a condition under which consent is not fully valid. But we should not see this condition as specifying the explanatory grounds of why the consent is not fully valid.

Just as we can construct the General Consent-Receiver Principle from the Subjective Consent-Receiver Principle, we can also construct the General Third Party Principle from the Subjective Third Party Principle and the General Social Norm Principle from the Subjective Social Norm Principle. And we could use similar reasoning as above to conclude that the objective and subjective versions of the Third Party Principle and the Social Norm Principle can be merged into these more general principles. Similarly, we could posit a General Constraint Principle that is constructed from the Subjective Constraint Principle. So, if you accept all of the principles that I have defended in this book, then I invite you to accept these General Principles as the more fundamental principles from which they are derived.

10.4 Summary

In this Chapter, we have asked: which principles govern the lack of full validity of consent under duress with an unknown future? To answer this question, I have defended the Subjective Principles. These are counterparts of the objective principles that I have defended earlier in the book—i.e., the Consent-Receiver Principle, the Third Party Principle, the Natural Causes Principle, the Social Norm Principle, and the Constraint Principle. We can construct the subjective counterpart of each objective principle using the following recipe. We consider the objective principle's "triggering condition," which concerns the relevant type of duress. For example, in the case of the Consent-Receiver Principle, the triggering condition is that the consent-receiver will impose a penalty on the consent-giver for withholding consent. Each counterpart subjective principle replaces this with the "doxastic condition" that the consent-giver believes or has a credence that this triggering condition is met. Each subjective principle states that if this belief or credence causes the consent, and the other conditions of its counterpart objective principle are met (e.g., the penalty is illegitimate), then the consent is not fully valid.

Consent under Duress. Tom Dougherty, Oxford University Press. © Tom Dougherty 2024.
DOI: 10.1093/9780198922360.003.0012

11

Against the Intention, Causal, and Epistemic Principles

In Chapter 10, I defended Subjective Principles that govern consent that is given when someone is unsure or misinformed about the duress that they face. According to these principles, whether someone's consent is invalidated depends on their beliefs or credences about this duress. For example, if someone consents because they mistakenly believe that the consent-receiver will violently attack them if they do not consent, then these principles imply that their consent is not fully valid. Controversially, the principles imply this even if the consent-receiver does not intend the consent-giver to have this mistaken belief, has done nothing to cause the belief, and is unaware of it.

My positive argument for the Subjective Principles is not irresistible, and so my defense of these principles also involves criticizing rival principles. This Chapter provides this criticism. In Section 11.1, I argue against rival principles that place importance on the consent-receiver's intentions for the consent-giver's beliefs and credences. In Section 11.2, I argue against rival principles that place importance on the causal contributions that the consent-receiver has made to the consent-giver's beliefs or credences. In Section 11.3, I argue against rival principles that place importance on the consent-receiver's specific evidence about the consent-giver's beliefs or credences. Then, in Section 11.4, I argue against rival principles that place importance on the consent-receiver's generic evidence about the consent-giver's beliefs or credences. Finally, in Section 11.5, I argue against principles that require that the consent-giver's beliefs or credences are supported by their evidence.

11.1 The Consent-Receiver's Intentions

The Subjective Principles focus only on the doxastic attitudes of the consent-giver. In this Section, I will argue against rival principles that also place importance on the consent-receiver's intentions for these doxastic attitudes.

The Subjective Principles do not mention the consent-receiver's intentions. Consequently, there are rival principles that add the following condition as part of their sufficient condition for when consent is not fully valid:

> Intention Condition. The consent-receiver intends the consent-giver to have the relevant belief or credence.

For this condition and subsequent conditions, what counts as the relevant belief or credence depends on the principle. For example, in the case of duress from the consent-receiver, it would be the belief or credence that the consent-receiver will impose a certain penalty if consent is withheld. To illustrate the addition of the Intention Condition, consider the principle governing duress from a consent-receiver:

> Intention Consent-Receiver Principle. Under conditions of partial ignorance, X's consent to Y performing action A is not fully valid if:
>
> (i) X either believes or has a credence that Y will impose a penalty on X's withholding consent to A;
> (ii) this belief or credence causes X to consent to A;
> (iii) X would have a legitimate complaint against the way that Y has conditioned this penalty on X's withholding consent;
> (iv) this complaint would concern the way that the penalty alters X's incentives for withholding consent; and
> (v) **Y intends X to have this belief or credence.**

The bold text indicates what has been added to the Subjective Consent-Receiver Principle. Apart from this addition, the Intention Consent-Receiver Principle and the Subjective Consent-Receiver Principle are identical. We could similarly formulate the Intention Third Party Principle, the Intention Natural Causes Principle, the Intention Social Norm Principle, and the Intention Constraint Principle by adding the same Intention Condition to their Subjective counterparts. Let us call the principles that add the Intention Condition the "Intention Principles."

By adding this condition, the Intention Principles state sufficient conditions that are narrower than the sufficient conditions stated by the Subjective Principles. Accordingly, the Intention Principles are rivals of the

Subjective Principles in two respects. First, if the Intention Principles can explain all the explananda, then we do not need the stronger Subjective Principles to explain these. In that respect, the Intention Principles threaten to leave the Subjective Principles inadequately motivated. Second, if the Subjective Principles and the Intention Principles are interpreted as explanatory principles that specify the grounds of the invalidity of someone's consent, then these principles disagree concerning these grounds. Specifically, they disagree about whether a certain intention of the consent-receiver is among these grounds.

The Intention Principles could be motivated by appealing to the view that coercion is objectionable because it involves manipulating someone or using them as a mere means. That is because to manipulate or use someone is an intentional endeavor: it is to make someone else into a tool for pursuing one's own ends. This is a characteristically Kantian objection to coercion.[1] In Chapter 1, I have already argued against these motivations in the case of consent that is given under conditions of full information. But my argument there proceeded by counterexamples concerning cases involving consent-givers who knew what would happen if they did not consent. So, it is open to an opponent to argue that intentions do not matter under conditions of full information, but they do matter for conditions of partial motivation.

Whether or not this is a plausible motivation, we should reject the Intention Principles because they cannot handle certain cases in which the consent-receiver is unaware that they are causing someone to fear a penalty. There are various reasons why a consent-receiver might underestimate how much fear they inspire in others. For example, a violent spouse could think of themselves as fundamentally a decent person, who is occasionally provoked into uncharacteristic anger (Stark 2007, 246). Because they have a distorted self-image, they could fail to realize that their partner fears violence in response to withholding consent. Second, a consent-receiver might fail to empathize with what it is like to be disempowered. Suppose that a boss engages in *quid pro quo* sexual harassment by offering an employee an undeserved work benefit in return for sex. A proposal like this often also connotes an implicit threat, whether the threat is intended or not (Schulhofer 1998). For example, the employee may think, "If my boss is prepared to break workplace rules to get me to have sex with them, then they might break other

[1] For Kantian accounts of coercion, see O'Neill (1985, 262–3) and Korsgaard (1996, 139–41). For the view that consent is invalidated when someone exercises illegitimate control over another person's decision, see Bromwich and Millum (2018).

rules if I refuse. Maybe my boss will make my life harder at work or even fire me." As a result, the employee might agree to have sex, not because they want the undeserved work benefit, but instead because they want to avoid the risk of the boss penalizing them for refusing to consent. The employee could consent for this reason even if the boss never intended them to fear being penalized.

In cases like these, someone's consent would not be fully valid, even though the consent-receiver does not intend for them to face a penalty for withholding consent. We can illustrate this point with a simplified case:

> *Breadmaker*. Leo comes across the following note from their new roommate Ally: "I'm off to my meditation retreat now, and I can't be contacted until it is over. I'm not generally inclined to let people use my stuff. However, in the last apartment that I lived in, I didn't let people share my things, and I got bullied as a result. Since I don't want to go through all that again, I am letting you borrow the breadmaker." This comes as a surprise to Leo, who has been exemplary in their behavior towards Ally and has done nothing to cause Ally to fear bullying. Since Leo can no longer communicate with Ally, Leo cannot causally affect Ally's beliefs or credences.

Leo does not intend and has never intended Ally to believe that Ally faces a penalty for withholding consent. Therefore, the Intention Consent-Receiver Principle does not imply that Ally does not give fully valid consent. However, I take it to be clear that Leo lacks Ally's fully valid consent: once Ally reads that Leo is only consenting to avoid being bullied, then that settles that Leo's consent is not fully valid. So, to explain why Leo's consent is not fully valid, we would need a different principle from the Intention Consent-Receiver Principle.

11.2 The Causal Role of the Consent-Receiver

The *Breadmaker* case also causes trouble for principles that place importance on the consent-receiver's causal contributions to the consent-giver's doxastic attitudes. For example, there are rival principles that add the following condition to the Subjective Principles:

> Causation Condition. The consent-receiver has causally contributed to the consent-giver having the relevant belief or credence.

Let us call the principles that add this condition the "Causation Principles." The Causation Principles allow that consent is invalidated in virtue of the consent-receiver's causal relation to the consent-giver's doxastic attitude, even if the consent-receiver neither intends this relation to hold nor is aware that it does hold.

One motivation for the Causation Principles is that they may seem to be a fair way to take into account the consent-receiver's interest in avoiding wrongdoing: by omitting the causal contributions that their actions made to the belief or credence, they could have avoided receiving consent that is less than fully valid.[2]

Can the Causation Principles explain why Ally's consent is not fully valid in the *Breadmaker* case? At the time at which Leo decides whether to use the breadmaker, Leo cannot causally influence Ally's doxastic attitudes. So a proponent of the principles would have to appeal to Leo's causal role before Ally gave consent. Since Leo has done nothing to cause Ally to be fearful, the only option is to appeal to Leo's omissions of actions that would have reassured Ally before leaving for the retreat.

But this maneuver leads to a separate worry that the Consent-Receiver Causation Condition is vacuous: if all that is required for a causal connection is that there was something that the consent-receiver could have done to reassure the consent-giver, then the condition obtains nearly all the time.

We can press this point by considering a case in which a consent-receiver had no prior contact with the consent-giver:

> *Hermit.* Out of the blue, you receive a long letter addressed from Hermit inviting you to stay in their cabin in a remote mountainside. At first, this letter charms, but flummoxes, you because you have neither met Hermit nor heard of their mountainside—you have to look it up on a map. As you read on, you are distressed to discover that Hermit is inviting you because Hermit is worried that otherwise you will harm them. You begin to realize that a villain has been impersonating you to menace Hermit.

[2] Another way to motivate the Causation Consent-Receiver Principle is to appeal to two ideas. The first is the idea that someone can wrong another person by causing them to believe or have a credence that they face an illegitimate penalty if they withhold consent. The second is David Owens's (2007) Injury Account, according to which someone's consent is invalidated when the consent-receiver wrongs the consent-giver in virtue of how the consent-receiver obtains their consent. I discuss this motivation in Dougherty (2021c).

Since Hermit is consenting because they believe that you will otherwise harm them, you do not have Hermit's fully valid consent to stay with them. Now, over the course of your life, you have omitted various actions that would have made Hermit believe that you would not harm them. For example, last year, you could have traveled to their mountainside, met with Hermit, and reassured Hermit of your gentle nature. But given that you had no idea of Hermit's existence prior to receiving the letter, it is hard to believe that your omitting this course of action has anything to do with why Hermit's consent is not fully valid. But if that is right, then we must turn our backs on the Causation Principles as explanatory principles that specify the grounds of why consent is not fully valid when it is given under duress with an unknown future.

11.3 The Specific Evidence of the Consent-Receiver

In this Section, let us now consider rival principles that place importance on the consent-receiver's *evidence* concerning the consent-giver's doxastic attitudes.

To formulate specific rival principles, let us distinguish two types of evidence that a consent-receiver might have. On the one hand, the consent-receiver can have *generic* evidence that there is always some chance that the consent-giver is consenting under duress. This evidence is generic in the sense that it is not based on any particular evidence about the specific circumstances that the consent-receiver and consent-giver are in. Instead, it is evidence about the activity of giving and receiving consent in general. (By analogy, we have evidence that in general the activity of driving imposes a risk of harm on pedestrians.) On the other hand, the consent-receiver can have *specific* evidence that this particular consent-giver is consenting under duress. For example, the consent-giver might be looking fearful, or the consent-receiver might have a reputation for being violent. This evidence is specific in the sense that it pertains to the identity of the consent-giver, the identity of the consent-receiver, or the particular situation that they are in. (By analogy, we can have evidence that a specific instance of driving imposes a particularly high risk of harm on pedestrians, e.g., because weather conditions are bad.)

Having drawn this distinction, we can see that there are two extra evidential conditions that could be posited by rival principles. Let us start with rival principles that add to the Subjective Principles the following condition:

Specific Evidence Condition. The consent-receiver has specific evidence that the consent-giver is consenting because they have the relevant belief or credence.

Again, the relevant belief or credence depends on the principle in question. For example, with respect to the Subjective Consent-Receiver Principle, it would be the consent-giver's belief or credence that the consent-receiver will impose the penalty for withholding consent. Let us call the principles that add this condition the "Specific Evidence Principles."

The Specific Evidence Principles could be motivated by the idea that "at the very least, [an agent] must be able to track the facts about whether [a consent-giver] has given her a permission" to perform a certain action (Bolinger 2019, 188–9).[3] This idea would imply that the consent-receiver must be able to track whether they are receiving consent that is not fully valid because the consent is given under duress. This would require the consent-receiver to have specific evidence about the duress that the consent-giver took themselves to be facing.

The Specific Evidence Principles could also be motivated by appealing to the ethics of risk imposition. Many everyday actions have minuscule risks of harm. But so long as an agent has no specific evidence that harm will arise from performing an everyday action, it may seem permissible for them to perform the action—even if the harm does in fact arise (Thomson 1986, 177–8).[4] Similarly, we may think that so long as an agent has no specific evidence that the consent that they receive is given under duress, the risks are low enough that it is permissible for them to act on the consent.

However, the Specific Evidence Condition is implausible. To see this, recall a real-world case of third-party duress that we encountered in Chapter 7:

Burnham. In the context of an abusive relationship, Victor Burnham threatened Rebecca Burnham with violence unless she attempted to stop passing motorists and solicit sex from them.

[3] Renée Jorgensen, writing as Renée Jorgensen Bolinger (2019, 187–8), appeals to this idea to argue that consent must be observable in order to distribute risks between people. But since consent distributes risks only when it is valid, Jorgensen's argument would also apply to the considerations that bear on whether consent is fully valid.

[4] For defense of a view along these lines, according to which an agent's obligations and a patient's rights depend on the agent's evidence, see Zimmerman (2008, xii, 33–41, 80, 87; 2014, 113–40).

Because Rebecca Burnham consented to avoid a violent attack, her consent was fully invalid. This result would hold even if we supposed that Rebecca Burnham was such a convincing actor that a motorist had no specific evidence that she was motivated by a background threat. If the roadside location of the solicitation seems suspicious, then we can imagine a variant of the case in which an abuser threatens their victim into soliciting sex at a bar that people often visit in order to seek casual sexual encounters. If we fill in the background details of the case in a certain way, then a consent-receiver may have no specific reason to suspect that the consent-giver is subject to duress from a third party. This ignorance would excuse the consent-receiver from blame. But the ignorance would not render the consent fully (or even partially) valid.

To press this point, note that third-party duress is only one of several problems along these lines. We just considered two motivations for the Specific Evidence Condition. One motivation appealed to the idea that an agent must have epistemic access to whether they have been given a permission, while the other motivation appealed to the idea that it is not excessively risky for an agent to act on consent when they have no specific evidence that the consent is given under duress. These motivations did not specifically address duress, as opposed to any of the other necessary conditions for consent's validity. Therefore, if these motivations support the view that a consent-receiver must have specific evidence that the consent-giver acts under duress, then these motivations would equally support similar views concerning the other necessary conditions for valid consent. One of these is the necessary condition that the consent-giver must have sufficient capacity. For example, in the case of sexual consent, consent is not fully valid when given by a minor. Yet a consent-receiver could have sex with someone while lacking evidence that they are a minor:

> *Minor.* Minor has the physical appearance of someone ten years older than them, and Minor has shown Adult a fake passport that looks so much like the real thing that it would convince an immigration official. Minor consents to sex with Adult.

Adult lacks specific evidence that they are having sex without Minor's valid consent. Yet the consent is not fully valid because it comes from someone who is underage.

11.4 The Generic Evidence of the Consent-Receiver

I take both the *Burnham* case and the *Minor* case to undermine the motivations that we considered for the Specific Evidence Condition, and I take the *Burnham* case to show that we should reject the condition. However, these cases do not undermine including an alternative principle that places importance on the consent-receiver's generic evidence:

> Generic Evidence Condition. The consent-receiver has generic evidence that there is always some chance that any consent-giver is consenting because they have the relevant belief or credence that they are under duress.

Let us call the principles that add this condition the "Generic Evidence Principles."

The Generic Evidence Condition might be motivated by appealing to the idea that an agent wrongs a patient with their action only if they are responsible for this action.[5] This idea might lead us to hold that a consent-receiver is responsible for wronging a consent-giver if they negligently fail to attend to the generic evidence of the tiny risk that any consent-giver is under duress. This position would accommodate the fact that in the *Burnham* case, Rebecca Burnham does not validly consent even if the motorists lack specific evidence of Victor Burnham's duress. These motorists would still have evidence that there is some chance that any consent-giver is consenting because they believe that they are subject to third-party duress.

Since this generic evidence is universally available, the Generic Evidence Condition is trivially satisfied. Consequently, the Generic Evidence Principles have dovetailed with the Subjective Principles, in the sense that both sets of principles have the same substantive implications about when consent is not fully valid. This is because the principles differ only in the respect that the Generic Evidence Principles contain the additional Generic Evidence Condition, and this condition is universally satisfied. There remains a difference between the principles insofar as they should be interpreted as explanatory principles that specify the grounds of the invalidity of someone's consent. Unlike the Subjective Principles, the Generic Evidence

[5] For defense of this idea in the context of theorizing the ethics of self-defense, see McMahan (2005, 394, 397, 401).

Principles imply that the lack of validity of the consent would be partly grounded in the fact that a consent-receiver has evidence that there is a tiny risk that the consent-giver is motivated by a belief or credence that they are under duress.

Given the extensional convergence between the Subjective Principles and the Generic Epistemic Principles, not much hangs on our choice between them. Consequently, it seems improbable that there are arguments that will decisively tell in favor of one set of principles over the other, especially if these arguments stay local to considerations concerning consent. Still, I think that we can find some reason to reject the Generic Epistemic Principles by changing topics to innocent misappropriations of others' property. Typically, when we make use of an item of our own property, we do so while oblivious of the tiny risk that it has been replaced by a qualitatively identical object that belongs to someone else. Yet it is conceivable that this scenario obtains. Consider:

> *Jacket Mixup*. You have an electric blue leather jacket with distinctive wearing. You attend a house party and throw it on a pile of coats in the host's spare bedroom. Against all odds, another guest leaves an identical electric blue leather jacket with the same distinctive wearing. You accidentally put this on when you leave the party, discovering your mistake only when you later find the guest's wallet in an inner pocket.

Because you made an innocent mistake, you are blameless. But even so, you infringed another person's property right by taking home their coat. Not only is this the intuitive way to describe walking off with someone else's property, but it is also reflected by the fact that you are obliged to bear the costs of undoing the effects of your action: you would have to return the coat rather than say that the guest has to come to meet you to pick it up. It seems artificial to say that the fact that you infringe the guest's property right is explained by the fact that you ought to be aware that there is always a tiny risk that what clearly appears to be your jacket is in fact someone else's. Instead, the more natural thing to say is that this is wholly explained by the fact that the jacket belongs to the guest. But if we take this view of the grounds of an accidental infringement of a property right, then we should take a similar view of the grounds of an accidental right-infringement that occurs in virtue of someone giving consent that is not fully valid. Just as your generic evidence that there is a tiny risk that the jacket belongs to someone else is not part of the grounds of why you infringe the owner's property right, so too is a consent-receiver's generic evidence that there is a tiny risk that the consent-giver is under duress not part of the grounds of why the consent-receiver infringes a right of the consent-giver by acting on the consent.

11.5 The Consent-Giver's Evidence

Finally, let me say why my Subjective Principles do better than rival principles that also focus on the consent-giver.

The Subjective Principles cater to the consent-giver's lack of descriptive knowledge, e.g., concerning what will happen if they do not consent. We could also formulate principles that cater to the consent-giver's lack of normative knowledge. For example, consider the Subjective Consent-Receiver Principle. Its condition (iii) concerns whether the penalty is *in fact* illegitimate. We could reach a principle that caters even further to the consent-giver by substituting a condition like:

(iii*) the consent-giver believes that this penalty would be illegitimate.

This would yield a principle that is even more subjective insofar as it also lets the consent-giver's normative beliefs bear on whether their consent is fully valid.

However, it is implausible that if a consent-giver has a true descriptive belief that they face a penalty for withholding consent, but they have a false normative belief that this penalty is illegitimate, then this false normative belief invalidates their consent (Alexander 1996, 171–2; Liberto 2022). Consider a variant of an earlier case:

> *Unreasonable Steroids.* Player is refusing to take part in steroids testing. Coach threatens to cut them from the team unless they take the test. Since Player falsely believes that Coach would be usurping their authority by dropping Player from the team, Player believes that Coach is imposing an illegitimate penalty on their withholding consent. Nonetheless, Player consents to the test.

Player has false normative beliefs about whether Coach's penalty is legitimate. These false normative beliefs do not prevent Player's consent from being fully valid. Indeed, these beliefs would not do so even if Player had good evidence for their belief—perhaps, a reputable source has misled them about the terms of Coach's contract.

As an aside, this reinforces Chapter 1's result that a consent-giver is not always in a position to know whether they are consenting sufficiently freely from duress and hence whether they are giving valid consent at the time at which they give consent. That conclusion might seem surprising, but it is the right one to draw. If Player later learned that Coach did have the authority to drop them, then they would have to accept that their consent to the test was valid even though they did not appreciate this at the time.

In addition, we could arrive at a rival principle by adding the following condition:

> Evidential Support Condition. The consent-giver's belief or credence is appropriately supported by their evidence.

By adding this condition, a rival principle would avoid implying that someone's consent is invalidated when they have made a mistake when forming their beliefs or credences about the penalties that they face. The mistake could be that they form a belief in a penalty when their evidence does not support this belief. Or their mistake could be that their credence in the penalty is higher than the credence that would be supported by their evidence. This is not uncommon. We can become anxious about the future turning out badly, and anxiety can cause us to overestimate risks.

There are reasons to add the Evidential Support Condition. On the grounds that the consent-giver is responsible for making a mistake, we might conclude that the mistake should not disadvantage the consent-receiver. Since the consent-receiver would be disadvantaged by their moral freedom being constrained in virtue of their receiving consent that is not fully valid, we might conclude that the consent-giver's mistake should not prevent their consent from being fully valid.

This line of argument is particularly forceful when the consent-giver's mistake is morally criticizable. Consider the following case:

> *Racist*. Racist has internalized a racist stereotype of people from a marginalized racial group as dangerous and violent. Minority belongs to this group. Minority asks Racist whether they want to have sex. Minority has done nothing to make Racist feel fearful. In addition, Racist has not indicated to Minority that they are fearful (or racist for that matter). Nonetheless, Racist is privately scared that Minority will respond violently if they refuse, and this motivates Racist to consent.

Some people will not want to say that Minority has sex with Racist while Racist gives fully invalid consent. Moreover, they may find it unjust if a moral theory implies as much. The background racism is already an injustice that Minority suffers. Some will see this as aggravated if Minority's moral freedom is further constrained by a moral principle that implies that Racist gives fully invalid consent.

However, there is another way to analyze the case. We could say that Minority acts impermissibly but innocently. Minority is innocent because Minority has no evidence that Racist does not give fully valid consent. In addition, if we agree that it is unjust that Minority has innocently been made into the agent of an impermissible action, then we need not put this at the feet of a moral theory that implies that Racist's consent is fully invalid. Instead, we can attribute this injustice to Racist's prejudice and the background racism in Minority's society that has shaped Racist's attitudes.

Although this is a finely balanced issue, I think that we should accept the latter analysis. My argument for this conclusion begins by considering the following variant of the case:

> *Trembling Racist.* Racist has internalized a racist stereotype of people from a marginalized racial group as dangerous and violent. Minority is a member of this group. Minority knows that this stereotype is widespread in their society. Minority asks Racist whether they want to have sex. Minority has done nothing to make Racist feel fearful. However, Racist is visibly trembling and showing other forms of fear because they are scared that Minority will respond violently if they refuse. This fear motivates Racist to consent. Minority correctly infers that Racist is motivated to consent by the racist stereotype.

In this case, I take it to be clear that Minority cannot permissibly have sex with Racist. It would obviously not do for them to reason, "I know that Racist is consenting because they are afraid that I will violently attack them if they refuse to consent. But I know that I will not attack them, and they have no evidence that I will. They have just made a mistake when forming their false belief, and this mistake is based on their racism. So, it is ok for me to have sex with them." This reasoning is not cogent. Once Minority grants that Racist consents to avoid violence, that settles the fact that Minority cannot justify acting on the consent. This is the case even though Racist lacks evidence to support their belief and Racist is motivated by racism.

The difference between the *Racist* case and the *Trembling Racist* case concerns the specific evidence and beliefs of Minority, the consent-receiver. In particular, the cases differ with respect to whether Minority has specific evidence that Racist is consenting out of fear of violence and whether Minority believes that Racist is consenting out of this fear. The *Burnham* case illustrates that the consent-receiver's beliefs do not bear on the validity of the consent. And in Section 11.3, we just saw that the consent-receiver's specific evidence does not bear on whether the consent is fully valid. Since it is clear that Racist's consent is fully invalid in *Trembling Racist*, and since the consent-receiver's specific evidence does not bear on the validity of consent, we should conclude that Racist's consent is fully invalid in *Racist* too.

We could run a similar argument for any case involving a consent-giver who, without supporting evidence, believes or has a credence that they are under duress (whether this mistake is explained by racism, epistemic irrationality, or anything else). We could construct a parallel case in which the consent-receiver has evidence that the consent-giver has made this mistake and is consenting because they take themselves to be under duress. In that parallel case, it is clear that the consent is not fully valid. Since the parallel case and the initial case differ only with respect to the consent-receiver's evidence and beliefs, and since the consent-receiver's evidence and beliefs do not bear on the validity of the consent, we should conclude that the consent is not fully valid in the initial case. Since this is a fully generalizable argument, we should conclude that any consent-giver's doxastic attitude need not be supported by the evidence in order for it to prevent their consent from being fully valid. Accordingly, we should not add the Evidential Support Condition to our Subjective Principles.

11.6 Summary

This Chapter has continued my defense of the Subjective Principles. These principles state conditions that are jointly sufficient for consent not being fully valid. Among these is the condition that the consent-giver believes or has a credence that they are under duress. In this Chapter, I argued against rival principles that include further conditions among those that are jointly sufficient for the consent to be not fully valid.

One set of rival principles adds the condition that the consent-receiver intends the consent-giver to have the relevant belief or credence that they are under duress. I argued that these Intention Principles fail to imply the correct result that consent is not fully valid in key cases. For example, in the *Breadmaker* case, Leo learns that their housemate Ally is consenting to Leo using their breadmaker out of a fear that Leo will otherwise bully them. Even though Leo never intended Ally to have a credence that Leo will bully them, Ally's consent is not fully valid.

The *Breadmaker* case also caused trouble for a different set of rival principles that add the condition that the consent-receiver has caused the consent-giver to have the relevant belief or credence. These Causal Principles fail to handle the case because Ally's fear is not based on Leo's behavior but rather on the basis of Ally's previous experiences with other housemates.

The remaining sets of rival principles add the condition that the consent-receiver has certain evidence. We can subdivide these sets of principles according to the type of evidence in question. On the one hand, there are the Generic Evidence Principles. These add the condition that the consent-receiver has the generic evidence that any consent-giver might have a belief or credence that they are under duress. Since this condition is trivially satisfied, the Generic Evidence Principles dovetail with my Subjective Principles with respect to their implications for cases. Accordingly, there is not much at stake in our choice between them, and it is hard to choose between them. Still, I argued that we should prefer my Subjective Principles on the basis that they have more plausible implications about the explanatory grounds of the lack of full validity of someone's consent.

On the other hand, there are the Specific Evidence Principles. These add the condition that the consent-receiver has specific evidence that the consent-giver has the relevant belief or credence that they are under duress. For this evidence to be specific, it is not enough that it is evidence that any consent-giver might take themselves to be under duress. Instead, the evidence must concern the identity of the consent-giver, the identity of the consent-receiver, or the particular situation that they are in. Against these principles, I argued that in general it is implausible that the consent-receiver's evidence or beliefs bear on the validity of someone's consent. This can be seen by considering versions of the *Burnham* case, in which Rebecca Burnham is subject to third-party duress, or the *Minor* case, in which someone has misleading evidence that their sexual partner is old enough to give fully valid consent.

Finally, I argued that we should not add the Epistemic Support Condition to the Subjective Principles. The Epistemic Support Condition is the condition that the consent-giver's belief or credence is appropriately based on the evidence that is available to them. I argued that if a consent-receiver is aware that the consent-giver is consenting because of this belief or credence, then it is clear that the consent is not fully valid. But since the consent-receiver's awareness does not bear on the validity of consent, we should equally conclude that the consent is not fully valid even when the consent-receiver is unaware.

Consent under Duress. Tom Dougherty, Oxford University Press. © Tom Dougherty 2024.
DOI: 10.1093/9780198922360.003.0013

Conclusion—Cat Person Revisited

In this book, I have defended a set of principles that offer us new ways of thinking about consent under duress. To illustrate how they can shine light on sexual encounters, let us conclude by returning to a scene from Kristen Roupenian's (2017) "Cat Person":

> Margot sat on the bed while Robert took off his shirt and unbuckled his pants, pulling them down to his ankles before realizing that he was still wearing his shoes and bending over to untie them. Looking at him like that, so awkwardly bent, his belly thick and soft and covered with hair, Margot recoiled. But the thought of what it would take to stop what she had set in motion was overwhelming; it would require an amount of tact and gentleness that she felt was impossible to summon. It wasn't that she was scared he would try to force her to do something against her will but that insisting that they stop now, after everything she'd done to push this forward, would make her seem spoiled and capricious, as if she'd ordered something at a restaurant and then, once the food arrived, had changed her mind and sent it back.

When most readers encounter this scene, I imagine that they find it troubling, but I doubt that they think that Margot does not properly consent. I speculate that often the reason is that they endorse a binary view of consent that involves a key pair of claims. The first claim is that sexual encounters can be divided into consensual and non-consensual encounters. The second claim is that non-consensual encounters involve serious sexual violations. On the assumption that Robert does not commit a serious sexual violation, this pair of claims leads to the conclusion that the sex was consensual. Of course, that conclusion is consistent with evaluating the sex as bad in other respects. But that evaluation would not concern Margot's consent.

And yet I argue that it is Margot's reasons for consenting that should trouble us. After all, if we had to explain to Robert why he should not proceed to have sex with Margot, we would point to the fact that, although she would ideally prefer to avoid having sex with him, she feels pressured into continuing a chain of actions that she feels that she has set in motion. That pressure is, I submit, a type of duress. So, our concern with this case is ultimately a concern with consent under duress. And a view with a sharp binary of consensual and non-consensual sex fails to let us see the case that way.

Fortunately, there is a better way to think about the ethics of sexual consent. On the view that I have defended, we can allow that there is a spectrum of sexual misconduct that varies in its gravity. While particularly grave misconduct results from the use of major coercion to obtain consent, there is also less grave misconduct that results from consent being undermined in less egregious ways. As some people may like to put the idea: rather than there being a sharp binary of consensual and non-consensual sex, it is more illuminating to think of sexual encounters as more or less consensual.[1] Or as I prefer to put the idea, consent can be partially valid to a greater or lesser degree. If someone receives partially valid consent, then this does not prevent them from committing misconduct. But the partially valid consent does reduce the gravity of this misconduct.

These are the ideas that are central to my scalar approach from Part 2 of this book. The scalar approach places moral significance on the fact that duress comes in different degrees, and consequently, it allows that consent can be morally undermined to different degrees. Using this approach, we can give a better account of the sexual scene in "Cat Person." Since Margot is subject to minor duress, her consent is partially valid. The upshot is that Robert wrongs Margot by having sex with her, even though he does not commit a serious sexual violation on a par with rape. And I suggest that on reflection, this is an intuitively attractive way to think of what is going on.

The scalar approach is one of the two distinctive approaches of this book that I flagged in the Introduction. The other is my expansive approach. This casts a wide net over misconduct that is wrongful in virtue of the victim's consent being undermined by duress. Following this approach, I have developed an account of how social norms can prevent consent from being fully valid. This account can explain why Margot's consent is only partially valid. By going back to Robert's house and making out with him, Margot feels that she has given Robert a legitimate expectation of sex and that she is

[1] This is how Kimberly Ferzan (2018) interprets a view like the one that I defend. Ferzan's interpretation is natural if we use "consent" as a moral success term, such that consent is necessarily morally efficacious. Personally, I prefer not to use "consent" in this way and instead to leave room for the idea that consent can be morally inefficacious.

obliged to meet this expectation. That's why Margot feels that refusing sex would be like sending back a dish that she had ordered. It is understandable that Margot feels this way, given the prevailing social norms in her culture. But these norms objectionably place Margot in a double bind: she must choose between unwanted sex and coming across as capricious. Given Margot's interest in sexual freedom, she is entitled to be free from the double bind, and she has no genuine obligation to meet Robert's sexual expectations. And so, if she consents for this reason, then her consent is not fully valid.[2] Or at least that is the implication of the Social Norm Principle that I defended in Part 3.

In this analysis, I am making claims only about expectations for which someone can be held morally accountable by another person. I accept that in a purely epistemic sense it may well be appropriate for Robert to think that sex is more likely given that Margot has gone back to his place and made out with him. But evidentially licensing a purely epistemic prediction is not the same as entering into a contractual obligation. Continuing Margot's restaurant theme, we can imagine that a group of restaurant diners have finished off a bottle of wine with their starters. This behavior would make it reasonable for their server to predict that the diners will order another bottle. In that purely epistemic sense, the server may be given an expectation that the diners will order another bottle. But this is not an expectation for which the diners can be held morally accountable. If the diners decide not to order any more wine, then they do not wrong the server. In this respect, the options of "cooling down" and "escalating" their wine consumption are equally open to them. Similarly, I claim that Margot's prior behavior should leave her free either to cool down or to escalate her sexual encounter. As it happens, Margot's social world implies otherwise, by making it the case that breaking things off will count as "having led Robert on." But this is a respect in which Margot's society's culture has let her down, as she is entitled to be free from this double bind.

For all we know, Margot may also take herself to be subject to duress from Robert himself. We are told that Margot is not scared that Robert will "force her to do something against her will." But that leaves open other ways that he might react negatively to her breaking off their encounter. There are various clues that this may be his reaction. During their date, Margot has

[2] Here I am implicitly assuming that Margot is not sincerely expressing a preference that, of the options open to and not excessively costly for Robert, she prefers Robert to act on this consent.

had images of violence. For example, when Robert picked Margot up, "it occurred to her that he could take her someplace and rape and murder her." And when Margot enters his house, fear still has a "hold on her" and "she had the brief wild idea that . . . all the other rooms in the house were empty, or full of horrors: corpses or kidnap victims or chains." Moreover, for much of their time together, Margot has been trying to manage Robert's mood—she has interpreted him as angry at various points and tried to minimize this type of reaction. The narrative of "Cat Person" does not state that these fears are among Margot's reasons for having sex. But it would be understandable if Margot were keen to avoid an angry backlash to breaking off their encounter. Since Margot would have a legitimate complaint against this backlash, Part 1's Consent-Receiver Principle implies that her consent would not be fully valid if she gave it to avoid this backlash.

Indeed, Margot's consent would be impaired if she mistakenly thought there might be an angry backlash, even if Robert would not in fact react angrily. That is an implication of Part 4, where I argued that it is a consent-giver's perception of duress (rather than the duress's existence in reality) that matters for whether their consent is not fully valid.

Of course, Robert is himself in an epistemically limited position. He has little insight into Margot's private thoughts. Indeed, he would be horrified to learn of how he is repulsing and amusing her as they have sex. But I have argued that Robert's own ignorance does not make a difference to the validity of Margot's consent. At most—and this is debatable[3]—it could furnish him with an excuse for having acted wrongly.

[3] It is not at all clear to me that Robert has this excuse. We get a clue as to how Robert is viewing sex with Margot in light of how their sexual encounter unfolds:

> When she was on top, he slapped her thigh and said, "Yeah, yeah, you like that," with an intonation that made it impossible to tell whether he meant it as a question, an observation, or an order.

This behavior fits so neatly with representations of sex in pornography that a reasonable inference is that pornography is shaping Robert's assumptions about what Margot likes, particularly considering social science research findings that pornography influences people's sexual behaviors and attitudes toward sex (Sun et al. 2016). But if Robert's ignorance of Margot's duress results from him uncritically placing too much weight on pornographic representations of sex when forming his beliefs, then he would be to blame for his ignorance and hence be acting negligently. Moreover, Robert could be negligent in virtue of failing to consider evidence that Margot is consenting under duress or failing to take appropriate steps to check that Margot is not under duress. Indeed, part of the reason why Robert misinterprets Margot is that he spends so little effort looking for cues about her level of interest or explicitly communicating with her about what she wants. But if Robert is culpable for his ignorance of the duress that Margot is under, then this ignorance would not exculpate him from mistreating her.

That analysis relies on various substantive assumptions. In particular, I have assumed that Margot is entitled to be free to decline sex without counting as having "led Robert on," and I have assumed that Margot would have a legitimate complaint against Robert retaliating angrily. These assumptions strike me as plausible, and I hope that they appear that way to you too. But they are contestable and defending them goes beyond what I have attempted in this book. As a result, more is required to argue against people who endorse a different moral assessment of the encounter between Robert and Margot. And this encounter is not alone in this respect: for pretty much any controversy about a sexual encounter, the principles that I have defended will not have determinate implications without auxiliary assumptions that go beyond what I have defended here. But while this book leaves us with further work in these respects, it has offered progress in other respects. In particular, this book has developed an overarching and cohesive framework of moral principles that identify conditions under which consent is morally undermined by duress. This framework takes into account the fact that consent is often given under partial ignorance, and it allows us both to expand the class of sexual encounters undermined by duress and to recognize the differences made by degrees of duress.

Consent under Duress. Tom Dougherty, Oxford University Press. © Tom Dougherty 2024.
DOI: 10.1093/9780198922360.003.0014

Glossary of Principles

Authorization Principle. X gives fully valid consent to Y performing A if:

(i) X sincerely performs a speech-act that communicates that, out of the options that are available to Y and are not excessively costly for Y, X authorizes Y to perform A as an extension of X's own agency; and
(ii) all other validity conditions are met.

Adequate Position Principle. If Y's expressed choice is explained by the fact that Y is not in a sufficiently favorable position to make or express this choice, then X cannot appeal to this expressed choice to justify interfering with Y's personal domain, unless this expressed choice constitutes Y's sincere expression that, out of the options that are available to X and are not excessively costly for X, Y most prefers X to engage in this interference in the circumstances.

Consent-Receiver Principle. Under conditions of full information, X's consent to Y performing action A is not fully valid if:

(i) Y will impose a penalty on X's withholding consent to A;
(ii) the prospect of this penalty causes X to consent to A;
(iii) X has a legitimate complaint against Y conditioning this penalty on X's withholding consent; and
(iv) this complaint concerns the way that the penalty alters X's incentives for withholding consent.

Constraint Principle. X's consent to Y performing action A is not fully valid if:

(i) X will face a penalty if they do not consent to A;
(ii) the prospect of this penalty causes X to consent to A;
(iii) X has a legitimate complaint against the way that someone has conditioned this penalty on X's withholding consent;
(iv) this complaint concerns the way that the penalty alters X's incentives for withholding consent; and
(v) it is not the case that X has sincerely expressed that, out of the options that are available to and not excessively costly for Y, X most prefers Y to perform A in the circumstances.

Facilitative Duty Principle. If Y's expressed choice is explained by X's failure to discharge their duties to put Y in a sufficiently good position for making and expressing this choice, then X cannot appeal to this expressed choice in order to justify interfering with Y's personal domain.

Individualist Principle. For any penalty p that an individual X faces as a result of withholding consent, X's morally weighted interest in avoiding p is trumped if there is another individual Y who has a stronger morally weighted interest in p being imposed on X's withholding consent.

Natural Causes Principle. Under conditions of full information, X's consent to Y performing action A is not fully valid if:

(i) natural causes will impose a penalty on X's withholding consent to A;
(ii) the prospect of this penalty causes X to consent to A;
(iii) X has an untrumped interest in being free from consenting leading to this penalty;
(iv) this interest concerns how the penalty alters X's incentives for withholding consent; and
(v) it is not the case that X has sincerely expressed that, out of the options that are available to Y and are not excessively costly for Y, X most prefers Y to perform A in the circumstances.

Social Norm Principle. Under conditions of full information, X's consent to Y performing A is not fully valid if:

(i) a social norm makes it the case that X's withholding consent to A directly instantiates an adverse property;
(ii) the prospect of this property causes X to consent to A;
(iii) X is entitled to withhold consent to A without it being the case that withholding consent directly instantiates this property; and
(iv) it is not the case that X has sincerely expressed that, out of the options that are available to and not excessively costly for Y, X most prefers that Y perform A in the circumstances.

Subjective Consent-Receiver Principle. Under conditions of partial ignorance, X's consent to Y performing action A is not fully valid if:

(i) X either believes or has a credence that Y will impose a penalty on X's withholding consent to A;
(ii) this belief or credence causes X to consent to A;
(iii) if Y had imposed this penalty on X's withholding consent to A, then X would have a legitimate complaint against the way that Y has done so; and
(iv) this complaint would concern the way that the penalty alters X's incentives for withholding consent.

Subjective Constraint Principle. Under conditions of partial ignorance, X's consent to Y performing action A is not fully valid if:

(i) X either believes or has a credence that X will face a penalty if they do not consent to A;
(ii) this belief or credence causes X to consent to A;

(iii) X has a legitimate complaint against the way that someone has conditioned this penalty on X's withholding consent;
(iv) this complaint concerns the way that the penalty alters X's incentives for withholding consent; and
(v) it is not the case that X has sincerely expressed that, out of the options that are available to Y, X most prefers Y to perform A in the circumstances.

Subjective Natural Causes Principle. Under conditions of partial ignorance, X's consent to Y performing action A is not fully valid if:

(i) X believes or has a credence that natural causes will impose a penalty on X's withholding consent to A;
(ii) this belief or credence causes X to consent to A;
(iii) X has an untrumped interest in being free from consenting leading to this penalty;
(iv) this interest concerns how the penalty alters X's incentives for withholding consent; and
(v) it is not the case that X has sincerely expressed that, out of the options that are available to Y and are not excessively costly for Y, X most prefers Y to perform A in the circumstances.

Subjective Social Norm Principle. Under conditions of partial ignorance, X's consent to Y performing A is not fully valid if:

(i) X believes or has a credence that X's withholding consent to A would directly instantiate an adverse property;
(ii) the belief or credence causes X to consent to A;
(iii) a social norm would make it the case that withholding consent to A directly instantiates this property;
(iv) X would be entitled to withhold consent to A without it being the case that withholding consent directly instantiates this property; and
(v) it is not the case that X has sincerely expressed that, out of the options that are available to Y, X most prefers that Y perform A in the circumstances.

Third Party Principle. Under conditions of full information, X's consent to Y performing action A is not fully valid if:

(i) a third party Z will impose a penalty on X's withholding consent to A;
(ii) the prospect of this penalty causes X to consent to A;
(iii) X has a legitimate complaint against the way that Z has conditioned this penalty on X's withholding consent;
(iv) this complaint concerns the way that the penalty alters X's incentives for withholding consent; and
(v) it is not the case that X has sincerely expressed that, out of the options that are available to Y and are not excessively costly for Y, X most prefers Y to perform A in the circumstances.

References

Alexander, L. 1996. "The Moral Magic of Consent II," *Legal Theory 2*(3): 165–74.

Anderson, S. 2016. "Conceptualizing Rape as Coerced Sex," *Ethics 127*(1): 50–87.

Archard, D. 2007. "The Wrong of Rape," *The Philosophical Quarterly 57*(228): 374–93.

Bennett, J. and D. Jones. 2019. "45 Stories of Sex and Consent on Campus," in The New York Times Editorial Staff (eds.), *Defining Sexual Consent: Where the Law Falls Short*, New York NY: New York Times Educational Publishing, pp. 66–82.

Berkich, D. 2009. "A Heinous Act," *Philosophical Papers 38*(3): 381–99.

Berman, M. 2002. "The Normative Functions of Coercion Claims," *Legal Theory* 8(1): 45–89.

Berman, M. 2011. "Blackmail," in J. Deigh and D. Dolinko (eds.), *The Oxford Handbook of Philosophy of Criminal Law*, New York NY: Oxford University Press, pp. 37–106.

Bicchieri, C. 2006. *The Grammar of Society: The Nature and Dynamics of Social Norms*, Cambridge: Cambridge University Press.

Bolinger, R. 2019. "Moral Risk and Communicating Consent," *Philosophy and Public Affairs 47*(2): 179–207.

Brawley L. 2018. "Let's Be Honest about Aziz Ansari," *CNN*, 18 January [online]. https://www.cnn.com/2018/01/17/opinions/lets-be-honest-about-aziz-ansari-brawley/index.html (accessed 6 February 2021).

Brison, S. 2002. *Aftermath: Violence and the Remaking of a Self*, Princeton: Princeton University Press.

Bromwich, D. and J. Millum. 2018. "Lies, Control and Consent: A Reply to Dougherty and Manson," *Ethics 128*(2): 446–61.

Brown, C. 2020. "Sex Crimes and Misdemeanours," *Philosophical Studies 177*(5): 1363–79.

Conly, S. 2004. "Seduction, Rape and Coercion," *Ethics 115*(1): 96–121.

Cornell, N. 2015. "Wrongs, Rights, and Third-Parties," *Philosophy and Public Affairs 43*(2): 109–43.

Darwall, S. 2006. *The Second-Person Standpoint: Morality, Respect and Accountability*, Cambridge MA: Harvard University Press.

Dembroff, R. and D. Wodak. 2018. "He/She/They/Ze," *Ergo 5*(14): 371–406.

Dougherty, T. 2013. "Sex, Lies, and Consent," *Ethics 123*(4): 717–44.

Dougherty, T. 2015. "Yes Means Yes: Consent as Communication," *Philosophy and Public Affairs 43*(3): 224–53.

Dougherty, T. 2020. "Informed Consent, Disclosure, and Understanding," *Philosophy and Public Affairs 48*(2): 119–50.

Dougherty, T. 2021a. "Sexual Misconduct on a Scale: Gravity, Coercion, and Consent," *Ethics 131*(2): 319–44.

Dougherty, T. 2021b. "Why Does Duress Undermine Consent?" *Nous 55*(2): 317–33.

Dougherty, T. 2021c. "Coerced Consent with an Unknown Future," *Philosophy and Phenomenological Research 103*(2): 441–61.

Dougherty, T. 2021d. *The Scope of Consent*, Oxford: Oxford University Press.

Dougherty, T. 2022. "Social Constraints on Sexual Consent," *Politics, Philosophy, and Economics 21*(4): 393–414.

Dougherty, T. 2024. "Paradoxical Proposals and Consent," in M. Timmons (ed.), *Oxford Studies in Normative Ethics*, Oxford: Oxford University Press, pp. 9–30.

Feinberg, J. 1986. *Harm to Self*, Oxford: Oxford University Press.

Ferzan, K. 2016. "Consent, Culpability, and the Law of Rape," *Ohio State Journal of Criminal Law 13*(2): 397–439.

Ferzan, K. 2018. "Consent and Coercion," *Arizona State Law Journal 50*(4): 951–1007.

Ferzan, K. and P. Westen. 2017. "How to Think (Like a Lawyer) about Rape," *Criminal Law and Philosophy 11*(4): 759–800.

Flanagan, C. 2018. "The Humiliation of Aziz Ansari," *The Atlantic*, 14 January [online]. https://www.theatlantic.com/entertainment/archive/2018/01/the-humiliation-of-aziz-ansari/550541 (accessed 6 February 2021).

Foa, P. 1998. "What's Wrong with Rape," in R. Baker, F. Elliston, and K. Wininger (eds.), *Philosophy and Sex*, Amherst NY: Prometheus Books.

Frankfurt, H. 1988. *The Importance of What We Care About*, Cambridge: Cambridge University Press.

Freitas, D. 2018. *Consent on Campus: A Manifesto*, New York NY: Oxford University Press.

Frick, J. 2016. "What We Owe to Hypocrites: Contractualism and the Speaker-Relativity of Justification," *Philosophy and Public Affairs 44*(4): 223–65.

Fricker, M. 2007. *Epistemic Injustice*, Oxford: Oxford University Press.

Frye, M. and C. Shafer. 1977. "Rape and Respect," in M. Vetterlin-Braggin, F. Elliston, and J. English (eds.), *Feminism and Philosophy*, Lanham MD: Rowman & Littlefield Publishers, pp. 333–46.

Gardner, J. and S. Shute. 2000. "The Wrongness of Rape," in J. Horder (ed.), *Oxford Essays in Jurisprudence: Fourth Series*, Oxford: Oxford University Press, pp. 193–217.

Gerver, M. 2021. "Consent and Third-Party Coercion," *Ethics 131*(2): 246–69.

Gibert, S. 2023. "The Wrong of Wrongful Manipulation," *Philosophy and Public Affairs 51*(4): 329–449.

Hampton, J. 2001. Defining Wrong and Defining Rape," in K. Burgess Jackson (ed.), *A Most Detestable Crime: New Philosophical Essays on Rape*, New York NY: Oxford University Press, pp. 118–56.

Hänel, H. 2018. "What is a Sexist Ideology? Or: Why Grace Didn't Leave," *Ergo* 5(34): 899–921.

Hart, H. L. A. 1968. "Legal Responsibility and Excuses," in *Punishment and Responsibility*, Oxford: Oxford University Press, pp. 28–53.

Hart, H. L. A. 1982. *Essays on Bentham: Studies in Jurisprudence and Political Theory*, Oxford: Clarendon Press.

Haslanger, S. 2012. *Resisting Reality: Social Construction and Social Critique*, Oxford: Oxford University Press.

Hohfeld, W. 1923. *Fundamental Legal Conceptions*, New Haven, CT: Yale University Press.

Hurd, H. 1996. "The Moral Magic of Consent I," *Legal Theory* 2(2): 121–46.

Hyman, J. 2015. *Action, Knowledge, and Will*, Oxford: Oxford University Press.

Ichikawa, J. J. 2020. "Presupposition and Consent," *Feminist Philosophy Quarterly* 6(4): 1–32.

Johnson, M. 2010. *A Typology of Domestic Violence: Intimate Terrorism, Violent Resistance, and Situational Couple Violence*, Hanover: Northeastern University Press.

Julius, A. J. 2013. "The Possibility of Exchange," *Politics, Philosophy and Economics 12*(4): 361–74.

Kiener, M. 2022. "Consenting under Third-Party Coercion," *Journal of Moral Philosophy 19*(4): 361–89.

Kolodny, N. 2017. "What Makes Threats Wrong?" *Analytic Philosophy 58*(2): 87–118.
Korsgaard, C. 1996. *Creating the Kingdom of Ends*, Cambridge: Cambridge University Press.
Kukla, R. 2018. "That's What She Said: The Language of Sexual Negotiation," *Ethics 129*(1): 70–97.
Liberto, H. 2021. "Coercion, Consent, and the Mechanistic Question," *Ethics 131*(2): 210–45.
Liberto, H. 2022. *Green Light Ethics: A Theory of Permissive Consent and Its Moral Metaphysics*, New York NY: Oxford University Press.
Lindsey, M. 2018. "Silence is Not Consent: Sexual Assault and Aziz Ansari," *Columbia Daily Spectator*, 8 February [online]. https://www.columbiaspectator.com/opinion/2018/02/08/silence-is-not-consentsexual-assault-and-aziz-ansari (accessed 6 February 2021).
MacKinnon, C. 1989. *Towards a Feminist Theory of the State*, Cambridge MA: Harvard University Press.
MacKinnon, C. 2003. "A Sex Equality Approach to Sexual Assault," *Annals of the New York Academy of Sciences 989*(1): 267–75.
MacKinnon, C. 2016. "Rape Redefined," *Harvard Law and Policy Review 10*(2): 431–77.
Manne, K. 2018. *Down Girl: The Logic of Misogyny*, New York NY: Oxford University Press.
Manson N, and O. O'Neill. 2007. *Rethinking Informed Consent in Bioethics*, Cambridge MA: Cambridge University Press.
Martin, A. 2021. "Personal Bonds: Directed Obligations without Rights," *Philosophy and Phenomenological Research 102*(1): 65–86.
McMahan, J. 2005. "The Basis of Moral Liability to Defensive Killing," *Philosophical Issues 15*(1): 386–405.
Miller, F. and A. Wertheimer (eds.). 2010. *The Ethics of Consent*, Oxford: Oxford University Press, pp. 79–105.
Millum, J. 2014. "Consent Under Pressure: The Puzzle of Third-Party Coercion," *Ethical Theory and Moral Practice 17*(1): 113–27.
O'Neill, O. 1985. "Between Consenting Adults," *Philosophy and Public Affairs 14*(3): 252–77.
Owens, D. 2007. "Duress, Deception, and the Validity of a Promise," *Mind 116*(462): 293–315.
Owens, D. 2012. *Shaping the Normative Landscape*, Oxford: Oxford University Press.
Pallikkathayil, J. 2011. "The Possibility of Choice: Three Accounts of the Problem with Coercion," *Philosophers' Imprint 11*(16): 1–20.
Price, D. 2018. "A Few Words About Sexual Coercion, in the Wake of the Aziz Ansari Accusations," *Medium*, accessed on 7/27/20 at https://medium.com/@dr_eprice/a-few-words-about-sexual-coercion-in-the-wake-of-the-aziz-ansari-accusations-7db015c1cde5.
Roupenian, K. 2017. "Cat Person," *The New Yorker*, 4 December [online]. https://www.newyorker.com/magazine/2017/12/11/cat-person (accessed 6 February 2021).
Rubenfeld, J. 2013. "The Riddle of Rape-by-Deception and the Myth of Sexual Autonomy," *Yale Law Journal 122*(6): 1372–442.
Salzberger, M. 2020. *The Meaning and Moral Significance of Domestic Violence*, PhD Thesis, University of North Carolina at Chapel Hill.
Scanlon, T. M. 1986. *The Significance of Choice, The Tanner Lectures on Human Values*, Brasenose College, Oxford University, https://tannerlectures.utah.edu/_documents/a-to-z/s/scanlon88.pdf (accessed 6 June 2020).
Scanlon, T. M. 1998. *What We Owe to Each Other*, Cambridge MA: Harvard University Press.

Scanlon, T. M. 2008. *Moral Dimensions*, Cambridge MA: Harvard University Press.

Scanlon, T. M. 2013. "Responsibility and the Value of Choice," *Think 12*(33): 9–16.

Schank, R. and R. Abelson. 1977. *Scripts, Plans, Goals and Understanding: An Inquiry into Human Knowledge Structures*, Hillsdale NJ: Lawrence Erlbaum Associates.

Schulhofer, S. 1998. *Unwanted Sex*, Cambridge MA: Harvard University Press.

Shaw, J. 2012. "The Morality of Blackmail," *Philosophy and Public Affairs 40*(3): 165–96.

Sidgwick, H. 1893. *The Methods of Ethics*, 5th ed., London: Macmillan.

Sreenivasan, G. 2010. "Duties and Their Direction," *Ethics 120*(3): 465–94.

Stark, E. 2007. *Coercive Control: The Entrapment of Women in Personal Life*, Oxford: Oxford University Press.

Strawson, P. 1962. "Freedom and Resentment," *Proceedings of the British Academy* 48: 1–25.

Sun, C., A. Bridges, J. Johnson, and M. Ezzell. 2016. "Pornography and the Male Sexual Script: An Analysis of Consumption and Sexual Relations," *Archives of Sexual Behavior 45*(4): 983–94.

Tadros, V. 2016. *Wrongs and Crimes*, Oxford: Oxford University Press.

Tadros, V. 2021. "Consent to Sex in an Unjust World," *Ethics 31*(2): 293–318.

Thompson, M. 2004. "What Is It to Wrong Someone? A Puzzle about Justice," in R. J. Wallace, P. Pettit, S. Scheffler, and M. Smith (eds.), *Reason and Value: Themes from the Moral Philosophy of Joseph Raz*, Oxford: Clarendon Press, pp. 333–84.

Thomson, J. J. 1986. *Rights, Restitution, and Risk*, Cambridge MA: Harvard University Press.

Thomson, J. J. 1990. *The Realm of Rights*, Cambridge MA: Harvard University Press.

Walker, L. 1979. *The Battered Woman*, New York NY: Harper and Row.

Wallace, R. J. 2019. *The Moral Nexus*, Princeton NJ: Princeton University Press.

Way, K. 2018. "I Went on a Date with Aziz Ansari. It Turned into the Worst Night of My Life," *Babe*, [online]. https://babe.net/2018/01/13/aziz-ansari-28355 (accessed 6 February 2021).

Weiss, B. 2018. "Opinion: Aziz Ansari is Guilty. Of Not Being a Mind Reader," *New York Times*, 15 January [online]. https://www.nytimes.com/2018/01/15/opinion/aziz-ansari-babe-sexual-harassment.html (accessed 6 February 2021).

Wertheimer, A. 2001. "Intoxicated Consent to Sexual Relations," *Law and Philosophy 20*(4): 373–401.

Wertheimer, A. 2003. *Consent to Sexual Relations*, Cambridge: Cambridge University Press.

Wertheimer, A. 2010. "Consent to Sexual Relations," in F. Miller and A. Wertheimer (eds.), *The Ethics of Consent*, Oxford: Oxford University Press, pp. 195–220.

West, R. 2010. "Sex, Law, and Harm," in F. Miller and A. Wertheimer (eds.), *The Ethics of Consent*, Oxford: Oxford University Press, pp. 221–50.

Westen, P. 2004. *The Logic of Consent*, Ashgate: Ashgate Publishing.

Whisnant, R. 2017. "Feminist Perspectives on Rape," in Edward N. Zalta (ed.), *The Stanford Encyclopedia of Philosophy*, https://plato.stanford.edu/archives/fall2017/entries/feminism-rape.

White, S. 2017. "On the Moral Objection to Coercion," *Philosophy and Public Affairs 45*(3): 199–231.

Zimmerman, M. 2008. *Living with Uncertainty: The Moral Significance of Ignorance*, Cambridge: Cambridge University Press.

Zimmerman, M. 2014. *Ignorance and Moral Obligation*, Oxford: Oxford University Press.

Index of Cases

Since the index has been created to work across multiple formats, indexed terms for which a page range is given (e.g., 52–53, 66–70, etc.) may occasionally appear only on some, but not all of the pages within the range.

Index of Topics

Since the index has been created to work across multiple formats, indexed terms for which a page range is given (e.g., 52–53, 66–70, etc.) may occasionally appear only on some, but not all of the pages within the range.